Bram Stoker and Russophobia

# Bram Stoker and Russophobia

*Evidence of the British Fear of Russia in* Dracula *and* The Lady of the Shroud

JIMMIE E. CAIN, JR.

McFarland & Company, Inc., Publishers
*Jefferson, North Carolina, and London*

An earlier version of Chapter Three appeared under the title "*With the Unspeakables*: Dracula and Russophobia — Tourism, Racism, and Imperialism" in Elizabeth Miller, ed., *Dracula: The Shade and the Shadow* (Essex: Desert Island Books, 1998).

An earlier version of Chapter Five appeared under the title "*The Lady and the Shroud*: A Novel of Balkan Anglicization" in *Balkanistica* 12 (1999).

LIBRARY OF CONGRESS CATALOGUING-IN-PUBLICATION DATA

Cain, Jimmie E., 1953–
    Bram Stoker and Russophobia : evidence of the British fear of Russia in Dracula and The lady of the shroud / Jimmie E. Cain, Jr.
      p.    cm.
    Includes bibliographical references and index.

    ISBN 0-7864-2407-9 (softcover : 50# alkaline paper)

    1. Stoker, Bram, 1847–1912 — Criticism and interpretation. 2. Russia — Foreign public opinion, British. 3. Public opinion — Great Britain. 4. Crimean War, 1853–1856 — Influence. 5. Stoker, Bram, 1847–1912. Dracula. 6. Stoker, Bram, 1847–1912. Lady of the shroud. 7. Horror tales, English — History and criticism. 8. Vampires in literature. I. Title.
PR6037.T617Z59   2006
823'.8 — dc22                        2005036407

British Library cataloguing data are available

On the cover: Portrait of Bram Stoker (*Personal Reminiscences of Henry Irving*, 1906); bear and globe illustration ©2006 Clipart.com

Manufactured in the United States of America

*McFarland & Company, Inc., Publishers*
*Box 611, Jefferson, North Carolina 28640*
*www.mcfarlandpub.com*

To the women in my life:
Edna Ann Dunlap, my mother,
who taught me the joys of reading;
Allison Wicker, my aunt,
who inspired me to write;
Lu-Ann Parks, my sister,
who keeps me connected to home and family;
and, most importantly, Betty, my wife,
without whose love and devotion
none of this would have been possible.

# Table of Contents

# Preface

This book investigates the role that Russophobia, a deep-seated mistrust and fear of Russia, played in the formation of Bram Stoker's fictional works, in particular his novels *Dracula* and *The Lady of the Shroud*. Much has been written concerning the origins of *Dracula*. The first book-length study of the novel was Raymond McNally's and Radu Florescu's *In Search of Dracula: The History of Dracula and Vampires*, which appeared in 1972 and again in a revised edition in 1994. Clive Leatherdale, drawing conclusions often at odds with those of McNally and Florescu, made significant contributions to *Dracula* studies in the 1980's. His *Dracula: The Novel and the Legend*, 1985, and *The Origins of Dracula: The Background to Bram Stoker's Gothic Masterpiece*, 1987, explored the folkloric and historical backgrounds of the novel and the development of the vampire legend in Europe; the latter also provided readers with excerpts from Stoker's original print sources for the novel. More recently, Elizabeth Miller has added three important studies: *Reflections on Dracula*, 1997; *Dracula: The Shade and the Shadow*, 1998; and *Dracula: Sense and Nonsense*, 2000.

All of these works draw attention to the Germanic influences on Stoker. McNally and Florescu list among their primary sources two pamphlets printed in German: *Die Geschicht Dracole Waide*, 1488, and *Ein wunderlich und erschroliche Hystorie*, 1491. Leatherdale writes

> Abetted by the early labours of their academic countrymen, it was the poets of Germany who first realized the potential of the vampire, and who transported the undead from Church-dominated superstition into the respectable channels of verse [*Dracula: The Novel and the Legend* 46].

Miller's *Dracula: The Shade and the Shadow*, a critical anthology of papers presented at "Dracula 97," a centenary celebration held in Los Angeles in August 1997, dedicates an entire section to "Dracula and the Germans." Up to now, however, scant attention has been paid to possible Russian influences on the author and his novels. McNally and Florescu include a translation of a fifteenth century "Story about Dracula" while Leatherdale traces the derivation of the term vampire "from the Magyar *vampir* and Slavic derivatives: *vapir* in Bulgaria, *upir* in Russia" (*Dracula: The Novel and the Legend* 20). Miller's collection contains but one entry suggesting a Russian connection, my own essay "'With the Unspeakables': Dracula and Russophobia — Tourism, Racism and Imperialism," the essay out of which this book developed.

Growing out of doctoral research initiated at Georgia State University, this volume attempts to establish a clear link between the anti–Russian sentiments prevalent in nineteenth century England and Stoker's two tales of vampires, *Dracula*, 1897, and *The Lady of the Shroud*, 1909. That hostility toward Russia animated both British public and governmental discourse in the era has been demonstrated by John Howes Gleason in his 1950 book *The Origins of Russophobia in Great Britain: A Study of the Interaction of Policy and Opinion*. Following Gleason's lead, this work examines how Russophobia was manifested in Victorian popular culture, politics, and foreign policy. It traces the course of Russophobia from its inception in the eighteenth century, through the Crimean War of 1854–1856, and up to World War I. Relying on Stoker's own fiction and non-fiction writings and those of his friends, family, and contemporaries, it argues that Stoker lived in a milieu rich in antagonism toward Russia and that his novels about vampires exhibit the symptoms of this worldview.

This work would not have been possible without access to the resources of institutions in the United States, Britain, and Ireland. For print sources, I am indebted to the William Pullen Library at Georgia State University, the Main Library at the University of Georgia, the Horace W. Sturgis Library at Kennesaw State University, the Robert W. Woodruff Library and the Pitts Theology Library at Emory University, the Francis A. Countway Library of Medicine at Harvard Medical School, and the James E. Walker Library at Middle Tennessee State University. Illustrations were provided by the National Library of Ireland, the British Library, the Royal Collection, the Manchester City Galleries, the National Geographic Society, and the *Punch* Cartoon Library.

A number of colleagues and students also played instrumental roles in this project. Elizabeth Miller kindly offered guidance and encouragement from the very outset. Nick Roberts at the *Punch* Cartoon Library proved particularly helpful in locating and acquiring the bulk of the illustrations in the book. Paul Schmidt, Randy Malamud, William Sessions, and Tom McHanney mentored me through early drafts during my doctoral studies at Georgia State University. Bill Connelly, David Lavery, and Larry

Mapp, colleagues in the English department at Middle Tennessee State University, graciously gave of themselves, helping me secure release time for writing, reading and offering comments on various pieces of the larger manuscript, and providing computer assistance. Gaylord Brewer, another colleague in the department, kindly gave permission for use of his poem "Vampire Western," taken from his 1999 collection *Devilfish*, published by Red Hen Press of Los Angeles. Reuben Kyle, professor of economics at Middle Tennessee State University, brought to my attention print sources documenting a personal connection between Stoker and Rudyard Kipling. The Creative Activity and Research Committee at Middle Tennessee State University saw fit to grant me release time on two separate occasions and to grant a substantial monetary award to help defray the cost of the illustrations included herein.

Four students at Middle Tennessee State University also performed tasks essential to the completion of the manuscript. Jeremy Brown sorted through dozens of nineteenth century illustrations and determined how best to acquire them for publication. Mary Tarsi logged countless hours typing and organizing passages from the books and articles cited herein. Stan Williams identified and recorded the relevant works of Rudyard Kipling. Quan Mark Ha provided invaluable assistant indexing. Without their tireless efforts, this project might well never have reached fruition.

# Introduction

In Thomas Pynchon's novel *V.*, an elaborate array of English intelligence operatives are employed in safeguarding England's colonies and commercial interests in Africa and the Middle East just prior to the outbreak of World War I. Constrained by the demands of what they euphemistically term the "Situation," these agents must live the lives of perpetual tourists. Thus, Sidney Stencil, one of their number, envisions himself stepping "into Baedeker land" on each mission, becoming a "sort of vagrant who exists ... entirely within the Baedeker world — as much a feature of the topography as the other automata: waiters, porters, cabmen, clerks," a party to "an almost perfectly arranged tourist-state" (59). Unlike holiday travelers, however, Stencil has a much more vested, permanent interest in the distant lands he visits. As one of his colleagues suggests, while simple voyeurism "sends English reeling all over the globe in the mad dances called Cook's tours" so as to see "the skin of a place," those pursuing the *Situation* "want its heart" (188). In a way, then, Pynchon's novel can be read as something of a travelogue, as a document that not merely notes sites of interest and affordable accommodations, but one that also describes loci of political intrigue, places where empires collide.

I would argue that Bram Stoker's novels *Dracula* and *The Lady of the Shroud* may likewise be read as political, imperial travelogues.[1] Stephen Arata has suggested as much about *Dracula*, interpreting the novel as a "travel narrative [which] clearly displays aspects of imperial ideology" (626). Taken as what Arata terms an "Occidental Tourist," Dracula makes preparations not just for a sojourn in England, but rather for a permanent residence there. In Arata's view, the Count is an invader who enacts a "reverse colonization" (623) or what Carol Senf denotes as "a kind of reverse imperialism, the threat of the primitive trying to colonize the civilized world"

("Face in the Mirror" 97). Although I concur with Arata and Senf, I would argue that *Dracula* is much more than merely a manifestation of Victorian fears of invasion by generalized primitives from England's far-flung colonies.

Specifically, I contend that in *Dracula* the Eastern menace facing England should be read as Russia, England's greatest imperial rival of the nineteenth century, and her hereditary allies amongst the Slavic peoples of the Balkans.[2] In the groundbreaking 1950 study *The Genesis of Russophobia in Great Britain*, John Howes Gleason has argued that early on in the nineteenth century the English public developed "an antipathy toward Russia which soon became the most pronounced and enduring element on the national outlook on the world abroad" (1). Spurred on by imperial rivalry in the Near East and Central Asia, Russophobia, Gleason contends, was a defining feature of English foreign policy and military planning, eventuating in the ill-fated Crimean War of 1854–1856. Russophobia would continue to influence the English worldview well into the twentieth century.[3]

Responding to Russia's challenge to English hegemony, Bram Stoker both illustrates the threat and fictionalizes a remedy to the danger it poses to the nation. In doing so, Stoker engages in what David Glover, drawing on the work of Jean-Jacques Lecercle, terms a type of myth making that "should be read as a species of ideology which provides an imaginary solution to real and insoluble contradictions" (*Vampires, Mummies, and Liberals* 138). Lecercle, writes Glover,

> argues that *Dracula* belonged to ("il refletait") a difficult historical moment in which the beginning of Britain's decline was signaled politically by setbacks during the First Boer War (1880–81), economically by the Great Depression between 1873 and 1896, and culturally by a pervasive sense that the high point of the Victorian era was now past and the signs of decadence were plainly visible for anyone to see [139].

Russian imperial expansion presented real "insoluble contradictions" to the maintenance of the empire and English imperial designs in the East, and Bram Stoker offered an "imaginary solution" to them. *Dracula* performs the salubrious feat of ameliorating the stain on England's reputation eventuating from her problematic incursion against Russia in the Crimean War and of dissipating the anxieties engendered by Russia's designs on British India and Central Asia. It does so by portraying a force of imperial warriors pledged to England who defeat a primitive Eastern invader, pursue him to his homeland, and destroy him on his native soil. Furthermore, Stoker's next vampire novel, *The Lady of the Shroud*, continues the imperial narrative begun in *Dracula*; in this instance, a group of English imperial warriors establish a permanent English colony and a Slavic client state in the Balkans. Not only does this move frustrate Russian ambitions in the region, but it also provides England a means of blocking advances in the Balkans by Turkey, who at the time of the novel was aligned with England's great rival after the turn of the century, Germany.

In my estimation, therefore, these novels are what Edward Said terms "cultural forms [...] important in the formation of imperial attitudes, references, and experiences" (*Culture and Imperialism* xii); this study will examine how they echo imperial attitudes toward Russia and the Balkans. It will further show that these attitudes were formulated in no small part by the political and cultural environment that spawned the Crimean War, especially accounts of Russia and the war in the popular press; the propaganda the war engendered; and the representations of the war on the stage and in painting. Moreover, *Dracula* and *The Lady of the Shroud* will be shown to reflect the social changes brought about by the war and the racial discourse surrounding the Russian and Balkan Jews who flooded England toward the end of the nineteenth century.

Travel literature also played a significant role in fomenting Russophobia among nineteenth century English readers. Paul Fussell, in his 1980 study *Abroad: British Literary Traveling Between the Wars*, posits that travel and travel writing are uniquely English pursuits, a consequence of England's early "industrialization and urbanization":

> The tedium of industrial work made "vacation" necessary, while the unwholesomeness of England's great soot-caked cities made any place abroad, by flagrant contrast, appear almost mystically salubrious, especially in an age of rampant tuberculosis [73].

Aside from escaping the blight of industrialization and urbanization, England's "geographical and linguistic insularity" and "two centuries of wildly successful emperialism" (74) made travel an appealing pastime to the English citizenry. Fussell further argues that imperial success bred a pronounced "national snobbery," culminating in a "half-disdainful awareness of outsiders" (74). Some years later, in his anthology *The Norton Book of Travel*, Fussell writes, "Successful travel literature mediates between two poles: The individual physical things it describes, on the one hand, and the larger theme that it is 'about' on the other" (126). Reflecting Fussell's position, Casey Blanton suggests that

> What travel books are "about" is the interplay between observer and observed, between a traveler's own philosophical biases and preconceptions and the tests those ideas and prejudices endure as a result of the journey [5].

Contemporary studies of nineteenth century travel literature suggest that, for the most part, travel did little to shake the prejudices and biases of English writers and readers.

Amanda Gilroy, for one, echoes Fussell's postulation that a "national snobbery" informed travel writing in England in the 1800s. She asserts that "the circulating discourse of travel secured self-identity and reaffirmed existing convictions of cultural superiority for the authors and the readers" alike (1). Mary Louise Pratt conceives of such solipsistic travel literature as integral to the growth of imperial states in Europe. Her interest is in

> how travel books by Europeans about non-European parts of the world went (and go) about creating the "domestic subject" of Euroimperialism; how they have engaged metropolitan reading publics with (or to) expansionist enterprises whose material benefits accrued mainly to the very few [4].

Pratt sees two events in 1735, the publication of Carl Linnaeus's *Systema Naturae* and the first major European scientific attempt to graph the exact shape of the earth, as essential in forming what she terms the Eurocentric "hegemonic reflex," whereby "European elites' understanding of themselves and their relation to the rest of the globe" articulates cultural superiority by describing and objectifying non-Europeans solely from the vantage point of European rationalist and scientific perspectives (15).

Jaundiced views of Eastern Europe penned by English travel writers certainly affected Bram Stoker. As Clive Leatherdale has established in *The Origins of Dracula*, Stoker, who traveled widely in the United States and Europe, drew extensively on such travelogues as William Wilkinson's *An Account of the Principalities of Wallachia and Moldavia: with various Political Observations Relating to Them* and Major E. C. Johnson's *On the Track of the Crescent: Erratic Notes from the Piraeus to Pesth* in his preparations for writing *Dracula*. Of perhaps more significance, however, is a little known travelogue entitled *With the Unspeakables*,[4] written by George Stoker with his older brother Bram's assistance. An account of George's travels and activities during the Russo-Turkish War of 1877–1878, the book focused Bram's attention on Russia as a great threat to English imperial hegemony; reinforced the negative stereotypes about Jews, Russians, and Slavs he held in common with the general public; and possibly provided him with the physical descriptions for the setting in both *Dracula* and *The Lady of the Shroud*.

The political and military struggle between England and Russia for control of Central Asia — the "Great Game" as it came to be known — further agitated English anxieties about Russia and provided another possible source for Stoker's decision to locate a threat to English imperial hegemony in Eastern Europe. During Stoker's lifetime, a number of studies about the menace that Russian incursions in Central Asia posed to India were published. Many of the authors of these studies later went on speaking tours to promote their works, frequently sharing their alarm about Russian intentions with English audiences. One writer in particular, Arminius Vambery, was a personal acquaintance of Stoker's. He not only is mentioned in Stoker's memoir of the great actor Henry Irving, but he also appears as a character in *Dracula*. Reinforcing and complementing these voices of alarm raised about the Russian threat in Central Asia, Rudyard Kipling, an acquaintance of Stoker's, both in verse and fiction portrayed Russia as hostile to England.

It should come as no surprise that Stoker enunciates English imperial desires and fears. Arata even goes so far as to suggest that a "concern with questions of empire and colonization can be found in nearly all of Stoker's fiction" (625). As an Anglo-Irishman, the son of a reputable, if not prosperous, middle-class Protestant bureaucrat, a member of a minority descended from the original English colonizers of an "unwashed" multitude of Irish Catholics, Stoker was himself an appropriated agent of the imperial dominion of England.[5] Cannon Schmitt argues that Stoker, "a human legacy of England's seven hundred years of colonial involvement in Ireland" (34), expresses in *Dracula* Anglo-Irish anxieties at the end of the century:

> What frightens the Anglo-Irish in the 1890s is the specter of absorption. The dominance enjoyed by the Protestant Ascendancy was based in control of Irish land, which they had been given in the Williamite and Cromwellian settlements of the seventeenth century, and in the position held by the Anglican Church as the established Church of Ireland. Both sites of privilege, land and church, came under assault in the last thirty years of the nineteenth century [35].

Stoker, who was at best ambivalent[6] to the idea of Home Rule for Ireland, thus exposes in his narratives distress over the apparent dismantling of England's colonial empire and the colonist's apprehension at losing the plantation. The descriptions he read in George's book of despondent and mournful Turkish colonists forced by rebellious Bulgarians and Russian troops to leave behind their farms and homes in Bulgaria must have therefore filled him with a similar sense of distrust and loathing for Russia as he felt for those in Ireland who promoted independence from England.

Toward the end of the nineteenth century, England addressed challenges to her empire in two ways. One, toward the end of the nineteenth century, was a call for "unlimited expansion as justified by racial superiority, manifest destiny and divine mission" (qtd. in Garnett 33). In other words, the nation could secure its imperial status and commercial vigor by constantly enlarging its colonial holdings. Cecil Rhodes best summed up this view when he remarked that "History has taught me that expansion is everything" (qtd. in Garnett 37). Such an attitude resulted in expeditionary campaigns in the Sudan and Egypt at about the same time as the publication of *Dracula*.

However, expansion came at the cost of grievous losses in men, materiel, and revenues. And, even more alarming, it threatened "widespread armed conflict among European nations over territorial possessions" (Schmitt 30). England had learned from the Crimean War that conflicts between imperial superpowers were not only ruinous, but more often than not, they also yielded few tangible gains, if any. Although the Treaty of Paris, signed on 15 April 1856, ended the hostilities in the Crimea and ostensibly prohibited Russia from maintaining a naval presence in the Black Sea, seemingly fulfilling England's chief ambition in waging the war, by 1878, the year of the publication of George Stoker's travelogue *With the Unspeakables*, Russia had reclaimed all territorial losses, renewed its war with Turkey, and returned to the Black Sea (Norman Rich 197–199).

In practical terms, one of the costliest wars in English history had resulted in nothing better than a stalemate and at worst a defeat of England's imperial designs in the Balkans and Black Sea region. Faced with such obstacles to continued expansion of the empire in a world more and more divided into competing spheres of colonial domination, Victorian imperial desire had to be channeled into less problematic arenas. As Patrick Brantlinger suggests, these desires found expression in the "Imperial Gothic" fiction of the late nineteenth century (227). Imperial Gothic, as defined by Brantlinger, shares many qualities with what Kathleen Spencer identifies as "the 'romance revival' of the 1880s and 1890s— more explicitly, the species of romance called 'the fantastic'" (198). To Brantlinger, such works as *The War of the Worlds* and *Dracula* express "anxieties about the waning of opportunities for heroic adventure," anxieties which led writers like Wells and Stoker to seek such opportunities "in the unreal world of romance, dreams, and imagination" (239). As Nicholas Daly contends, the romance revival also had a nationalist dimension. He suggests that the renewed interest in the romance and the gothic in the late nineteenth century comes about in reaction to the rise of continental realism, which "was very often represented as essentially a noxious weed of foreign growth [...] imported into Britain by American expatriates like James and Howells" [17].

The romance, unlike the works of French and American realism, was seen to have "links to [ ... ] a grand tradition of native British fiction" (Daly 17). Moreover, late Victorian romance fiction, unlike its counterpart, eighteenth century gothic fiction, was viewed as an essentially masculinist enterprise:

> If the romance offered an alternative to unhealthy foreign realism, it was also welcomed as putting an end to the rule of the home-grown realism of the domestic novel. Again, the romance was presented as restoring the manhood of British fiction, too long tied to the apron strings of the domestic novel [19].

Operating much as "a narrative dream-machine" the romance worked "to satisfy the reader's 'nameless longings,'" in this instance for an imagined loss of male control in both the artistic and domestic spheres. In an era when the emergence of what came to be known as the New Woman threatened the status quo, fiction offered a soothing balm. The fates of the principal female characters in *Dracula* and *The Lady of the Shroud* attest to Stoker's personal anxieties about this emerging threat to male hegemony.

Likewise, such works helped to palliate anxieties spawned by imperial rivals to English hegemony in Asia and Africa. Robert Mighall argues that the "'Gothic,' by definition is about history and geography"(xiv). As a literary trope, the term gothic reinforces cultural and regional prejudices directed against a series of ostensibly lesser peoples and cultures. Originally, gothic "denoted to the Classical mind Germanic uncouthness and unreason" (xvii), but over time, the term came to signify an ever expanding and changing host of despicable others:

> Long after [the Goths] disappeared into the ethnic melting-pots of the northern Mediterranean, their fearful name was taken and used to prop up one side of that set of cultural oppositions by which the Renaissance and its heirs defined and claimed possession of European civilization: Northern versus Southern, Gothic versus Graeco-Roman, Dark Ages versus the Age of Enlightenment, medieval versus modern, barbarity versus civility, superstition versus Reason. As revised by northern Protestant nationalisms, the "map" of these countries would be turned about so that the southern Catholic cultures could be represented as the barbarously superstitious antagonist; but the essential shape of the polarity would persist as the founding mythology of modern Europe and its internal tensions [xvii].

Even though nations and peoples targeted as gothic shifted over time, in every case the term applied to those deemed superannuated.[7] Mighall therefore situates the gothicness of Dracula in "the fact that the vampire aristocrat is four hundred years old, and thus out of place in nineteenth century London" (xx). As will be shown later, Russia's anachronistic ties to autocracy and feudalism made it an object of ridicule to western Europeans of the period.

Another feature of Imperial Gothic fiction is an interest in occultism and spiritualism. This interest had a twofold purpose:

> Not only were occultists seeking proofs of immortality and of a spiritual realm above or beneath the material one, they were also seeking adventure. The fantasy element in such adventure seeking is its most obvious feature, as it is also in the literary turn away from realism to romanticism [Brantlinger 240].

In a world where imperial expansion and colonization are limited by superpower politics, tourism replaces adventure, and the "Briton clutching a

Baedeker or a Cook's travel guide" (238) displaces the imperial explorer and colonizer. Only through the "subjectivism of [Imperial] Gothic romance" (245) can the late Victorian experience the adventure of his colonial predecessors. Thus for Brantlinger, "Africa, India, and the other dark places of the earth become a terrain upon which the political unconscious of imperialism maps its own desires, its own fantastic longitudes and latitudes" (246). As I hope to demonstrate, Stoker "maps" Imperial Gothic fantasies about Russia and the Balkans in both *Dracula* and *The Lady of the Shroud*. In both novels, English tourism and spiritualism mask a colonial agenda in a corner of the real world outside the empire's grasp.

As has already been noted, Stoker's Anglo-Irish heritage made him particularly sensitive to the position of the Protestant Irish Ascendancy. No less influential on Stoker's artistic temperament and political worldview, however, was a childhood steeped in romantic fantasies and gothic horrors. In her biography of Stoker, Barbara Belford argues that the genesis of Stoker's interest "in the gothic tradition, in the preternatural, can be traced back to these early years" (15). Stoker was born in 1847 into a world of blight and pestilence during one of "the nightmare years" of the Irish potato famine (Belford 17). Almost appropriately, he was a sickly child who did not even walk until age seven. In the course of his long illness, Stoker passed his most pleasant hours listening to his mother's many ghoulish tales about the plague[8] that had decimated County Sligo in her infancy—events he later recounted in the story "The Invisible Giant"—to her retelling of Irish myths, and to his father's accounts of his English forefather's military exploits.

Later in the course of his formal education, especially at Trinity College in Dublin, he evinced a particular interest in such gothicized romantic works as Goethe's "The Bride of Corinth," Coleridge's "The Rime of the Ancient Mariner," and in the poetry of Shelley, Byron, and Keats. Keats' "La Belle Dame sans Merci" and Irish tales "of the succubus, who seduces young men in their sleep, and her male counterpart, the incubus," certainly gave him models for Lucy Westenra and Dracula (Belford 257–258). Another clear sign of his romantic sensibilities and tastes was his early championing of Walt Whitman. Rumor has it that Stoker first encountered the American bard when he picked up an edition of *Leaves of Grass* that a fellow student had contemptuously flung away. After a first reading, Stoker was enthralled, so much so that he had the temerity to write impassioned letters to Whitman, thus beginning a correspondence that would lead to a close friendship between the two and to Stoker's vociferous defense of Whitman before a gathering of prominent intellectuals at the Fortnightly Club in Dublin (Belford 39–45). So close was his affection for Whitman that in the thinking of one critic, Stoker has Dracula speak in the characteristic rhythms of Whitman's poetry, models Dracula after Whitman's physique, and "was also affected by the pervasive death imagery throughout Whitman's poetry" (Perry 30).

My point here is that Stoker came to write *Dracula* and later *The Lady of the Shroud* with an intellectual inclination toward romantic and gothic themes and images and an abiding interest in the occult — he was even rumored to have practiced ritualistic magic as a member of the secret society the Hermetic Order of the Golden Dawn in the late 1880s (Bedford 211–213). Combined with his allegiance to English imperial hegemony and his sense as a late Victorian of the dangers to that hegemony, namely the denial of further colonial acquisitions by superpower politics and the threat of a reverse colonization by the primitive, his penchant for gothic literature and the occult rendered him ideally suited to become a practitioner of "Imperial Gothic" fiction. Stoker's experiences during his years as an acting manager at Henry Irving's Lyceum Theatre reinforced his hostility toward Russia and the Balkans, rendering the region in his mind a fit "terrain upon which the political unconscious of imperialism maps its own desires" (Brantlinger 246).

Shortly after he had established himself at the Lyceum, Stoker married Florence Balcombe. His marriage is one point at which the Crimean War enters his consciousness. His wife, the daughter of Lt. Colonel James Balcombe, late of the Indian colonial army and veteran of the Crimean War, was named for Florence Nightingale (Belford 83–84), a figure who helped to publicize the suffering of British troops in the Crimea and who came to represent the New Woman challenging male economic and political dominance at the time. Moreover, according to Harry Ludlam, the author of the first definitive biography of Stoker, during his courtship of Florence and his subsequent marriage, Stoker was "a ready listener" to the Colonel's tales of the horrific battles of Inkerman, Alma, and Sebastopol in the Crimean campaign (48).

Another point of contact with the Crimean War would certainly have been his conversations with Alfred Lord Tennyson and William Ewart Gladstone. As members of the inner circle of Irving's friends and acquaintances invited to dine in the exclusive Beef Steak Room at the Lyceum, Tennyson and Gladstone spent many an intimate evening at table with Stoker (Belford 130–131). The poet of such stirring patriotic verse as "The Charge of the Light Brigade" and *Maud*[9] and the chancellor of the exchequer in the Aberdeen administration which launched England's entry into the war undoubtedly discussed the war's causes, aims, ends, and the bravery of English arms in Stoker's presence, embedding a seed mixture of noble intentions, military and governmental blunders, Russian savagery and ineptitude, exotic Euro-Asiatic locales, and blunted imperial ambitions in Stoker's fertile imagination. In an episode that may well have given Stoker the inspiration for Dr. Seward and reinforced his impressions of the Crimean War, Stoker had occasion to hear Tennyson reading "The Charge of the Heavy Brigade at Balaclava" on a recorded cylinder in preparations for the staging of Tennyson's *Beckett* at the Lyceum (Belford 232).

When Stoker began to write *Dracula*, then, he came to the story well equipped by heritage, education, literary predilection, and social position to articulate imperial desires and fears in Imperial Gothic fiction. Moreover, he was writing at a time when attitudes toward the Crimean War had softened and, as is so often the case with perspectives many years removed from the actual event, when images of English glory, bravery, and nobility began to supersede earlier images of tragedy and defeat in the collective national imagination. Although English arms could not conclusively defeat Russia or permanently curtail her expansion into Europe and Asia, English fiction could keep the forces of the East at bay and secure the empire. *The Lady of the Shroud*, written some twelve years after *Dracula*, completes the Imperial Gothic fantasy by planting an English colony in the Balkans to permanently block Russia and forestall nascent German expansion.

In a highly revealing passage from his *Personal Reminiscences of Henry Irving* describing a celebration of the 1902 Coronation at the Lyceum, Stoker describes a list of colonial dignitaries paying homage to the new king. What is most striking about this passage is that it makes clear for all to see his devotion to the empire[10] and his jingoism toward "lesser" peoples:

> They were from every part of the world and of every race under the sun. In type and colour they would have illustrated a discourse on ethnology, or craniology. Some were from the centre of wildest Africa, not long come under the dominion of Britain [339].

Like any good practitioner of colonial discourse, Stoker here evidences the nineteenth century notion that racially determined biological features demarcate inferior species, species whose savagery makes them appropriate objects for the civilizing ministrations of English domination.[11] However, in the places where this domination is denied or challenged, imperial Gothic fiction fills the void. Therefore, in *Dracula* and *The Lady of the Shroud* Stoker accomplishes what English imperial strategy and arms could not do: satisfactorily erase the taint of England's failure in the Crimea, curtail Russian expansionism, and block German interests in the Balkans.

Where is the countenance that could burn a village?

Or melt the daughter while her daddy weeps?
Think about the Man Inside, held merely,
you reckon, in stupid mortal clay. And anyway

as the box of native soil is discovered at sunrise
and the last good woman in town marries your brother,
you're above it all, you're really laughing.

From "Vampire Western" by
Gaylord Brewer*

*Reprinted from his collection *Devilfish* (Los Angeles: Red Hen Press, 1999). Used by permission.

# ONE

# Russophobia and the Crimean War

In describing the Vietnam Memorial in Washington, D.C., Stanley Karnow writes

> The names of the dead engraved on the granite record more than lives lost in battle: they represent a sacrifice to a failed crusade, however noble or illusory its motives. In a larger sense they symbolize a faded hope — or perhaps the birth of a new awareness. They bear witness to the end of America's absolute confidence in its moral exclusivity, its military invincibility, its manifest destiny. They are the price, paid in blood and sorrow, for America's awakening to maturity, to the recognition of its limitations [9].

Karnow might well be describing here England's experiences in the Crimean War. England had waged war on Russia for many of the same reasons that America entered, to borrow David Halberstam's apt phrase, the quagmire of Vietnam: to halt Russian imperial expansion, to guarantee the ostensible freedom of a weaker nation, and, most importantly, to protect commercial interests in Asia.[1] The consequences of these wars also bear striking similarities: tactical victories coupled with overall strategic stalemates, rampant inflation, far-reaching social upheavals, and a protracted "cold war" fought between clandestine forces,[2] both local and foreign, operating in border territories separating imperial dominions.

Moreover, the two nations experienced pronouncedly similar social changes. Both witnessed a vocal condemnation of the government that had led the nation to war and a popular demand for the reform of the military establishment that had governed the conduct of the war.[3] New voices, especially those of the commercial middle class and of women, came to dominate political discourse. The two countries likewise saw the influx of waves of immigrants who, rightly or wrongly, were portrayed as parasites, criminals, and disease carriers. Finally, both confronted, toward the end of the centuries during which their respective wars had been waged, what many perceived as cultural and moral degeneration.[4]

Dracula responds to just such fears. More precisely, the novel addresses the anxieties that spawned the Crimean War and those the conflict was thought to have engendered, namely the real and imagined dangers posed by the threat of oriental autocracy to middle-class economics and democracy, by the rise of the New Woman and her challenge to traditional patriarchy, by what were considered racially suspect Eastern European immigrants, and by the complexities of maintaining a commercial empire in an era of ever-contentious imperial competition. Furthermore, Dracula performs the salubrious duty, as have many revisionist appraisals of America's involvement in Vietnam, of assuaging the nation's sense of loss and of bolstering national pride.[5] For all of these reasons, Dracula should be seen as a reflection of the Russophobia and superpower politics that led England into the Crimean War and of the social changes resulting from the war.

When the Crimean War began in 1854, Stoker was seven years old. At that age, as his first photograph suggests (Belford 16), he was a precocious lad who was, according to Belford, keenly aware of the "Protestant bourgeoisie" fears and prejudices of his caste (23). Through his parents' stories, their conversations with friends and neighbors, and what he saw and read in the press, especially the illustrated newspapers and journals, he would have learned that Russia threatened his personal safety and freedom and that England was engaged in a holy crusade against almost inhuman forces of barbarism and absolutism. Moreover, his mother's accounts of the cholera epidemic of 1832 and his many hours with uncle William Stoker, a physician at Dublin's Fever Hospital (Belford 18–19), would have rendered the newspaper reports of the ravages of cholera, typhus, and dysentery on the troops in the Crimea all the more real and frightening for Stoker. Even well after the war, an adult Stoker would still encounter its images in political tracts and the arts. In 1874, for example, the Royal Academy prominently exhibited a Crimean War painting, and paintings of the war were popular well into the 1880s (Lalumia 136).

The Crimean War reminded late Victorians of the limitations of their commercial and military power, of their precarious place in a world of hostile imperial forces. Their culture's art and literature offered, however, a refuge from such anxieties. Thus in the works of authors like Wells and Stoker, English courage, intelligence, righteousness, and technology defeat whatever perils or enemies confront the nation. In the case of Dracula, that enemy is a sinister, monstrous, and insatiable denizen of Slavic Eastern Europe aligned to Russia. As such, Dracula articulates anxieties consequent to a long-standing, generalized Russophobia and to the Crimean War it helped to foment. To fully understand how widespread and pervasive anti–Russian sentiments were in England during Stoker's lifetime and how susceptible he would have been to a generalized anti–Russian hostility permeating English society, at this point it is helpful to review the genesis and course of the Russophobia that influenced Stoker's fiction.

## The Roots of War

The historical origins of the conflict between Russia and England reside in large part in two treaties ending wars between Russia and Turkey. The first, signed in the Bulgarian village of Kutchuk-Kainardji on 21 July 1774, resolved to Russia's distinct advantage a war initiated by Turkey in 1768. Its provisions allowed Russia to annex "the Kuban and Terek areas in the Black Sea steppe which had hitherto, as parts of the vassal Khanate of Crimea, been under Turkish suzerainty," thus gaining Russia the right to unmolested navigation in the Black Sea and the right to build an Orthodox church in Constantinople (M. S. Anderson xi). Moreover, the treaty contained provisions for Russia to intercede on the behalf of Ottoman Christians, clauses that David Goldfrank terms "a potential timebomb" (42). Prominent among these was Russia's prerogative "to petition on behalf of the Romanian Principalities," namely Orthodox Moldavia and Wallachia,[6] notably Dracula's homeland, territories that Catherine the Great dreamed would one day comprise the kingdom of Dacia and, with the collapse of Turkey, the core of a new Byzantine Empire (Goldfrank 42).

Further consolidating Russian influence in Moldavia and Wallachia was the Treaty of Adrianople signed in 1829. The treaty enlarged Russia's political and commercial rights in the Black Sea and specified that the rulers of the Romanian Principalities, the Hospodars, were to be "Romanians appointed for life by the Sultan with Russian approval and have full power within the confines of established treaties and charters" (Goldfrank 45). An entrenched Russian presence in Romania spelled certain trouble for Turkey and her Balkan possessions, for it promoted the growth of nationalism and, even more ominous, Panslavism, which carried the "implication of Russian dominance of east-central and south-eastern Europe" (M. S. Anderson 150).

For England, this expansion of the Russian Empire posed a grave threat. According to John Howes Gleason,

> The decline and incipient disintegration of the Ottoman empire induced apprehension lest the tsar be the chief heir of the sick man of Europe [Turkey]. It was feared in England that Russia's control of the Straits would endanger Britain's Levantine trade, her naval power in the Mediterranean, and her position in India. It might even upset the European balance of power [2].

English fears were not unfounded. Between 1716 and 1718, Peter the Great established fortifications in Central Asia after learning of the existence of gold deposits along the River Oxus and, more importantly, after Russian travelers described for him the riches of India, a land just beyond the deserts and mountains of Central Asia. Peter also recognized, argues Peter Hopkirk, a leading authority on the Great Game, the nineteenth century struggle between Britain and Russia for control of Central Asia, that the wealth of India was

> already being carried away on a massive scale by his European rivals, and by the British in particular. His fertile brain now conceived a plan for getting his hands on both the gold of Central Asia and his share of India's treasure [16].

Peter was to die before accomplishing his plan, but forty years later, Catherine the Great would cast a longing look toward India again.

Inflamed with the same expansionist zeal as her predecessor Peter the Great, Catherine dreamed of wresting Constantinople from Turkish rule so as to "give her fleet access to the Mediterranean, then very much a British lake, from the Black Sea, still very much a Turkish one" (Hopkirk 21). In 1791 she took under consideration a plan to seize control of India. Although she eventually abandoned her designs on India, Catherine did add the Caucasus and the Crimean to the Russian empire, thus gaining a permanent port on the Black Sea. The presence of the Russian navy on the Black Sea alarmed senior officials with the East India Company (Hopkirk 22).

The emerging threat posed by Napoleon shifted English attention away from Russian expansion. However, Russian interest in India continued. In 1808 Alexander I entertained a proposal by Napoleon to divide the Ottoman Empire between them and thence to advance on India via Constantinople and Asia Minor (M. S. Anderson 42–43). But, Napoleon's disastrous invasion of Russia and subsequent defeat at Waterloo by the combined arms of England, Russia,[7] Prussia, and Austria temporarily restored Anglo-Russian amity. But, these good relations were to be short lived. English opposition to Russian dominance in Poland and her growing ties, both military and commercial, with Turkey assured strained relationships during the years leading up to the Crimean War. Thus, according to Goldfrank, ensued

> a rivalry based on the fact that British commercial and imperial expansion, with two loci of power, England and India, as well as commerce with the Americas as a logistical reserve, threatened to carry British influence to most of Russia's borders [48].

Gleason further argues that the political and diplomatic hostility between Russia and England that grew out of this expansion of the Russian empire engendered in England an intense and bitter Russophobia that "was the fruit of competitive ambitions which in the nineteenth century transformed into neighbors in the colonial world two powers hitherto remote" (1). This antipathy hastened, as will be shown, England's entry into the Crimean War and continued to animate government policy and public sentiment into the next century, certainly some years beyond the publication of *Dracula*.

Gleason contends that English fears of Russian military and commercial expansion grew out the spirit of liberalism after the Napoleonic wars, "the intellectual atmosphere in which Romanticism and Utilitarianism flourished" (16). The radical architects of the 1832 Reform Bill, led in large measure by Jeremy Bentham and guided by the principles of Utilitarianism, found "little in the institutions or policies of Russia which could merit [...] approbation" (20), especially "the autocratic regime of Russia — the corrupt judicial system, political secret police, arbitrary and cruel punishments, and serfdom" (22).

Romanticism, Gleason argues, also played a signal part in shaping popular hostility toward Russia. As the works of Blake, Wordsworth, Byron, and Shelley make abundantly clear, the Romantic "condemnation of the restraint which the neoclassical ideal placed upon individual self-expression [...] frequently extended beyond the limits of the arts and became a revolt against authority in general" (22). As Gleason notes,

> the political implications of Romanticism were liberal and the polity of the tsars inevitably must have excited antipathy in the minds of those Englishmen who were sympathetic to the general intellectual currents of the early nineteenth century. The Romantic movement, actually quite in harmony with the English tradition of individual and national freedom, belongs both in its essential and in its incidental character among the factors which disposed Englishmen to condemn Russia. It played a part in the transfer to her of the hostility which France had so long excited [25].

In conjunction with criticisms of monarchial absolutism, Romanticism created a widespread interest in the exotic, the distant,[8] and thereby engendered a "plethora of travel literature" that gave the ordinary English citizen access to the "most inaccessible parts of the world" (22). Furthermore, as Edward Said has suggested, such literature transformed the East, the Orient, into "almost a European invention [...] a place of romance, exotic beings, haunting memories and landscapes, remarkable experiences" (*Orientalism* 1).[9]

Moreover, as Jane Stabler suggests in a recent study of Romantic travel writers, travel abroad, beginning with the emergence in the eighteenth century of the Grand Tour as an element in the formal education of the privileged classes, "provided an opportunity to reflect on the advantages of being English" and to demonstrate "English cultural authority" (225). From this ostensible position of authority, English Romantic travel writers could not help but conceive of the lands they visited except as they related to England, the *sine qua non* of the civilized world, especially to England's "commercial and political interests" (228). In all but rare instances, the country or people being described failed miserably in the comparison.

Saree Makdisi's reading of Shelley's *Alastor* provides a useful explanation for the debasement of native peoples and cultures that was a regular feature of Romantic travelogues. For Makdisi, *Alastor* offers a picture of the East as "a region and a space that did not and does not exist as such, but that had to be endlessly reinvented by its symbiotically related opposite term, 'the West,' during the long and bloody history of imperialism" (240). In the system of Romantic travel writing, the non-western world apparently has no value in and unto itself; it acquires meaning and value only when appropriated by the West:

> This Orient, in other words, is a vacancy and an absence to be filled in (a "land without people," to cite the planners of a later episode in the region's colonial history) to be brought to life by the European, who alone can fulfil its hidden potential and make this symbolic desert "bloom." Unlocking this Orient's potential wealth, both material and figurative, in other words, fundamentally requires the intervention of Europe, without which this wealth would go unappreciated and hence unexploited [246].

One stratagem of appropriation occurs "through the invention and spatial production of a certain version of the Orient as Europe's source of origin ('the birthplace of all that is wise and beautiful')" (248).

Nigel Leask provides a most compelling example of just how this stratagem plays out. He recounts the story of one Francis Wilford, an associate of the Asiatic Society of Bengal and lecturer in Sanskrit at Banares College, India. Starting in 1799, Wilford published a series of articles about Hindu geography and mythology. Most striking was Wilford's attempt "to confirm the historicity of revelation and of the ethnology of Genesis from external sources, namely the records of Hindu (or other pagan) religions" (206–207). In the essay "On the Sacred Isles in the West," Wilford argued that the "source of 'all the fundamental and mysterious transactions of [the Hindu] religion' were none other than the British Isles [...] the remote northern islands of the colonial motherland itself" (212). Wilford further claimed that in Sanskrit texts "the coming of a saviour from the West is often foretold" (qtd. in Leask 213). Summing up Wilford's putative discoveries, later disavowed for having been based on forged documents, Leask describes Wilford's work as "an orientalized (in Edward Said's sense of the word) version of British national and imperial ideology":

In the guise of Hindu "scripture," we have representations of the following national myths: Britain as bearer of the civilising mission to corrupt Asiatic states, and above all the bringer of justice to its colonial subjects, long over-shadowed by Asiatic despotism; British national identity defined by an unwritten ("orally delivered") constitution in contrast to, say, Napoleonic France; an account of the immutability of British political institutions ("este perpetua"), resisting the Polybian cycle of birth, maturity, and decay [213].

In such co-opted Eastern realms, European travelers and travel writers were not only empowered to assume ideological and cultural superiority, but they could also, according to Joseph Boone, "project fantasies of illicit sexuality and unbridled excess" (89).

The first significant appearance of the vampire in English literature, *The Vampyre* in 1818, was written by John Polidori, the personal physician of the great Romantic poet and libertine Lord Byron, while vacationing in Switzerland. The tale, appropriately, foregrounds both tourism and illicit desire. Carol Senf describes the central characters of the story as "young men who set off on the continental Grand Tour together. One is the naïve but honorable narrator while the other, Lord Ruthven, might have been modeled on Mr. B. Lovelace, or any of the other rakes in eighteenth-century literature" (*The Vampire in Nineteenth-Century English Literature* 24). Senf goes on to claim that "Polidori is the first to present the vampire as an aristocratic threat" (34).

Complementing Senf, Robert Morrison and Chris Baldick, editors of *The Vampyre and Other Tales of the Macabre*, assert that

> the significance of Polidori's momentous transformation of the figure of the vampire from bestial ghoul to glamorous aristocrat cannot be fully grasped without recognizing that his Lord Ruthven is really the conventional rakehell or libertine with a few vampire attributes grafted onto him [xix].

According to Morrison and Baldick, *The Vampyre* and the other tales in their collection were thought of at the time as "moral tales" meant to illustrate "the thoughtlessness of the fashionable and dissolute young rake or libertine" (xviii), especially "middle-class resentment against the sexual allure of the noble *roue*" (xiii). Count Dracula is himself an object of middle-class scorn because he shares with Lord Ruthven, his literary kin, the same noble vice: wanton sexual promiscuity. But Dracula was a far more frightening figure than Lord Ruthven to Victorian readers, for he combines in the image of the dissolute aristocratic rakehell the threat that Arata has enunciated as "reverse colonization." In other words, Dracula threatens to do to England what the English have done to others in the name of tourism and imperialism.

*Dracula*, therefore, creates a lasting image of Eastern Europe as an exotic, yet terrifying realm and place of imperial intrigue. From the many reports of diplomatic and private visitors to the East, the general public formed ideas "about Russia and her potential challenge to the political and economic position of Great Britain," ideas advanced by "men who suspected before they visited that region, that Russia was a serious threat" (Gleason 24).

## Russophobia and the Popular Press

The twin forces of liberalism and Romanticism coalesced to form a powerful image of Russia as a locus of social danger, corruption, and tyranny. Legitimizing and furthering hostile attitudes toward Russia and her Eastern European colleague states were the popular press. In the twenty odd years leading up to the Crimean War, the "suspicion and fear of Russia [...] vigorously stoked by journalists" (Norman Rich 3) became markedly influential throughout English society. This universalization of Russophobia was especially true after 1830 when, as Patricia Anderson demonstrates, the readership of the popular press expanded as never before to include both the middle and working classes, not just the monied and educated elite. Advances in printing technology had much to do with this growth in the reading population, for the

> introduction into England of mechanized paper-making (1803), the steam-powered press (1814), and multiple-cylinder stereotype printing (1827) permitted the low-cost, high-speed dissemination of the printed word. The same technological advances also made possible the profitable, high-quality mass reproduction of diverse imagery. As a result, illustrations of art, nature, technical processes, famous people, foreign lands, and many other subjects for the first time became widely available and affordable [2].

Moreover, reductions in the newspaper tax and the paper duty during the 1830s gave a wide audience of readers access to a broad range of affordable periodical literature (9).

Aside from considerations of cost, the most important factor contributing to increased readership was the "increasingly pictorial character" of most of this literature, a fact that "represented a cultural break with the past, for it demanded neither a formal education nor even basic literacy" (2–3). Thus the whole citizenry, the gentry through the lowest paid semi-illiterate worker, could be made aware of recent domestic and foreign events. Even more significant is the fact that middle and working class readers could be more easily swayed by the opinions of commercial and governmental leaders, for low cost newspapers and periodicals "were among the many cultural forms and processes through which the economically and politically powerful members of society [...] exercised their social, moral, and intellectual leadership" (5).

Kingsley Martin has shown how effectively Victorian politicians, particularly Henry John Temple, Viscount Palmerston, lord of the admiralty, secretary of war, foreign secretary, home secretary, prime minister during the Crimean War, and a committed Russophobe, used the press to whip up anti–Russian feelings and to portray the impending war with Russia "as a struggle for democracy against tyranny," fostering the impression that a war in support of Islamic Turkey was really "'a war for Christianity'" and, therefore, "a just war" (20). Though an aristocrat and a long-standing member of the inner most circles of parliament, Palmerston broke ranks with his class and political cronies by making personal appeals to the public through the popular press (56). In the manner of contemporary politicians, Palmerston

> never missed an opportunity of appearing to advantage in a daily paper. Every political group employed some newspaper to represent its point of view, and even on occasion, to make official statements on its behalf, but Palmerston was probably the first British statesman who deliberately ingratiated himself with papers of all shades of opinion [55].

More so than any other politician of his time, Palmerston understood, Martin argues, "that the English were not really interested in foreign politics but in individuals" and that visual images and tropes appealed to a broad public (53). Thus he commonly described himself and his actions in the language of sport, especially that of boxing. For example, shortly after the coup d'etat by Napoleon III, he said that "'I have been so busy ... fighting my battle with France that I have been obliged to put off for a time taking up my skirmish with Russia'" (qtd. in Martin 53). At a later time when circumstances called for a less bellicose posture (France and Russia were negotiating with Turkey over the protection of Ottoman Christians) he once again made use of boxing imagery, referring to himself as the "'judicious bottle-holder'" (qtd. in Martin 54). *Punch* magazine quickly picked up on the remark and published a sketch of Palmerston in a pub decorated with pictures of boxing matches. At the tables sit representations of the parties engaged in the dispute. Palmerston stands in the foreground in a jaunty pose, his hat rakishly cocked over one eye, a straw in his mouth, a rock labelled PROTOCOL held in his right hand, and his left thumb extended derisively toward those seated. The caption reads, "THE 'JUDICIOUS BOTTLE-HOLDER;' OR, DOWNING STREET PET. 'BLESS YOU! IT'S ALL CHAFF—WON'T COME TO A FIGHT. OLD NICK'S GOT NO CONSTITUTION—AND THEN I'M BOTTLE-HOLDER ON T'OTHER SIDE, TOO!'" It is important to note here that Palmerston directs his derisive remarks specifically at Czar Nicholas, "Old Nick."

# THE "JUDICIOUS BOTTLE-HOLDER;"
## Or, Downing Street Pet.

" BLESS YOU! IT'S ALL CHAFF—WON'T COME TO A FIGHT. OLD NICK'S GOT NO CONSTITOOTION—AND THEN I'M
BOTTLE-HOLDER ON T' OTHER SIDE, TOO! "

Lord Palmerston, prime minister during Crimean War, was one of the first
English politicians to appeal to the masses through the popular press, often
allowing himself to be depicted engaged in sporting events, especially boxing,
to sway public opinion. (*Punch*, Vol. 21, July–December 1851. *Punch* Cartoon
Library.)

As Anglo-Russian relations took a decided turn for the worse at mid century, *Punch* sketches graphically projected staunchly anti–Russian sentiments such as those held by Palmerston. Thus shortly before England's invasion of the Crimea, *Punch* published a sketch entitled "SAINT NICHOLAS OF RUSSIA." In this portrayal, the czar sits in state, but implements of war have been substituted for his usual regalia. Instead of a scepter,

## SAINT NICHOLAS OF RUSSIA.

In a typical example of renderings of the czar in the Russophobic press just prior to the outbreak of the Crimean War, Nicholas is depicted both as a military menace and something of a buffoon. (*Punch*, Vol. 26, January–June 1854. *Punch* Cartoon Library.)

he holds in one hand a ramrod while in the other he holds a spear. In place of a crown rests a helmet fashioned from a mortar, and about his head is an aureole made up of bayonets rather than beams of light. Finally, he sits upon a pile of cannon balls rather than a throne. A *Punch* poem from an earlier issue captures the essence of the sketch, emphasizing the tyranny of the czar, who exercises absolute power in Russia by means of military might, as opposed to the social liberties enjoyed by English citizens living in a parliamentary monarchy:

> Ordnance the subject multitude for ordinance obey;
> The bullet and the bayonet debate at once allay:
> The mouth is gagg'd, the Press is stopp'd, and we remain alone
> With power our thoughts to utter, or to call our souls our own [qtd. in Olive Anderson 7].

Further emphasizing the tyranny and evil of Russia and the good ministrations of England and her ally France, the illustration "A CONSULTATION ABOUT THE STATE OF TURKEY" depicts Turkey as a gravely ill patient confined to bed. Beside the bed sit representations of John Bull and his French counterpart, here pictured as physicians deliberating upon a suitable therapy. Hovering over the patient is a spectral image of the czar, rendered as a winged skeleton adorned with a plumed helmet and brandishing a cat of nine in one hand while the other hand menacingly reaches out toward the recumbent patient. Significantly, the image of the czar recalls Dracula's associations with bats and death, his ability to emerge from mists and miasmas, and his power to absorb living creatures.

At the onset of hostilities in 1854, the associations of Czar Nicholas with such images became more pronounced. For example, in "A LITTLE GALE," the Russian menace to Europe is expressed metaphorically in an image of the czar, who, much like a threatening storm cloud, drifts from east to west across the face of Europe. The rendering is extraordinarily ghostlike. As the czar floats above the earth, his cloak trails in dark folds, intermingled with the smoke of a blazing torch he brandishes in one hand. Most importantly, however, the shadow the czar casts takes the form of a deformed human skull, its sinister outline threatening to consume western Europe. These representations of the czar as a spectral menace bear striking similarities with the illustration that adorned the cover of Stoker's first collection of stories, *Under the Sunset*. Titled "The Invisible Giant," the illustration, drawn by the Rev. William Fitzgerald, a fellow Trinity graduate (Belford 140), depicts a huge shrouded figure hovering diaphanously over a city, ostensibly Dublin. The city's residents, akin to the innocents of western Europe, go about their daily business unaware of the ghoul about to descend upon them. Belford even argues that *Under the Sunset* signals "the beginning

CONSULTATION ABOUT THE STATE OF TURKEY.

In the run up to the war, this allegorical sketch depicts England and France as physicians overseeing the treatment of a weakened Turkey, called the "sick man of Europe" by Czar Nicholas I. Of particular significance is that the czar emerges from a vapor as a skeletal figure adorned with bat wings, recalling Dracula's associations with mists, bats, and death. (*Punch*, Vol. 25, July–December 1853. *Punch* Cartoon Library.)

of [Stoker's] vampiric motif," that the invisible giant, which "represents the plague," is a "harbinger of the sickness of the Un-Dead" (139).

Other depictions reiterate the image of the czar as a bat, clearly an intentional parody of the dynastic symbol of the Romanovs, the dual-headed

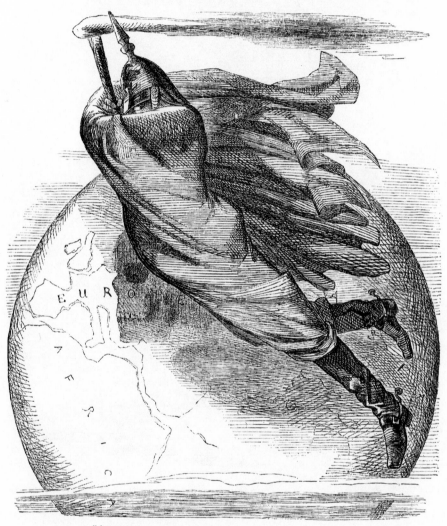

"A LITTLE GALE WILL SOON DISPERSE THAT CLOUD,
AND BLOW IT TO THE SOURCE FROM WHENCE IT CAME."—*Shakspere.*

Russia had been described in the press as "a secret, stealthy mass" threatening England and Europe. Here the czar drifts ghostlike from east to west, casting a ghoulish shadow, sinking western civilization into barbarous darkness. (*Punch*, Vol. 26, January–June 1854. *Punch* Cartoon Library.)

eagle. In "TE DEUM!" the czar sits at a church organ, perhaps providing musical accompaniment to the hymn the title implies. The illustration, however, suggests two possible alternative readings. For one, the title might indicate solipsism, the czar's assumption that he is a god himself, an idea reinforced by the figure's bearing and arrogant smirk. Another equally pos-

"The Invisible Giant," an illustration by the Rev. William Fitzgerald— used on the cover of Stoker's first collection of stories, *Under the Sunset* (second edition, 1882). This shrouded figure, representing a plague, hovers diaphanously over a city, threatening death and contagion, much like the figure of the czar in the *Punch* cartoon "A little gale." Barbara Belford suggests that the figure is a "harbinger of the sickness of the Un-Dead."(National Library of Ireland.)

sible assessment is that the czar is appealing for God's assistance in the war, for he is dressed in military uniform and armed with a sabre and protected by an elegant helmet. Whatever the act being depicted, the important feature of the illustration is that the czar is pictured with wings, unmistakably the wings of a large bat.

The illustration "THE LION, THE EAGLE, AND THE BAT" continues the theme. An allegorical display, the image includes a lion, attired in the uniform of a Royal Navy sailor, engaged in personal combat with a figure dressed in the military costume of the czar but with twin eagle heads surmounted with crowns, rather than a normal human head. Hovering above the fray is a bat, also wearing the same type of crown and holding

This illustration TE DEUM encodes the sinister designs of Czar Nicholas I by portraying him adorned with bat wings. (*Punch*, Vol. 26, January–June 1854. *Punch* Cartoon Library.)

an orb and scepter in its outstretched claws. As imagined, England is winning the fight, for the lion advances upon a wary and presumably retreating Russia, aided in the struggle by the bat. Undoubtedly, the message here is that Russia, governed by a feudal autocrat, is no match for England, a land governed by law, where all citizens, ostensibly, have equal representation in the state and are willing to defend their rights.

Representations of England stress, on the other hand, the nation's valor, courage, righteousness, devotion, and purity. They also gave pictorial substance to Palmerston's convictions, stated before Parliament, "that the real policy of England is to be the champion of justice and right" (qtd. in Martin 54) and that an English subject "should be able to say '*Civis Romanus sum*' and, in whatever land he might be, feel 'Confident that the watchful eye and the strong arm of England will protect him against injustice and wrong'" (qtd. in Martin 61–62). For example, in "RIGHT AGAINST WRONG," a maiden

THE LION, THE EAGLE, AND THE BAT.

*Vide* Æsop's Fables.

This image parodies the dynastic symbol of the Romanovs, a two-headed eagle, and a recurrent association of the czar, like Dracula, with bats. (*Punch*, Vol. 26, January–June 1854. *Punch* Cartoon Library.)

outfitted in Hellenic battle dress, a sword in one hand, a flag in the other, stands next to a stately lion. The two symbols of English prowess and virtue stare menacingly to the viewer's left — perhaps toward an approaching enemy and assuredly toward Russia. Another sketch, entitled "ENGLAND'S WAR VIGIL," demonstrates England's Christian duty in fighting Russia. Attired in medieval armor, a maiden kneels before an altar emblazoned with the crucifix. She extends, ostensibly toward a minister, a sword to be blessed for the upcoming battle. Here is a dramatic contrast to the czar as depicted in "TE DEUM!"

Russophobia elicited equally virulent expressions in print as well as in illustrations. Beginning in the 1820s, a number of pamphlets and books appeared sounding the alarm about the impending danger to England posed by imperial Russian expansion.[10] In 1828, Colonel George de Lacy published

"RIGHT AGAINST WRONG."

Unlike Russia and the czar as portrayed in the popular press, England was equated with both classical and Christian virtues, depicted as a valorous maiden set forth to battle the despotic forces threatening civilization. (*Punch*, Vol. 26, January–June 1854. *Punch* Cartoon Library.)

## ENGLAND'S WAR VIGIL.

Another association of England with classical and Christian virtues, the noble
warrior arrayed against a bestial Eastern menace. (*Punch,* Vol. 26, January–June
1854. *Punch* Cartoon Library.)

*On the Design of Russia,* claiming "that St. Petersburgh was planning, before
very long, to attack India and other British possessions." Soon thereafter,
in 1829, de Lacy published another alarming tract, *On the Practicability of
an Invasion of British India,* arguing that Russia's aim, at first, would not
be to actually invade India, but, rather, "to destabilise British rule there"
by fomenting dissent among the Indian population. This was a fearful
prospect to the East India Company, which feared "trouble with the natives
who so vastly outnumbered the British in their midst" (Hopkirk 116).

David Urquhart, a diplomat, pamphleteer, and editorialist for the *Morning Advertiser*, gained widespread fame prophesying Russian treachery. As an assistant to the British ambassador to the Porte, the seat of the Turkish government in Constantinople, Urquhart had published in 1834 the pamphlet *England, France, Russia, and Turkey*. In this work Urquhart expounded the theory that the underlying purpose for Russian involvement in the Balkans and Turkey was to acquire Constantinople and the Dardanelles. He further contended that a Russian conquest of Turkey held perilous consequences for England:

> The force, the arms, the frontiers, the fortresses, the treasures, and the ships of Turkey now placed against Russia, will be against us—disciplined, combined, and directed by her [Russia] [qtd. in Gleason 174].

In a series of editorials beginning in August of 1853, Urquhart reiterated these themes and bitterly attacked Russia and those in England who opposed a war against Russia. He singled out for attack the members of the Aberdeen administration who wished to partition Turkey with Russia and also *The Times*, which under the editorship of J. T. Delane initially opposed the war. Moreover, Urquhart rendered Russia even more sinister by portraying Turkey innocently as "an earthly paradise. [...] a nation ideally tolerant and enlightened" (Gleason 31–32).

Sir John McNeill joined the fray in 1836 with the appearance of the pamphlet *The Progress and Present Position of Russia in the East*. Originally published anonymously at the urging of Palmerston, it was reissued under the author's name in 1854 with a plea for an immediate invasion of Russia (Small 45–46). Employing statistics to make his argument, McNeill demonstrated the rapacity of the Russian threat, noting that

> between 1689 and 1825, the Russian Empire's population had grown from fifteen million to fifty eight million as a result of conquest of territories previously belonging to Sweden, Turkey, Poland, Persia, and Tartary. The Russian frontier had advanced 700 miles toward Berlin, 500 towards Constantinople, 600 towards Stockholm, and 1000 towards Tehran... [Small 45].

It also contained a large fold out map graphing the expansion of the Russian empire since the beginning of the seventeenth century. In the pamphlet McNeill asserted that

> Every portion of these vast acquisitions has been obtained in opposition to the views the wishes and the interests of England. The dismemberment of Sweden, the partition of Poland, the conquest of the Turkish provinces and those severed from Persia, have all been injurious to British interests [qtd in Hopkirk 163].

McNeill went on to conjecture that should Russia conquer Turkey, "it would gravely threaten Britain's interests in Europe and the Mediterranean, while

Russia's occupation of Persia would very likely seal the fate of India" (Hopkirk 164).

In the run up to the Crimean War and early in the conflict itself, such propaganda became widespread. Also, foreign journalists writing in the English press offered serious analyses of Russia's real threat to European peace and prosperity. For example, Karl Marx, who while living and writing in England served as a European observer for the *New York Tribune*, voiced the opinion that England had a manifest commercial interest in Turkey and the Dardanelles and that Russian control of the Black Sea would only catalyze Russian expansion. As a result,

> the Black Sea would be more properly a Russian lake than even the Lake of Ladoga, situated in its very heart. The resistance of the Caucasians would be starved out at once; Trebizond would be a Russian port; the Danube a Russian river [17].

Should Russia take Constantinople, the Turkish Empire would be severed, thus leaving Macedonia, Thessaly, Albania, and the rest of the Balkans open to Russia (17–18). Convinced that "the foundations of Russian society were those of an Oriental despotism" (Goldfrank 20), Marx too envisioned a war with Russia as necessary to save nascent European and established English democracy:

> The maintenance of Turkish independence, or, in case of a possible dissolution of the Ottoman Empire, the arrest of the Russian scheme of annexation, is a matter of the highest moment. In this instance the interests of the revolutionary Democracy and of England go hand in hand. Neither can permit the czar to make Constantinople one of his capitals [...] [19].

Another notable foreign journalist whose first-hand knowldege of Russian despotism won him widespread public appeal was Louis Kossuth, a Hungarian nationalist who had sought asylum in Turkey when Austria and Russia crushed the Hungarian revolt of 1849. When he immigrated to England in 1851, Kossuth commenced a campaign to raise English awareness of the horrors committed by Russia in Hungary and to reveal the czar as a manifest tyrant and despot (Martin 52). By 1855 he had won the ear of Palmerston and become a regular contributor to the *Sunday Times* and the radical newspaper *The Atlas* (Haraszti 11). Though a highly skilled polemicist, Kossuth had learned English in a very short time, primarily "from reading Shakespeare" (Haraszti 15), and therefore suffered as a journalist from a highly irregular prose style and from a rather unusual command of the English language. Another intriguing connection to *Dracula* here is that Kossuth's English is as non-idiomatic and syntactically flawed as Dr. Van Helsing's, the Dutch leader of Dracula's adversaries.

In his articles, Kossuth relentlessly challenged the folly of those groups urging peace with what he saw as an essentially evil and tyrannical ruler. A piece titled "An Answer to the Christian Appeal of the Society of Friends in Great Britain," for example, refutes the claim that under the Gospel all war is unlawful by arguing that God justifies the use of righteous force:

> Like as we see in Geology, that the work of creation is still going on, hour by hour incessantly, just so we see a revelation of His will incessantly propounded in history. Know ye of one single people delivered from thraldom by some other means than the sword? [...] It is therefore the Lord says "I came not to send peace, but a sword" [84].

When Czar Nicholas I died toward the end of the war in 1855, thus raising hopes for a quick Russian surrender, Kossuth warned in "Nicholas Dead — What Is the Change?" against a hastily arranged peace that failed to arrest Russian expansion in the Balkans and Asia Minor. For Kossuth, the whole of Russian history could be condensed into one phrase, "A continual struggle for power":

> this struggle is clearly divided into two acts. The first: Struggle for national unity; and the second act, still going on: Struggle for the extension of dominion down to the open seas. The first act a preparatory for the second; and the second act an instrumentality of the aim, which, like an immovable thought presides over the history of Russia. And that aim is: Power [108].

Thus the Black Sea, the scene of the present conflict, had to be recognized as only "an intermediary station, not a terminus" in Russia's march to the Mediterranean (109). The Crimean War, then, must be viewed as just another proof of Russia's implacable expansionist designs, designs necessitated by Russian autocracy:

> Russian aristocracy must strive for extending its dominion to the Mediterranean Sea, and thus give to the Russian nation power and preponderance abroad, or else it could not prevent liberty at home. A nation of sixty-five millions must have, and will have, something. Either liberty, or power and glory — there is no help against it, even at St. Petersburg [111].

Once Russia controls the Mediterranean, Kossuth argues, "the world will have a master" (111). Therefore, a negotiated peace is but a fanciful illusion, for to be lasting "it must be gained by the sword" (112).

Before the war Kossuth had won support in most of the leading journals of the day as well as in the cheap Sunday papers, such as the illustrated *Reynold's Weekly*, read by the working class; thus he helped to sway public opinion in all ranks of society (Martin 93). By the fall of 1853, the eve of the war, "there was complete unity in the Press" (135) for aiding Turkey by fighting Russia. Moreover, pro–Turkey and anti–Russian sentiments found expression in numerous public meetings, sermons, pamphlets, broadsides, poems, and popular songs condemning Russian aggression. Some ministers interpreted the war as an approaching Armageddon in which England was "destined to be a great instrument in preparing the world for that unspeakably glorious event" (qtd. in Martin 206–207). The Anglican luminary Charles Kingsley published a pamphlet, *Brave Words to Brave Soldiers*, to assure the troops that they would be "fighting on God's side" (qtd. in Martin 207).

On the other hand, secular writers stressed England's military superiority. For example, in *The Shores of the Black Sea*, Laurence Oliphant contended that the Russian army was no more than an "Imperial plaything" (qtd. in Martin 166). Nevertheless, he called for action lest Russia threaten trade with India. However, England's task would be made easier because "from the Baltic to the Black Sea, from the shores of the Danube to the banks of the Pheisis, extends an indissoluble band of sympathy — a deeply rooted hatred of Russia" (qtd. in Martin 166). A typical popular song of the time reflects such sentiments:

> And did he say the Turk was sick
> And that the Turk should die?
> There's 50,000 Englishmen
> Will know the reason why! [qtd. in Martin 187].

By 1853 "pamphlets, verses, letters, and newspapers throughout the country" had created an image of Russia as a barbarous nation "led by the Tsar and his Scythian hordes"[11] confronted by "the forces of civilization [led] by Palmerston and the troops of Turkey, England, and France" (Martin 199). Inciting public outrage were daily reports of Russian atrocities committed against Turkish subjects. When the war actually came in 1854, the Russian army had acquired monstrous qualities in the public mind.

The illustrators at *Punch*, once again, provided pictorial examples of Russian monstrosity. Early on in the war, the illustration "THE RUSSIAN FRANKENSTEIN AND HIS MONSTER" appeared, reifying the popular notion of the Russian army. The czar, the creator, leads his creation, a hideous creature with an outsized, deformed human head and arms surmounting a torso and legs crafted from artillery pieces, in an assault against England and her allies. Brandishing a sword dripping with blood and a flaming torch, the monster leaves a path of broken bodies and destroyed buildings in its wake. Another illustration from later in the war, titled "RUSSIAN SAVAGES PREPARING TO RECEIVE A FLAG OF TRUCE," further reinforces the image of Russian bestiality. It depicts a group of Russian soldiers luring an English dingy flying a white flag of truce into an ambush. The faces of the Russian troops not only are drawn with malicious grins, denoting the treachery about to unfold, but they also verge on the subhuman in appearance, almost porcine in nature, perhaps a mockery of the Slavic and Asiatic features common among the Russian army. Finally, in a cartoon celebrating Czar Nicholas's death, "'GENERAL FEVRIER' TURNED TRAITOR," the artist ridicules the czar's misplaced

## THE RUSSIAN FRANKENSTEIN AND HIS MONSTER.

Once the war began, the czar and his forces were presented as either subhuman savages (as was the case in Nazi propaganda some ninety years later) or as inhuman monsters unleashed on the world by a mad creator. (*Punch,* Vol. 27, July–December 1854. *Punch* Cartoon Library.)

trust in what he termed Generals January and February, the infamous Russian winter that had defeated Napoleon and would later add to Hitler's failures in Russia. Here, February appears as a human skeleton, dressed in the uniform of the late czar, over whom he stands amidst a driving snowstorm. Clearly, the monster has turned on itself.

RUSSIAN SAVAGES PREPARING TO RECEIVE A FLAG OF TRUCE.

Lacking the virtues of civilized British and French forces in the Crimea, Russian troops were shown to be deceitful and treacherous, even going so far as to fire upon a flag of truce. (*Punch*, Vol. 28, January–June 1855. *Punch* Cartoon Library.)

A contemporary description of the Russian army by the writer T. Pearce captures the popular conception of the Russian forces that took hold among the English public as the war approached:

> Then comes the horrid image of a secret, stealthy, creeping mass, slowly dragging its enormous bulk like some reptile, towards that noble, that devoted band of paladins [qtd. in Martin 199].

Here is an apt description of the battle at the heart of *Dracula* as well, a group of honorable, western-oriented crusaders battling a stealthy, inhuman, shape-shifting Eastern evil to preserve all that is noble and good. However, the actual misfortunes, miscalculations, and horrors of the war itself were soon to dispel English enthusiasm for the war and to shake the very foundations of English society. They would also confirm Russia as a fearsome, implacable enemy and source of anxiety in the public's, and Stoker's, imagination.

## "GENERAL FÉVRIER" TURNED TRAITOR.

**"RUSSIA HAS TWO GENERALS IN WHOM SHE CAN CONFIDE—GENERALS JANVIER AND FÉVRIER,"**—*Speech of the late Emperor of Russia.*

Nicholas I died just as the war was turning against Russia, prompting the wry observation that the Russian winter, which decimated both Napoleon's and Hitler's armies, had turned on the sovereign, perhaps suggesting that duplicity is endemic to the people and the land itself. (*Punch*, Vol. 28, January–June 1855. *Punch* Cartoon Library.)

# "Where Ignorant Armies Clash
by Night": The Crimean War

The event that most inflamed anti–Russian opinion in England was the Russian naval victory over Turkey at Sinope[12] on November 30, 1853 (M. S. Anderson 129–130 and Martin 170). The Russian attack followed a formal declaration of war by Turkey on October 4, an action prompted by Russian investment of Moldavia and Wallachia under the provisions of standing treaties. Nevertheless, just as the Tonkin Gulf incident of 1965, contrived as it may have been,[13] spurred popular support for direct American intervention in South Vietnam, Sinope became a *causus belli* for England. Now Urquhart and the other voices raised in alarm about Russia seemed justified. Also, England appeared to be disgraced for having stood by while the Sultan's sailors were slaughtered, and the ministers of the Aberdeen administration who had cautioned peace were ostensibly shown to be "treacherous agents of the Tsar" (Martin 170–171). In less than four months, on March 27–28, 1854, England and France declared war on Russia. To the news of the declaration of war, the public responded enthusiastically. The troops were cheered as they marched to their debarkation points, and the Queen gave a farewell address to her palace guard (Lalumia 42).[14] Theatrical productions at the time, such as *Iran Safferi, or the Sultan and the Czar*, portrayed the troops as gallant freedom fighters going forth to defeat tyranny while satirically characterizing the Russians as groveling cowards and liars who fed their infantry and prisoners on candles and train-oil (Bratton 120–124). On the whole, the world's most technologically[15] advanced nation blithely anticipated a swift and easy victory over an incompetent enemy:

> The modernists expected, therefore, a war which might indeed be bloody, but which would certainly be rapid and decisive. The electric telegraph, railways, shell-firing guns, rifled and breech-loaded gun barrels, innumerable inventions ranging from daguerreotype pictures and gutta-percha bivouacs to the most significant development of all in English eyes, the screw-propeller steamship, convinced them that a new and impressive chapter in the history of warfare was about to be written [Olive Anderson 2–3].

Once British troops were on foreign soil, however, events proved such optimism in technology unfounded and dreams of a quick and decisive victory illusory.

From almost the very beginning of the enterprise, things went woefully wrong. When war was declared in 1854, British forces were not organized or prepared for battle. At the time there was no official war department to oversee the military, and the British army had not fought in a major battle on foreign soil since the battle of Waterloo some forty years earlier. Moreover, the general designated as commander in chief, the sixty-five-year-old Lord Raglan, the Duke of Wellington's military secretary, had never commanded as much as a company in battle. He was, in the words of Florence Nightingale biographer Barbara Dossey, "a bureaucrat, not a general" (104). According to Phillip Knightley, his command and logistical staff were even less qualified and prepared for battle than he:

> [Raglan] was hampered by perhaps the worst collection of subordinate
> officers ever concentrated in one army, including the Earl of Cardigan, the
> hard-drinking commander of the Light Brigade. The British officers brought a
> French chef, Kaffir servants, their favourite horses and wine, their shotguns,
> dogs, and, in some cases, their wives [5].

The British officer corps, "an outmoded bastion of aristocratic privilege," was clearly not prepared for the rigors of a modern war (Dossey 104).

Although the initial British landings in June of 1854 in Bulgaria, at Varna, and Turkey, at Scutari, went off without incident, it soon became apparent that evil days lay ahead. The bivouac site at Varna proved to be inhospitable. Although an advance team from the army's Medical Department had reported that "the existing buildings were infested with rodents and other vermin and that the nearby countryside was low and swampy," the high command ignored their warnings. Soon the summer heat and unhealthy location took a toll. By August over 20 percent of the expeditionary force had fallen ill to such maladies as cholera, diarrhea, and dysentery. Before the first engagement, "nearly 1,000 lives were lost," and "over 600 British troops died in one night from cholera" (Dossey 105). Weakened by disease, British forces took two days to march the ten miles from their camp in Varna to the embarkation point for the trip to the Crimea.

Once allied landings on the Crimean peninsula began in preparation for an attack on the major Russian stronghold on the Black Sea, Sebastopol, the inadequacy of the British supply system became evident:

> The French and Turkish troops made camp and unfurled their tents
> upon arriving at the beach; the British had only what each man could carry,
> no tents. A wind-driven rainstorm lashed the exposed British troops the
> entire night. It was later calculated that the addition of only two more ships
> to the existing fleet would have provided all the supplies the British needed
> [Dossey 105].

Despite their logistical failings, British troops performed well in the first major battle of the campaign, which occurred on September 20 on the Alma River north of Sebastopol. In the only "set-piece" encounter of the war, the English were completely victorious, routing the Russian forces arrayed against them and driving their broken remnants into Sebastopol (Lalumia 44 and Norman Rich 132–133).

Unfortunately, Lord Raglan did not pursue the fleeing Russians and make quick work of capturing Sebastopol. Rather, fearing a Russian counterattack, Raglan marched his forces to the south of the city, ensconcing them in the nearby port town of Balaclava to facilitate provisioning by sea. In the most ill-fated decision of the war, one as ill fated as General Westmoreland's strategy of attrition in Vietnam, Raglan chose to lay siege to Sebastopol. By doing so, he thwarted what could have been "accomplished within the first fortnight of the Crimean campaign, [but] did not take place until after almost an entire year of grim and costly military operations" (Norman Rich 134).

Unlike the Russians, who took the opportunity to fortify Sebastopol and to reinforce, the British did not expeditiously consolidate their position at Balaclava so that when the Russians counterattacked on October 25, they were almost driven into the sea. If not for the heroic efforts of the 93rd Highland Regiment, known since as "the thin red line," all would have been lost. Nonetheless, the battle is most remembered for the tragic charge of the Light Brigade, "an action of errant folly resulting from confused orders transmitted by a confused orderly to an officer foolish enough to carry them out" (Norman Rich 134). Only 195 of the original 673 soldiers who made the charge "returned mounted and fit for battle" (Lalumia 45).

Again on November 5 the Russians attacked, this time at Inkerman Ridge to the east of Sebastopol. In perhaps the fiercest, most vicious battle of the war, a small British detachment — Raglan had not thought the position of strategic importance — fought off a much larger Russian force. The conflict was a hellish, close-fought affair of Dantesque proportions:

> There ensued a savage encounter battle in the mist and rain of early morning, in which British troops resisted the attack by instinct [...]. Many soldiers resorted to the bayonet, stones and fists when rain touched their cartridge powder. They fought without direction in a militarily primitive attempt to hold their ground, and to survive [Lalumia 46].

Between the battle of Inkerman Ridge and the final assault on Sebastopol, which began in the spring and concluded on September 11, 1855, British arms failed miserably as a result of poor command decisions. In two disastrous frontal assaults on the Russian fortress of Sebastopol, at Malakoff Tower on June 18 and at the Great Redan on September 8, the British suffered horrendous losses. Only by redoubled efforts were French forces able to save the day and eventually overwhelm the Russian bastion on September 11. Battle casualties accounted, however, for but a fraction of the British deaths. The suffering that disease and the Russian winter were to visit upon the British troops was to prove far more deadly than Russian arms.

Committing the same blunder as Napoleon some forty years before and Hitler some ninety years later, Raglan had invaded with visions of a swift victory and so did not make adequate provisions for a winter campaign. Moreover, when needed supplies of medicines and winter clothing did arrive, they sat on the docks at Balaclava,[16] some six miles from the fighting, because no suitable transportation was available. The ill clad and poorly provisioned troops soon fell prey to disease and exposure. Even Raglan himself succumbed to cholera a week after the assault on Malakoff Tower. In *A Contribution to the Sanitary History of the British Army During the Late War with Russia*, Florence Nightingale records the inefficiencies and deprivations afflicting the army:

> Nothing had been organized, either for sheltering, clothing, or feeding the troops. No scheme of diet or ration appears to have been intelligently considered; and no transport was organized either for bringing supplies, or for carrying away sick. [...] The fierce winter of the Russian steppe swept over the scene of military operations, and found the men unsheltered from its blasts. Blankets and clothing were piled up at Balaclava, while men were perishing from cold and frost-bit, six miles off [...]. Fortunately, the Commissariat had at its disposal salt beef and biscuit; otherwise the army might have perished from hunger. Unfortunately, it did not supply any other food, and the army all but perished from scorbutus [...] there was great difficulty in conveying the salt beef and biscuit to the front, and, even when it had arrived there, there were neither camp-kettles nor fuel to cook it with [...] [9].

What scant supplies there were proved wholly insufficient, a point Dossey makes abundantly clear:

> The few tents in the field were flimsy, lacked floors, and were of little use against the winds howling over the steppes. Most of the troops made do with wet blankets in the mud. Trenches were filled with water and ice; boots froze to the soldiers' feet and had to be boiled off, the skin coming off in huge patches [141].

At the end of *Dracula*, it should be noted, a battle between a valorous English force and an Eastern evil takes place in surroundings and weather conditions very similar to those described in accounts of the disastrous winter campaign before Sebastopol in 1855.

The fate of the sick and wounded was not much better. In another startling logistical and command failure, those charged with providing medical assistance had not secured and equipped adequate facilities for transporting the stricken or for caring for them once in hospital. Once again, supply problems proved disastrous. Although the army had shipped quantities of newly patented folding stretchers to the front, the legs and transverse supports that held the stretchers open had been shipped separately, rendering them useless (Small 33). As a consequence, the fallen were carried down to the harbor at Balaclava on the backs of Turkish laborers or on *cacolets*,[17] a contrivance of the French ambulance service consisting of two chairs strapped over the back of a mule (Small 23). In the event that the ill and injured survived the trip to Balaclava, their chances of survival were not greatly improved. Upon arriving at the harbor,

> they were either lifted aboard steamships at wharfside or rowed out into the harbor in small boats to be lifted onto the ships. Here they waited days or weeks without any care, lying on the hard wooden deck or on straw pallets, surrounded by filth, until the ships were full and ready to sail. They then faced the ordeal of an exhausting voyage lasting 2 days to 1 week (depending on the weather and the type of ship used) across the Black Sea to the Turkish hospitals with no medical or surgical care. On arrival at the dilapidated Scutari docks, they often had to lie for hours in pain, half-naked and in squalid conditions, before being unloaded once more into small boats, taken to the docks, and then assisted on foot, strapped to mules, or loaded in carts for the last agonizing journey to the military hospitals [Dossey 107].

The hospitals in Scutari that eventually received the sick and wounded were ill suited for the task and contributed to the high mortality rate that prevailed among patients there. This was especially so in the case of the largest facility, known as the Barracks Hospital.

Originally designed to house 1,200 patients, the Barracks Hospital held more than 2,000 most of the time, with wards meant for 30 patients often accommodating as many as 72 (Dossey 108). Because of the overcrowding, every available corridor was lined on both sides with beds. The passage between these lines of beds was less than three feet in width (Small 24). Exacerbating these conditions was a wholesale lack of essential equipment and furniture. The Commissariat had failed to supply chamber pots, chairs, beds (patients lay on lice-infested straw mattresses),[18] tables, pots, plates, utensils, bathtubs (only 30 patients a day could be washed in the few available hip baths), combs, and soap. Making matters even worse, medicines, bandages, surgical supplies, and operating tables were rare if available at all (Dossey 107 and Small 22). Thomas Chenery, who covered Constantinople for the *London Times*, captured the conditions at Scutari in a dispatch from October 1854:

> [...] it is with feelings of surprise and anger that the public will learn that no sufficient medical preparations have been made for the proper care of the wounded. Not only are there not sufficient surgeons— that, it might be urged, was unavoidable — not only are there no dressers and nurses— that might be a defect of system for which no one is to blame — but what will be said when it is known that there is not even linen to make bandages for the wounded? The greatest commiseration prevails for the suffering of the unhappy inmates of

Scutari, and every family is giving sheets and old garments to supply their
want. But, why could not this clearly foreseen event have been supplied? [qtd.
in Kingsley 12].

The want of supplies was a result of the army's not setting up a central
warehouse for the receipt and dispatch of provisions. Instead, merchant
ships from England deposited their cargo with the Turkish Customs
House,[19] where supplies often disappeared or were outright stolen (Dossey
126).

Other deficiencies only added to the suffering of the patients. During
inclement weather, the windows were kept shut, trapping the stench of fes-
tering wounds, overflowing privies, and smoke from the stoves. Only coarse
canvas blankets had been issued, and no laundry facilities had been prepared, so patients commonly lay in the soiled, lice-ridden clothes and blankets brought with them from the front. Food preparation was equally
abominable. Cooking took place in the same large copper pots used for
brewing tea, and cooks identified what passed for pieces of meat, usually
more bone and gristle than flesh, with nails, buttons, and other items not
meant for consumption. Nor were vegetables in adequate supply even
though a nearby market could have met this need. And, despite endemic
scurvy amongst the patients, no one would issue the lime juice[20] stored on
ships at anchor in the harbor (Dossey 128).

It was only when Florence Nightingale and her fellow nurses appeared
on the scene that hygienic and dietary standards in field hospitals improved
and the mortality rate declined. Soon after her arrival in November 1854, she
made significant changes in the management of the hospital and the treatment of patients. First, she searched through the markets of Constantinople
for the foodstuffs and furnishings lacking at Scutari, often paying with her
own money or funds that had been raised by the London Times (Small 22).
Also, she had the unused portions of the hospital building renovated to alle-
viate crowding, subsidizing much of the remodeling (Small 32). The daily
treatment of the patients changed for the better as well.

Before her arrival in Scutari, the high command operated under the
assumption that soldiers were primarily responsible for caring for themselves. Thus what few orderlies and support staff that had been assigned to
the hospital usually consisted of pensioners, who had come out of retire-
ment and were most often unfit for the work, or drunken, malingering soldiers who were more interested in stealing from their charges than
comforting them (Dossey 144 and Small 25). Florence Nightingale and her
staff soon saw to it that the building was cleaned, the patients washed and
their bandages changed regularly, and their meals made wholesome and
delivered on time.

Nightingale's efforts, however, did not go unchallenged by the high command and presiding physicians at Scutari, many of whom thought of her group as "meddling outsiders" (Dossey 123). Perhaps the greatest source of friction between the medical corps and Florence Nightingale arose over her efforts to improve the lot of the common soldiers.[21] Among the high command and the officer corps, most of whom at the time were members of the aristocracy, there existed a general disregard, if not contempt, for the common soldier. This attitude manifested itself in a host of ways. For example, Commissary-General Filder refused to supply fuel to the soldiers at the front during the winter siege of Sebastopol because, he argued, no regulations required that he do so, that enlisted men were responsible for gathering their own fuel (Small 25).

Considering the enlisted man little more than a beast of burden,[22] the army command also made few if any provisions for the entertainment or intellectual growth of the troops. Thus when Florence Nightingale requested that reading rooms and writing materials be made available to soldiers recuperating from wounds or resting in base camp, Lord William Paulet, the commander at Scutari, complained that she was "spoiling the brutes" (qtd. in Small 44). It was further assumed that the enlisted ranks were naturally disposed to drunkenness, but Nightingale contended that drinking could be reduced if soldiers had better means of sending their pay home. When her letter to that effect written to Queen Victoria was read before Parliament, Lord Panmure, the Minister of War, complained that she "knew nothing of the British soldier" and wrote to Lord Raglan that the British soldier "is not a remitting animal." However, once provisions were in place for soldiers to more easily remit pay home, the number of remissions substantially eclipsed what had been predicted (Small 44).

More dramatic instances of aristocratic prejudice toward the soldiery could be found in the treatment of the ill and wounded. Prior to Nightingale's tenure at Scutari, amputations were performed in plain view of those awaiting surgery themselves. Moreover, Dr. John Hall, Inspector-General of Hospitals, encouraged surgeons to not employ chloroform during such procedures. He reasoned that the "smart of a knife is a powerful stimulant" and that anesthesia might induce death although just a year prior Queen Victoria had been administered chloroform during childbirth (Dossey 123). Fortunately, Florence Nightingale soon applied remedial measures, writing to a surgeon at home that she was

> getting a screen now for the amputations, for when one poor fellow, who is amputated tomorrow, sees his comrade today die under the knife it makes an impression — and diminishes his chances [qtd. in Small 26].

She and her staff somehow found time to rectify another command oversight: sending letters of condolence to the family of the slain[23] and writing letters for those too infirm or ill educated to do so (Dossey 128).

The improvements that Florence Nightingale and her colleagues accomplished in terms of facilities, sanitation, and patient care were truly spectacular. Although 10,000 soldiers had died of disease[24] during the first winter of the war, only 500 more died during the same period the next year of the war (Small 54). Henry Wadsworth Longfellow's poem "Santa Filomena" immortalized her efforts and extolled the goodly ministrations of the professional nurse, an occupation previously viewed with derision:

> A lady with a lamp shall stand
> In the great history of the land,
> A noble type of good,
> Heroic womanhood.

But, despite the great good Florence Nightingale achieved almost single handedly for the common soldier and patient at Scutari, she more significantly acted as a catalyst for far-reaching change in the army Medical Service, the status of women in Victorian society, and the emerging middle class as a whole.

Through her steady stream of letters home to Queen Victoria, the Prime Minister, the Minister of War, newspaper editors, and family, she raised public awareness about the conditions in the Crimea. As a result, the Palmerston administration dispatched in March 1855 two civilian commissions to the war zone that would not only do much to further Florence Nightingale's local reforms, but, in the long run, to effect much needed reforms in the army and eventually to reforms in the government as a whole. The Supply Commission charged with investigating why food and clothing were not being issued to the troops at the front was composed of two members, Sir John McNeill, diplomat, physician, and author of *The Progress and Present Position of Russia in the East*, and Colonel Alexander Tulloch, a statistician. The Sanitary Commission, given the task of cleaning up the camps in the Crimea and Turkey, included three members: John Sutherland and Hector Gavin, both doctors, and Robert Rawlinson, an engineer. This latter group immediately set about taking necessary sanitation measures:

> The commission discovered that the water source for the hospital was being contaminated by open privies that couldn't be flushed and had never been cleaned out. A horse carcass was even found in the fresh water supply. Beneath the Barrack Hospital were clogged sewers; the hospital literally sat atop a huge cesspool. Dead animals and hundreds of cartloads of rubbish were removed from under the hospital, and a system was installed to flush out the sewers. Openings were made in the roof to improve air circulation. Rotten shelves and floors were torn out eliminating breeding places for rats and mice. The inside walls and floors were painted with disinfectant [Dossey 151].

This group of professionals would come to play a significant role in bringing about lasting reforms in the provisioning and medical treatment of British soldiers and contribute to the social changes that the war would help to engender in the ensuing years. They are, moreover, a group that shares much in common with the five men, professionals for the most part themselves, who dispel contagion and evil from England in *Dracula*.

On March 30, 1856, the Treaty of Paris ended hostilities. Under the provisions of the treaty, future conflicts between Russia and Turkey were to be resolved by a third party; the Black Sea was opened to commercial vessels of all nations, but closed to all warships; and the Principalities, Moldavia and Wallachia, were removed from Russian protection and given ostensible independence (M. S. Anderson 143). Palmerston, then Prime Minister, wished to continue the war to exact greater concessions from Russia, but the French had had enough and demanded a brokered peace. As a result, the war, which cost England some 15,000 lives and millions of pounds, ended inconclusively. According to Norman Rich, "The Russian threat remained as though the Crimean War had never been fought" (201). However, although the war did not substantially alter the international balance of power, it did evoke a drastic realignment in domestic affairs in England. Here again the popular press played a central role.

# Two

## Spawn of War: The Consequences of the Crimean War and Post-Crimean Russophobia

Besides advanced weapons and modes of transportation, what made the Crimean War "the first war of the modern era" (Lalumia xx) were technological developments that allowed for almost instantaneous "publicity and disscusion" of the war at home (Olive Anderson 71). The war artist, photographer, and correspondent, transmitting daily reports telegraphically, were all "creations of the war" (Olive Anderson 71 and Rich 131). Like reporters during the Vietnam conflict, they provided the home front, and unfortunately the enemy, with up-to-date, blow-by-blow accounts of the fighting, and, as the military situation worsened, unfavorable critical analyses of the conduct of the war. As the war progressed, they had more and more bad news to report. The result was that by 1855, the public's attitude toward the war, the government, and the military command had undergone a complete reversal.

Foremost among those shaping public opinion regarding the war was William Howard Russell[1] of *The Times*. As Nicolas Bently attests,

> [...] it was due to Russell's despatches from the scene more than any other single factor that the British government's mishandling of affairs, and the gross negligence of the War Office in particular, came to light and that the resignation of Lord Aberdeen's cabinet was brought about. This same event, had it been delayed even for a little while longer, must have resulted inevitably in a disaster to the British army far worse than any that the Russians had succeeded in inflicting upon it [11].

A rather large and stocky Irishman, similar in physique to his fellow Irishman Bram Stoker, Russell came to the Crimea well prepared to cover a military campaign. In 1850 he had covered the war between Schleswig-Holstein and Denmark and had been wounded in the process. His injury, though minor, "left him acutely sensitive to the plight of the wounded and the sick" (Dossey 109). As a consequence, he paid special attention to the living conditions of the troops in the field and, with colleagues such as Edwin Godkin of *The London Daily News*, reported extensively on the suffering of wounded and diseased troops.

With his very first reports from Gallipoli, Russell began to disabuse the British public through accounts of military and governmental incompetency:

> The camps in the neighbourhood of Gallipoli extended and increased in numbers every day, and with the augmentation of the allied forces, the privations to which the men were at first exposed became greater, the inefficiency of our arrangements more evident [...]. Amid the multitude of complaints which met the ear from every side, the most prominent were charges against the commissariat; but the officers at Gallipoli were not to blame. The persons really culpable were those who sent them out without a proper staff and without the foresight or consideration [31].

Jonathan Harker might have filed a similar complaint against his employer, Mr. Hawkins, who is less than honest with him about the nature and duration of his stay in Transylvania. Unknown to Jonathan, Mr. Hawkins gives Dracula *carte blanche* to use Harker as he will, informing the Count in a sealed letter that his young protege "shall be ready to attend you when you will during his stay, and shall take your instructions in all matters."[2]

Russell found the authorities equally inept in choosing a bivouac site in Bulgaria:

> In the stagnant water which ripples almost imperceptibly on the shore there floated all forms of nastiness and corruption, which the prowling dogs, standing leg-deep as they wade about in search of offal, cannot destroy. The smell from the shore was noisome[...]. The slaughter-houses for the troops, erected by the sea-side, did not contribute, as may be readily imagined, to the cleanliness of this filthy beach, or the wholesomeness of the atmosphere [40].

Later, during the cholera epidemics that decimated the troops even before their departure for the front, he painted a realistic picture of the carnage that must certainly have shocked even the most stout hearted:

> Horrors occurred here every day which were shocking to think of. Walking by the beach one might see some straw sticking up through the sand, and on scraping it away with his stick, be horrified at bringing to light the face of a corpse which had been deposited there with a wisp of straw around it, a prey to dogs and vultures. Dead bodies rose up from the bottom in the harbour and bobbed grimly around in the water or floated in from sea and drifted

past the sickened gazers on board the ships—all buoyant, bolt upright, and hideous in the sun [56–57].

However, Russell's most memorable reports were posted after the battle was joined on the Crimean peninsula.[3] Especially poignant are his descriptions of the horrible winter spent in the siege of Sebastopol.[4] In unmistakable terms of disapprobation and condemnation, he made it plain for all to read that the government and military high command were guilty of negligence and incompetence:

> Rain kept pouring down—the skies were black as ink—the wind howled over the staggering tents—the trenches were turned into dikes—in the tents the water was sometimes a foot deep—our men had neither warm nor waterproof clothing—they were out for twelve hours at a time in the trenches— they were plunged into the inevitable miseries of a winter campaign—and not a soul seemed to care for their comfort, or even for their lives. These were hard truths, which sooner or later must have come to the ears of the people of England. It was right they should know that the wretched beggar who wandered about the streets of London in the rain led the life of a prince compared with the British soldiers who were fighting for their country, and who, we were complacently assured by the home authorities, were the best appointed army in Europe [151].

Such reporting brought Russell and *The London Times*[5] in direct conflict with the government and the military authorities, who felt the press should "stimulate patriotism"[6] and maintain "the country's prestige abroad by [exercising] discretion in publicizing defeats and moderation in criticism of the country's leaders" (Olive Anderson 74). Lord Raglan retaliated by refusing to supply correspondents with rations or housing. At one point, Russell's tent was ordered to be cut down when he placed it among those of the troops. Later, after he had taken up residence in a ramshackle house with "Turkish soldiers, their horses and cattle, and the decomposing body of a Tartar in the only well," he was moved out to make room for other soldiers (Knightley 7 & 11).

The immediate result of Russell's dispatches was the resignation of the Aberdeen cabinet.[7] However, the long-range consequence of revelations of incompetence among the highest orders of the government and military was that the aristocracy as a whole fell into disrepute and lost much of its prestige and power to the emerging middle class. Official investigations into the conduct of the war, especially those spearheaded by Florence Nightingale concerning the medical treatment provided the wounded and diseased, would hasten the process and bring women greater status. All told, the war would leave an indelible mark on the social fabric of the English nation.

By mid-century, the rising middle class, empowered by the Reform Bill of 1832, had acquired considerable material wealth, yet the landed gentry still controlled ministerial and military policy. Excluded from these bastions of privilege, many liberal politicians and middle class industrialists and merchants were openly hostile to and contemptuous of the aristocracy. Olive Anderson contends that the war offered the aristocracy an opportunity to ameliorate such animosities. Many hoped that middle class resentment "would be stilled as war demonstrated once again that only the aristocratic spirit and aristocratic leadership could guide a nation and army to victory" (101). It was soon evident, though, that "personal bravery and leadership" were not enough to win a modern war of "supply and demand [...] organization and administration and the manipulation of material resources" (104).

During the winter of 1854-1855, such middle-class groups as the Administrative Reform Association, with the support of *The London Times*, the *Morning Chronicle*, and *Punch*, aligned against the aristocracy not out of "envy of wealth or rank," but because the aristocracy had failed to adapt to the "new military techniques, new weapons, and new administrative methods" required in a modern war (Olive Anderson 106–107). They had proven not to be the one thing that the new middle class demanded, "practical" (107). As a result, the argument was advanced that competent men of business and the professions were best suited to manage future wars:

> War was equated with a commercial undertaking or a specialized profession, not with an amateur sport or a moral crusade, and by the same token could be claimed as properly a middle-class and not an aristocratic preserve [Olive Anderson 107].

In May of 1855, *Punch* ran a poem, "Madrigal of Administrative Reform," that summed up the reform spirit of the times:

> No more will we be ruled by men
> Whose sole qualification
> Is not ability and ken;
> But lies in rank and station:
> None shall this land
> Henceforth command
> No men will we submit to,
> But those who business understand;
> Practical men of ditto [qtd. in Olive Anderson 112].

Proof of the credibility of this new doctrine was provided in 1855 when a civilian contractor laid over thirty-nine miles of railroad track connecting Balaclava with all the theaters of operations around Sebastopol, a task at which the military had failed miserably (Olive Anderson 118).

By the end of the war, then, the aristocracy's monopoly of the military and government had been severely tested, and over the next two decades, military reform measures were passed, notwithstanding stiff aristocratic opposition, that introduced business practices and ameliorated the conditions of service for enlisted men. Among these was the abolishment of the purchase system of commissions and promotions which excluded all but the wealthiest from the officer corps. The life of the common soldier was improved by the elimination of flogging as a punishment, by shortened tours of duty, and by increased opportunities for advancement. Florence Nightingale's unrelenting crusade, in the face of opposition by the aristocratic military command, for reform of the military medical corps so as to insure that troops would receive adequate care in sanitary facilities both at the front and in base hospitals would not only go far in accomplishing this goal, but it would also secure middle-class, professional women positions and authority in the traditionally male-dominated medical community, both military and civilian.

Toward the end of hostilities in the Crimean, Florence Nightingale had fallen ill herself, leading the British public to grow anxious about her safety. News of her eventual recovery spawned national jubilation. Later, when her health improved, she resolved to stay at her post rather than to return home to convalesce, an act garnering her even greater adulation on the home front. She remained at Scutari until the last soldier had been shipped home (Small 52 & 54). Little did she know that upon her return to England in August 1856, she would become the focus of national controversy.

Soon after she set foot back on English soil, Florence Nightingale became embroiled in the struggle to reform the military high command, especially the Medical Service. Earlier in 1856 Palmerston had submitted to Parliament a report[8] drafted by McNeill and Tulloch which detailed how "the incompetence or inaction of identified senior officers had caused the deaths of thousands of common soldiers" (Small 56). Against the wishes of the Queen, who was titular head of the military, and the general staff, Palmerston brought forth the report in an effort to establish stricter civilian control over the armed forces. However, the outcome of the Board of Enquiry, seated in April 1856, was just the opposite. As might have been expected, the generals empanelled rejected the criticism leveled by McNeill and Tulloch and exonerated the accused officers of any guilt. All four were eventually promoted. Florence Nightingale, who had developed a profound respect for McNeill during his sanitary improvements at Scutari and elsewhere in the Crimean theatre of operations, was particularly incensed by the ruling. With encouragement from Palmerston and Colonel John Henry Lefroy, Panmure's aide-de-camp, she entered the fray (Small 68–70).

In September 1856, Florence Nightingale sought the Queen's blessing for a royal commission to investigate military hospital administration and to recommend reforms. She soon recognized, however, that the Queen had sided with the military high command and did not wish to pursue the matter. In an effort to circumvent the objections of the Queen, Palmerston and Panmure, who had lost his brother to cholera in the war, asked Florence Nightingale to draft a confidential report based on her experiences in Turkey and the Crimea. Others, too, worked with her to bring about reform in the military. For example, her long time supporter Sidney Herbert, Minister of War in the Aberdeen administration, who had convinced Florence Nightingale to go Turkey, in a speech before Parliament called on the Queen to reward the efforts of McNeill and Tulloch. Soon thereafter, Tulloch was knighted and McNeill created a Privy Councilor (Woodham-Smith 194–195). Those interested in the reform of the military came to see Florence Nightingale as not only a source of valuable information and popular support, but also as a leader. Such was her influence that when Panmure drafted a call for a royal commission to investigate the failings of the army hospital administration, he shared it with Florence Nightingale before presenting it to the Queen. The membership of the commission that was eventually seated reflected the extent of her authority. It was chaired by Herbert and included Dr. Sutherland, an original member of the Sanitary Commission sent by Palmerston to the Crimea. In an act of deference to her, Panmure asked Florence Nightingale to write the official list of duties presented to the commission (Woodham-Smith 195). Once gathered, the commission relied on her for guidance and information; she was dubbed "Commander-in-Chief" by its principal members (Woodham-Smith 199).

In addition to her many responsibilities with the commission, Florence Nightingale was busily at work on her confidential report, which came to be titled *Notes on Matters affecting the Health, Efficiency and Hospital Administration of the British Army*. An enormous volume, it covered every facet of the fate that had befallen the army in 1854:

> In six long and detailed sections she examines the causes; the course and the cure of the Crimean disaster, quoting facts and figures, giving tables, plans, diet sheets, proving conclusively that the hospital was more fatal than the battlefield, that bad food, inadequate clothing, insanitary conditions led inevitably to defeat, while good food, proper clothing, tolerable conditions restored discipline and efficiency [Woodham-Smith 203].

It was completed in July 1857, the same month she testified before the royal commission. Her testimony took up thirty pages of the commission's official report and was based on the findings set forth in her own report. Thus, though her confidential report was never published for public consumption, it figured large in the official report of the Royal Sanitary Commission on the Health of the Army (Woodham-Smith 203).

The official report of the Royal Sanitary Commission called for the creation of four civilian sub-commissions to carry out specified reforms in the delivery of medical services in the armed forces. These sub-commissions would

1. put the Barracks in sanitary order;
2. found a Statistical Department for the Army;
3. institute an Army Medical School;
4. completely reconstruct the Army Medical Department, revise the Hospital Regulations, and draw up a new Warrant for the Promotion of Medical Officers. (Woodham-Smith 206)

Panmure officially established these sub-commissions in December 1857. By May of that year, Parliament had approved their creation. In a letter to Florence Nightingale that month, John McNeill described to her the extent of the victory over aristocratic privilege: "To you more than to any other man or woman alive will henceforth be due the welfare and efficiency of the British Army. I thank God that I have lived to see your success" (qtd. in Woodham-Smith 215). Later in 1858, Florence Nightingale distributed copies of her confidential report to the Queen, her cabinet, officials at the War Office, and notable public figures. Among these latter was Harriet Martineau, a writer for the *London Daily News*. Martineau, in contrast to Nightingale, was an avowed supporter of the women's rights movement, and she used the report in a series of articles and later as the basis of her 1859 book *England and Her Soldiers* (Woodham-Smith 217–218).

But, for all intents and purposes, even though she did not sign her report or publicize her work with the Royal Sanitary Commission, Florence Nightingale came to be seen as the model for the emerging New Woman in Victorian society. She clearly wielded substantial political power and public appeal. Almost single-handedly she had challenged the authority of the male-dominated medical community, in the process elevating nursing to a profession. Such was her accomplishment that even her most famous detractor, Lytton Strachey, author of *Eminent Victorians*, acknowledged her prodigious accomplishments:

> For not only was it an almost unimaginable thing in those days for a woman of means to make her own way in the world and to live in independence, but the particular profession for which Florence was clearly marked out both by her instincts and her capacities was at that time a peculiarly disreputable one. A "nurse" meant then a coarse old woman, always ignorant, usually dirty, often brutal, a Mrs. Gamp, in bunched-up sordid garments, tippling at the brandy-bottle or indulging in worse irregularities. The nurses in the hospitals were especially notorious for immoral conduct; sobriety almost unknown among them; and they could hardly be trusted to carry out the simplest medical duties. Certainly, things have changed since those days;

and that they *have* changed is due, far more than to any other human being, to Miss Nightingale herself [138].

And, though she had written to Harriet Martineau that she was "brutally indifferent to the wrongs or rights of my sex" (qtd. in Woodham-Smith 217), a letter to her father written during the Crimean War reveals that Florence Nightingale rebelled against the traditional views of the role of women expressed in the conduct books of the day:

> Lord Raglan asked me if my father liked me coming out to the East. I said with pride that my father is not as other men are. He thinks that his daughters should serve their country as well as sons. He brought me up to think so; he has no sons, and therefore, he has sacrificed me to my country, and told me to come home with my shield or upon it. He thinks that God sent women, as well as men, into the world to be something more than "happy," "attentive" and "amusing." My father's religious and social ethics make us strive to be the pioneers of the human race, and let "happiness" and "amusement" take care of themselves [qtd. in Small 49].

Here, clearly, is a woman who defers to no man, save her father, or aristocratic authority that stands in the way of her serving the common good of all men and women.

All told, by failing to govern and to manage efficiently in the Crimean War, the aristocracy lost its prestige to the new men and women of industry, commerce, and science:

> The image of an aristocracy of born leaders confronting a middle class of pettifogging money-grubbers had been effectively blurred by the brief but spectacular superimposition of a very different vision — a vision of well-born bunglers, out of date and helpless, who had been obliged in a crisis of the very kind which they should have been best fitted to handle, to turn for salvation to the middle class, the competent, experienced self-reliant "men of the age." In the long run the significance of this was profound [Olive Anderson 124].

Reports from the front by Russell and other journalists chronicling aristocratic failings thus catalyzed profound changes in Victorian society. However, the words of these writers would not have carried as much weight had they not been accompanied by the startling visual texts of war artists and photographers.

In his comprehensive study of print images made during the conflict, Matthew Lalumia argues that abrupt changes occurred in the paint artist's "vision of [...] military events" during the Crimean War in response to the "coverage of the campaign in the press," especially the contributions of "specially commissioned war artists" working for the illustrated newspapers (xxi). The presence of photographic records of the fighting also demanded greater realism in painting. The focus of these changes was on "the subjects chosen and the manner in which they were treated" (xxi). What resulted was an "anti-heroic vision of war," one that reified the general belief that "the injustices of the social system" were to blame for the catastrophes in the Crimea and that recorded the public's renunciation of "its traditional deference to the 'ruling classes'" (xxi). Essentially, the art coming out of the war expressed the "nation's realization that the common soldier and the typical inhabitants of English villages and towns, not titled military leaders, bore the brunt of the war" (xxi).

The art and photography of the war and post-war period most clearly documented the aristocracy's diminished stature and the concomitant elevation of the common soldier, who before the Crimean War had virtually ranked with criminals on the social scale. Prior to the war, British battle art had "depicted war as the ultimate stage for the high-born, a showcase for national prestige" (Lalumia 150). Shrouding "war in glorious trappings," paintings such as West's *Death of Wolfe*, Copley's *Death of Major Pierson*, Atkinson's *Battle of Waterloo*, 1817, and Jones' *Battle of Waterloo*, 1820, extolled the sacrifices of aristocratic commanders in the "colonial dominions" or as champions "of the conservative order that had finally suppressed the forces of the French Revolution" (150). In all of these works, the pyramidal arrangement of the subjects elevates the aristocratic leader, whether it be Wolfe or Wellington, above the common soldiery and focuses attention on his presence to the virtual exclusion of all others.

Early depictions of the Crimean campaign followed suit. For example, the sketch "Battle of Alma: General Brown Leading on the 23rd Regiment to the Russian Batteries," appearing in *Cassell's Illustrated Family Paper* in 1854, adheres to the existing tradition by drawing attention to the exploits of the general. At the front of his seemingly dazed and dispirited troops, the general strikes a heroic pose; sword raised, he boldly strides toward the enemy all the while urging his men to follow. However, the tragedies that were to befall British forces soon after this initial success "wrenched contemporary art toward a Realist investigation of battle and its consequences" (Lalumia 151).

Leading the way were the popular illustrated journals and newspapers. Of these, the *Illustrated London News* provided the most extensive coverage. With a circulation of some 100,000 copies a week by the 1850s, the *Illustrated London News* had wide influence in all strata of society, especially the successful middle class (Lalumia 151). In a series of full-page sketches covering the battle of Malakoff Tower in 1855, the artists of the *Illustrated London News* brought home to their readers the stark realities of the war. Two sketches in particular, "Interior of Malakoff Bastion" and "Burial of the Dead before the Malakoff Tower," show fidelity to the carnage that marked so many Crimean actions. A sketch made after the horrific battle

"Battle of Alma: General Brown Leading on the 23rd Regiment to the Russian Batteries." In this illustration published shortly after the war in the Crimea began, the artist is faithful to traditional representations of war that, according to Matthew Lalumia, "depicted war as the ultimate stage for the highborn." (*Cassell's Illustrated Family Paper,* 1855. By permission of the British Library.)

at Inkerman Ridge, "Our Artist on the Battlefield of Inkerman," is more disturbing still. Dominating the scene, a somber civilian artist, Joseph Archer Crowe, stands over a dead British soldier who lies face down in the mud. All about him rest his fallen and wounded comrades. So plentiful is death's harvest that the artist and his mount must tread carefully so as to not step on the dead while crossing the field. Only in the distant background does one see, diminutive and almost inconsequential, what appears to be an officer of field rank.

The most scathing pictorial indictment of the commanding aristocracy appears in the sketch "A Group of English Generals during the Assault on the Great Redan" published in another popular illustrated journal of the time, the *Illustrated Times.* In the very first depiction of any of the army's commanders, the sketch presents the three generals presiding over the most painful defeat of the war. Clearly associated with the failed attack in press

THE SIEGE OF SEBASTOPOL—BURIAL OF THE DEAD IN FRONT OF THE MALAKOFF TOWER.

"Our Artist on the Battlefield of Inkerman," sketched by Joseph Archer Crowe for the *Illustrated London News*, 1855. (By permission of the British Library).

accounts of the assault, they are General James Simpson, the planner of the disastrous frontal charge; General Sir Harry Jones, the officer in charge of the conduct of the siege of Sebastopol; and General Richard Airey, the quartermaster general responsible for the inept provisioning of the troops (Lalumia 67). Significantly, as Lalumia describes, the depiction of the generals resonates with "physical incapacity" and passivity, for the artist

> portrayed the army's highest-ranking officers in garb and poses much in contrast to the traditional iconography of martial command. Airey's head was wrapped in a woman's kerchief. Jones required the help of an aide to raise a telescope to his eye, and viewed the battle from a day-bed. Simpson, all but invisible beneath a blanket and cloak, sat in a chair to watch his troops fail [67].

Stripped of all aristocratic pretense, the generals appear effeminately weak and irresolute and, as the sketch suggests, unsuited for command.

*Opposite Top*: "Interior of Malakoff Bastion," sketched by William Simpson in 1855 for the *Illustrated London News*. Breaking with the tradition of depicting "war in its glorious trappings," artists for this paper gave the readers at home images of the realities and horrors of modern warfare. (By permission of the British Library). *Opposite Bottom:* "Burial of the Dead before the Malakoff Tower," sketched by Edwin Morin for the *Illustrated London News*, 1855. (By permission of the British Library).

An attack on the purchase system which allowed the wealthy and noble born to purchase promotions. The practice often spelled disaster when incompetent officers were assigned to combat units. (*Punch*, February 24, 1955. *Punch* Cartoon Library.)

*Punch* joined the assault on aristocratic privilege and prestige by contrasting the suffering of troops to the wantonness of the officer corps. Beginning in 1855, the illustrated journal ran a series of cartoons inditing the behavior and incompetence of the officer corps. "SHOPPING," published in a February issue, illustrates the purchase system, under which the well to do could buy promotions. This practice offered promotion based not on experience and proven leadership potential and further soured the relationship between the common troops and the aristocratic laden officer ranks. In the Vietnam War, U.S. officers were rotated out of combat assignments after six months rather than the normal twelve to thirteen month tour of duty for enlisted soldiers in an attempt to give as many officers as possible combat experience and to improve their eligibility for promotion. This practice, as did the purchase system in the Crimean War, bred distrust among the troops, who came to question the command abilities of their leaders.

Later illustrations focused specifically on the failings of the general staff. "THE GENERAL FAST (ASLEEP). HUMILIATING — VERY!" of March 1855 condemns the indolence of the high command and, it seems obvious, Lord Raglan in particular. Playing up his age, the cartoon depicts Lord Raglan as an aged officer, napping comfortably in warm quarters, indifferent to the storm warnings signaled on the barometer above his head and the plight of the men under his command. Through the window next to which he slumbers, the viewer sees a snow covered field scattered with dead horses and the detritus of war. Struggling through the driving snow,

General Raglan, supreme commander of British forces in the Crimea, was 65 when the war began and had never commanded troops in the field. Under his watch troops suffered from a lack of provisions, medical care, and able leadership. ( *Punch*, March 10, 1855. *Punch* Cartoon Library).

Raglan's deputies overseeing the commissariat and the medical corps were seen by the public as equally incompetent, invoking even the queen's ire. (*Punch*, March 24, 1855. *Punch* Cartoon Library.)

two soldiers bear a third on a stretcher. An April installment of *Punch* featured another illustration disdainful of the high command. Titled "THE QUEEN VISITING THE IMBECILES OF THE CRIMEA," the sketch attacks the failings of the medical and commissariat commands. A highly metaphorical rendering, the piece depicts the general overseeing medical support in a figure composed of an odd assortment of broken graduated cylinders, vials, splints, bandages, and crutches. The cloak he wears bears the sardonic inscription "When taken, ought to be well shaken," a sentiment with which Florence Nightingale would well have concurred. The general in charge of the commissariat is represented by a creature with a turnip for a head, a padlocked can of green coffee beans for a neck, and a set of empty shelves for a torso. Florence Nightingale singled out the folly of distributing green coffee to poorly provisioned troops in her 1859 report "A Contribution to the Sanitary History of the British Army during the Late War with Russia." She writes

Another of the notable expedients of that time must not pass without record, that of sending out green coffee to men who had nothing whatever to roast or prepare it with. It was the crowning touch in that system of mismanagement which has lowered the prestige of England and which almost cost her her fair name [9].

A November cartoon, "GRAND MILITARY SPECTACLE. The Heroes of the Crimea Inspecting the Field-Marshals," sums up the popular image of the high command that eventuated from their misdeeds. In the sketch, a group of Crimean War veterans stand before two seated field marshals attired in parade regalia. Among the veterans are many who have lost limbs, walk with canes, or still suffer from unhealed wounds. They stare angrily at the generals, frail old men who greet the veterans with fatuous, senile smiles, the suggestion being that they are mentally infirm and out of their element in modern warfare. Clearly the meeting is confrontational. The demeanor of the veterans communicates their disdain of and contempt for the field marshals, attitudes that came to be shared by the general public.

Opposed to such examples of aristocratic privilege, pretense, and incompetence are depictions of the common soldier. These usually emphasize the sacrifice and suffering of the troops in contrast to the wantonness

GRAND MILITARY SPECTACLE.

**Wounded and disabled veterans of the Crimean War confront the superannuated aristocratic high command. The illustration reflects the public's growing disdain for the aristocracy. (*Punch*, April 14, 1855. *Punch* Cartoon Library.)**

A STRUGGLE BETWEEN DUTY AND INCLINATION.

The Reform Bill of 1832 had extended the franchise to the middle class. Increasingly distrustful of the aristocracy, middle-class volunteers in the Crimean War worried that their rights would be curtailed while they were in service. (*Punch*, Vol. 26, January–June 1854. *Punch* Cartoon Library.)

of the officer corps. A sketch from the onset of hostilities, for example, champions the patriotism and self-sacrifice of the common enlistee. In "A STRUGGLE BETWEEN DUTY AND INCLINATION," Gallant Little John, a new recruit, is foregrounded bidding farewell to his true love while his colleagues in the background assemble to march away. Rather than the beautiful young lady traditional to similar scenes, John prepares to plant a parting kiss on the 1832 Reform Bill, which extended the franchise to men in the middle class. Although he might be expected to stay in England to

THE NEW GAME OF FOLLOW MY LEADER.

A number of aristocractic officers, most notably the Earl of Cardigan who commanded the ill-fated Light Brigade, withdrew from service in the Crimea by requesting transfers home for reason of "urgent private affairs." In the ironic illustration, a drummer boy makes a similar request to General James Simpson, Raglan's second in command, for himself and a file of common soldiers. (*Punch*, Vol. 28, January–June 1855. *Punch* Cartoon Library.)

reap the benefits of the reforms and to protect his middle class privileges accorded under the bill, John instead volunteers to fight, unlike those members of the aristocracy who either chose not to fight or to pay others to take their places.

Ridiculing another aristocratic means of avoiding service, "The New Game of Follow My Leader" satirizes the practice of requesting early transfers under the pretense of "'urgent private affairs'" at home. A number of prominent socially elite officers (i.e. the Duke of Cambridge, the Earl of Cardigan, and Lord George Padget) availed themselves of this privilege (Lalumia 75). The sketch shows a diminutive drummer boy standing before long ranks of enlisted men. He is addressing General James Simpson, second in command, with the highly ironic question: "Please, general, may me and these other chaps have leave to go home on urgent *private affairs*." Another cartoon, "Well, Jack," illustrates the dire consequences of the failures of supply. Two ragged and emaciated soldiers stand guard in a driving snowstorm. Littering the scene are dead and decomposing horses and discarded equipment. One soldier says to the other, "Well, Jack! Here's good news from home. We're to have a medal" to which his companion replies, "That's very kind. Maybe one of these days we'll have a coat to stick it on?"

Similar complaints against aristocratic privilege were voiced in the theater as well. The *Fall of Sebastopol* performed in 1855, for example, attacks the purchase system lampooned in the sketch "SHOPPING." In one scene, an English soldier complains to a captured Russian officer that "If you had been in some countries I could name, you would have continued a Subaltern unless an old Aunt had died and left you a few hundred" (qtd. in Bratton 124). The incompetence of the high command comes under attack that same year in *The Siege of Sebastopol*. At one point, Florence Nightingale is introduced as a figure of "true heroism" who has been dispatched to the front "to solve the problems of the nation and the army," a "mere woman who rescues the nation's honour, at the risk of her own." In another scene, hungry, ragged soldiers complain of the cold and the filth both at the front and in the rear (Bratton 134).

The photographs made during the war also captured the carnage of

Highlighting the failures of the high command, this illustration poignantly depicts the deprivations suffered by the common soldiery while the officer corps enjoyed meals prepared by French chefs and slept in beds turned down by personal valets. (*Punch*, Vol. 28, January–June 1855. *Punch* Cartoon Library.)

battle and the plight of the common soldier. The first war photographer, Roger Fenton, was dispatched to the front under the auspices of the Aberdeen government and Prince Albert to take photographs "suggesting that the troops flourished in a well-run campaign" (118). Thus as subjects Fenton chose well groomed and accoutered officers at rest or apparently contented troops gathered about a well stocked company mess.[9] The next photographer to visit the war, James Robertson, eschewed such idyllic scenes. Rather, he photographed "soldiers raising tombstones or walking sentry duty at the officers' burial ground" (Lalumia 123). However, Robertson's most famous works detail the destruction visited upon the fortress and city of Sebastopol, pictures that anticipate footage of European cities blasted into rubble during World War II and of the city of Hue in Vietnam. At home, photographers Joseph Cundall and Robert Howlett focused on the wounded recuperating in military hospitals. Their *Three Crimean Invalids* offers a poignant reminder of the consequences of war. Aligned on a tent bed are three amputees. The soldiers on either end are each missing one leg while the soldier in the middle has lost both. In a scene dripping with pathos, one examines the toes of his artificial leg.

War painting also "expressed the new apprehensions of war's least glorious face, the new esteem for the soldiery and the current anti-aristocratic feeling" (Lalumia 75). The first painter of note to emerge from the war years, Jerry Barrett, won popular acclaim with his 1856 piece *Queen Victoria's First Visit to Her Wounded Soldiers*. Not only did the painting gain sympathy and prestige for the war's victims, but it portrayed the new social standing of the common soldier as well. Barrett's next painting proved, however, to be much more popular. In *Mission of Mercy*, 1858, he lionized the most "popular heroine" of the war, Florence Nightingale, a person whose "industry and charity embodied the highest values of mid–Victorian society" (90). In the painting Nightingale, the prototype of the New Woman, commands a group of civilian nurses caring for a stream of wounded troops arriving at the Barracks Hospital in Scutari. Contributing to the popularity of the painting was the political controversy surrounding Nightingale's efforts to spur reform of the institutional obscurantism of the army medical service. The painting, then, as Lalumia suggests, combines a popular condemnation of the old guard with praise for the abilities of the middle class, both men and women:

> Nightingale supplanted the traditional protagonist of war-related art, as did the members of her retinue in Barrett's picture — other nurses, doctors and soldiers. These were denizens of everyday Victorian life elevated to a new status in art by the events of the Crimean War. [...] Their efforts sharpened impatience with a political hierarchy from which they and others of their ilk were excluded [90].

Appropriately, a female artist, Lady Elizabeth Thompson Butler, would create the definitive paintings of the Crimean War some fifteen years later, in the process gaining recognition for herself and helping to rekindle the nation's memories of the war and its aftermath.

## Post-Crimean Russophobia and Bram Stoker

As the child of a politically active mother and a father employed in governmental service, Stoker would not only have been cognizant of the anti–Russian sentiments that had led England to the Crimea and of the horrific accounts of the fighting there, but he also would have been conscious of the social changes swirling around him even in his youth. Moreover, in the years after the war, events would dramatize the profound social changes that followed the war and reinforce his conception of Russia as an aggressor state. In the realm of art, a resurgence of interest in Crimean War subjects in the 1870s reified the reordering of the class system. At its 1874 exhibit, the Royal Academy displayed, in "a most enviable location," Lady Elizabeth Thompson Butler's *Calling the Roll after an Engagement, Crimea.* So popular was the canvas that the Academy had to station a policeman in

*The Roll Call: Calling the Roll After an Engagement, Crimea,* by Elizabeth Thompson, Lady Butler, 1874. The featured painting at the Royal Academy's 1874 exhibit, *The Roll Call* drew throngs of viewers. Lady Butler had studied Russell's reports from the Crimea, which had recently been published in book form. The painting faithfully reproduced the harsh realities of battle and focused viewers' attention on the plight of the common soldier. (The Royal Collection © 2003, Her Majesty Queen Elizabeth II. RCIN 405915, OMV 185.)

front of it to keep the crowds from getting too close (Lalumia 136). The artist had made extensive studies of the war, especially of Russell's dispatches which had just recently been published in book form. The painting, appropriately, showed fidelity "to the harshest face of battle" (139–140) by presenting a motley group of combatants bloodied and demoralized by battle. Additionally, in keeping with the social awareness stemming from the war, "private soldiers dominated the canvas literally from one edge to the other" and the "horizontal disposition of the figures [...] replaced the carefully-constructed pyramidal format that once had been the norm for battle paintings" (140).

As a member of the art community resident in London,[10] Stoker probably either read the glowing reviews of the painting in the press or perhaps joined the crowds gathered before it. It is likewise probable that he would have been familiar with Butler's two other well publicized Crimean works, *Balaclava*, 1876, and *Inkerman*, 1877. The first of these, *Balaclava*, reiterates many of the same tropes displayed in *Roll Call*. Once more the common soldier dominates the field of view in this rendering of the remnants of Cardigan's Light Brigade after its disastrous charge. Although mounted troops occupy the frame on either side, the viewer is drawn to a standing figure dominating the center of the canvas. Though not physically injured, as are the many men depicted surrounding him, he bears the unmistakable

*Balaclava*, by Elizabeth Thompson, Lady Butler, 1876. A stark portrayal of the remnants of the battered Light Brigade, the painting captures in the face of the central figure the effects of psychological trauma or what would later be known as shell shock. (Manchester Art Gallery.)

psychological scars of war, as he stares vacantly at the viewer. His is what came to be known as the "thousand yard stare" during the Vietnam conflict, a sign of mental exhaustion, of the onset of what was termed in World War I "shell shock" under the unrelenting pressures of combat. In the 1880s, Stoker would have also been party to the "increasingly positive and nostalgic vision" (Lalumia 145) then beginning to characterize Britain's late war against Russia. Robert Gibb, who gained a reputation equal to Butler's as a painter of military subjects, won election to the Scottish Royal Academy in 1881 after exhibiting *The Thin Red Line*. Unlike Butler's portrayals of broken and wearied troops, Gibb's "image of Highland courage toppling Russian aggression reaffirmed British superiority at arms at the expense of a Realist treatment of battle" (146).

In later paintings about the charge of the Light Brigade at Balaclava, painters such as Gibb and Richard Woodville were to transform the tragedy into a glorious testament of British pluck and military daring[11] for viewers who "perceived the Crimean War through the rose-tinted lenses of time" (Lalumia 147). Flush with patriotic zeal over relatively easy victories in exotic colonial posts, Victorian audiences in the 1880s and 1890s demanded "imagery that suited the contemporary mood of confidence in the army's invincibility" (148). Such revisions merged Balaclava with Waterloo in "the glorious past" which Victorians "constructed for themselves" (147). *Dracula* enacts a similar revision, for the Eastern evil is not only defeated, but defeated in his own distant and exotic homeland.

Political and diplomatic events over the next forty or so years also kept memories of the war alive. Anglo-Russian disputes over Turkey and her Balkan dominions, particularly Bulgaria, in the 1860s and 1870s would continue to fuel Russophobia. Of special concern was the Russo-Turkish war of 1877, which brought England perilously close to another armed encounter with Russia over access to the Black Sea. When it appeared that Russia would capture Constantinople, Disraeli ordered the fleet into the Dardanelles in February 1878, a move which provoked an "intensification of Russophobia, principally in London"[12]:

> The Queen wished she "were a man" so that she could "go and give those horrid Russians a beating." Russia was warned that diplomatic relations would be broken off if Constantinople were entered [...] Disraeli called up the reserves and secretly ordered Indian troops to Malta with the object if necessary of seizing Cyprus [Seaman 214].

Although war was averted, English acrimony toward Russia did not abate. As the next chapter will demonstrate, Stoker had an intimate knowledge of the Russo-Turkish War of 1877–1878, one that certainly would have reinforced the stereotypes of the Russians he encountered in the press, theatre, and painting. His brother George had served as a volunteer physician to the Turkish army, and when he came to record his travels, he sought Bram's editorial assistance. As will be seen, George's travelogue *With the Unspeakables*, published in 1878, reinscribes English prejudices and fears centering on Russia and the Balkans.

Though not as dramatic and captivating as the threat of another international struggle such as the Crimean War, the long-smoldering, low intensity conflict known as the "Great Game" further helped to foment Russophobia during Stoker's lifetime. In the introduction to his 1977 book *The Struggle for Asia, 1828–1914*, David Gillard writes that a

> hundred years ago most politically conscious people in Great Britain and Russia regarded the other's government with fear and mistrust. A great political game seemed to be in progress. The prize would be political ascendancy in Asia; the losing empire would go into permanent decline. There was only one war, the Crimean, in which their armies were directly engaged against one another, but they fought or intimidated most of the peoples of Asia who lived precariously between their two empires. Even when the cause of these local conflicts seemed remote from the "Great Game," the outcome usually marked a crucial shift in the distribution of power and influence on which the "Game" turned [1].

Interest in the Great Game has risen sharply since the fall of the Soviet Union in 1989 and has accelerated even more after the attacks of September 11, 2001.[13] This interval has witnessed the publication of four significant books about the nineteenth century contest for supremacy in Central Asia between Britain and Russia. The most comprehensive chronological study, Peter Hopkirk's *The Great Game: The Struggle for Empire in Central Asia*, appeared in 1990. It was followed in 1999 by Karl Meyer's and Shareen Brysac's *Tournament of Shadows: The Great Game and the Race for Empire in Central Asia*. Although this work covers much of the same ground as Hopkirk's book, it extends the chronology of events up to the retreat of Soviet forces from Afghanistan and the demise of the Soviet Union. Meyer authored a second Great Game study, *The Dust of Empire: The Race for Mastery in the Asian Heartland*, in 2003. According to the dust jacket, this latest work is meant to provide "the context for America's war on terrorism, for Washington's search for friends and allies in an Islamic world rife with extremism, and for the new politics of pipelines and human rights in an area richer in the former than the latter." Tapping into the United State's recent preoccupation with the region, Ben MacIntyre published in 2004 *The Man Who Would Be King: The First American in Afghanistan*, the story of Josiah Harlan, a Pennsylvania Quaker who traveled and fought against the British in Afghanistan.

Just as the threat of terrorism preoccupies the minds of untold English citizens today, Russia served as a perennial source of anxiety for Englishmen in the nineteenth century. The two superpowers were "expansionist and their relationship hostile" (Gillard 2), a sure recipe for eventual conflict. The one major war fought between the two may not have been a direct result of "Great Game" calculations, but according to Hopkirk, even though the Crimean War was not specifically a consequence of the "Great Game," having been "fought by large armies on the open battlefield, far from the grim deserts of Central Asia and the lonely passes leading down into India," the

> ripples were soon to be felt by those responsible for India's defence. For just as British hawks saw the war as an opportunity to prise the Russians from their Caucasian base, and thereby reduce the potential threat to India, there were Russian strategists who believed that a march on India would help speed their victory in the Crimea [283–284].

Russophobia, as has been demonstrated, had a long history in England, dating from the eighteenth century. The "Great Game" would periodically bring to the fore the Russophobic tendencies in Britain that prevailed throughout the nineteenth century, and one of its most vocal proponents would come to befriend Bram Stoker toward the end of the century.

Events some few years after the Crimean War once again popularized the image of Russia as a hostile force challenging Britain for imperial supremacy. Czar Alexander II, heir to Nicholas I, looked to the expansion of his empire in Asia as a means of assuaging defeat in the Crimea and resuscitating Russian prestige in Europe.[14] To do so he turned to his like minded Minister of War, Count Dmitri Milyutin, and the Anglophobic officers under his command. Principal among this group who hoped to spearhead expansion in Asia was Count Nikolai Ignatiev. Ignatiev was a committed Anglophobe who, in Hopkirk's words, "burned to settle his country's score with the British" (295). While serving as a military attache in England during the Indian Mutiny of 1857–1858, Ignatiev encouraged his superiors in the ministry to invest territories in Central Asia bordering the Indian frontier while British forces were occupied in the Indian interior (295). Ignatiev himself led in 1858 a scouting party to determine the extent of British influence in Turkmenistan and Uzbekistan, regions explored some sixteen years earlier by British agents slaughtered for their efforts.[15]

Ignatiev survived and in 1859 was dispatched to Peking to acquire from the Chinese emperor official acknowledgement of Russian control of Siberia, territories recently wrested from China (Hopkirk 298). At the same time, his mission was meant to deny Britain, who was then engaged in the Second Opium War with China, a permanent presence in Peking that might threaten

Russia's Siberian conquests. At the completion of his Chinese mission, Ignatiev was recalled to St. Petersburg, where he received a permanent promotion to general, was awarded the prestigious Order of St. Vladimir, and given command of the newly established Asiatic Department of the Foreign Ministry (298–301).

Ignatiev there joined a group of influential Anglophobes who promoted further expansion in Asia. Aside from a desire "to expunge the memory of Crimean defeat" (Hopkirk 301), commercial and geopolitical concerns motivated them:

> Foremost was the fear of the British getting there first and monopolising the region's trade. Russian merchants and manufacturers had long had their eyes on the untapped markets and resources of Central Asia, especially its raw cotton. Then there was the question of imperial pride. Blocked in Europe and the Near East, the Russians sought to work off their frustration by demonstrating their military prowess through colonial conquest in Asia. After all, it was no more than the other European powers were doing, or had already done, almost everywhere else in the world. Finally there was the strategic factor. Just as the Baltic was Russia's Achilles' heel in the event of trouble with Britain, it had long been obvious that the latter's most vulnerable point was India. Therefore to have bases in Central Asia from which its frontiers could be threatened greatly increased Russia's bargaining power [Hopkirk 314–312].

Ignatiev, a vocal proponent of expansion, argued that the time was ripe for conquest in Central Asia, for Britain, the chief obstacle in Russia's march to the east, was reeling from costly wars in Afghanistan, Russia, Persia, and China as well as the bloody insurrection in India and was in no condition to block Russia's path. In 1864, as preparation for what would be a long and concerted program of expansion, the Russian foreign minister, Prince Gorchakov, issued a memorandum to embassies throughout Europe, one that raised eyebrows in England:

> The position of Russia in Central Asia is that of all civilised states which are brought into contact with half-savage nomad populations possessing no fixed social organisation. In such cases it always happens that the more civilised state is forced, in the interests of security of its frontiers and its commercial relations, to exercise a certain ascendancy over those whose turbulent and unsettled character make them undesirable neighbours [qtd. in Hopkirk 304].

Citing the example of other empires, Gorchakov went on to suggest that the "Russian government therefore had to choose between bringing civilisation to those suffering under barbarian rule and abandoning its frontiers to anarchy and bloodshed" (Hopkirk 304). In doing so, Russia was merely following the example "of every country which has found itself in a similar position" and was "irresistibly forced, less by ambition than by imperious necessity, into this onward march" (qtd. in Hopkirk 304).

By 1869, Russian forts had been established east of the Caspian Sea, within striking distance of the city of Herat, in Afghanistan, considered to be the "strategic key to India" (Hopkirk 318). Such was the state of the Russian menace to India that a number of government and military figures in England and British India called for immediate military action to halt the advance. One of these figures was Major-General Sir Henry Rawlinson, a member of the Advisory Council of India, which had replaced the East India Company in 1858, and president of the Royal Geographic Society, under whose auspices British spies roamed the Afghan frontier.[16] As early as 1865, Rawlinson had published two articles which chronicled the history of Russian expansion in Asia, described the political landscape in Central Asia, and called for direct action in Afghanistan and beyond to thwart Russian encroachment on India (Gillard 125).

In 1875, Rawlinson reprinted these articles in a larger collection of memoranda and reports written while he was serving as a British consul to India and Persia. Titled *England and Russia: A Series of Papers on the Political and Geographical Condition of Central Asia*,[17] the book, as Rawlinson states in the preface, "is intended to be a sort of Manual for students of the Eastern question." His reasons for reprinting and updating his observations are that "events of the last few years, and the giant strides which Russia is now making in the East, have revived public interest in the subject" (v). The event that most moves Rawlinson to go to print is Russia's seemingly ineluctable advance on Afghanistan, an event so alarming that should Russia

> overstep certain limits in her approach to India, she must be checked by armed resistance, even at the risk of producing war between the two countries. Herat, which has been justly named "the key to India," must, in my view, be secured against Russian occupation at all hazards, even though it should be necessary to march a force from India for its protection [viii].

Essentially Rawlinson is here enunciating the policy of the "Forward School," the position held by militant members of the government and military who "argued that the only way to halt the Russian advance was ... getting there first, either by invasion, or by creating compliant 'buffer' states, satellites astride the likely invasion routes" to India. Opposing this group was the Backward or "Masterly Inactivity" School, which maintained that India's natural physical barriers would so exhaust a Russian army who had breached them that it would be no match for the British army it eventually met in the field (Hopkirk 6).

Espousing what would today be considered a hawkish or neo-conservative foreign policy, Rawlinson dismisses such thinking as idealistic and impracticable. For instance, he points out the folly of those in the

Backward School who actually see advantages in a Russian presence in Afghanistan and Persia because

> we should then have a reasonable and respectable neighbor with whom to conduct political negotiations, instead of hordes of fanatical savages on whom no reliance can be placed; and secondly, because Central Asia, in a settled condition and under a European Government, would naturally be a better customer, both in regard to export and import trade of India, than the barbarians who now encircle our North-West frontier with transit duties and prohibitive tariffs [143].

Such thinking, as Rawlinson points out, fails to take into account that "India is a conquered country, where a certain amount of discontent must ever be smoldering which would be fanned into a chronic conflagration by the contiguity of a rival European power." In terms dripping in sarcasm, he goes on to offer this biting analogy:

> Let the advocates of Russian neighborhood consider what would be the effect in the French position in Algeria, if England were to occupy the conterminous territory of Morocco, and they will obtain some notion of our probable political embarrassments when confronted with Russia on the Indus [144].[18]

A Russian presence in Afghanistan would have an immediate and pernicious effect on British rule in India. It would specifically foment unrest among the indigenous peoples on the northern frontier:

> Every chief throughout Northern India who either has, or fancies he has, a grievance, or who is even cramped or incommoded by our orderly Government, will at once commence intriguing in the hopes of relieving himself from our oppressive shadow [279].

Rawlinson warns that the British are "living upon a volcano in India, which at any minute may explode and overwhelm us"; most to be feared are the "Mohamedan priesthood" in whom hostility to British rule "burns with an undying flame." His estimation of this group is chilling:

> I believe that not more fiercely does the tiger hunger for his prey than does the Mussulman fanatic throughout India thirst for the blood of the white infidel. All this may be very sad, but it is no use disguising a fact which is inevitable [281].

It is therefore necessary that "whatever the price" Britain must establish "a dominant position" in Afghanistan so as "to close the avenue of approach against Russia" (284).

Although most Forward School theorists believed that the route from Kabul through the Khyber Pass would be the most likely line of advance for an invading army, Rawlinson, who had served in Persia, emphasizes the danger posed by a Russian occupation of Herat. This city on Afghanistan's frontier with Persia presented a special threat to India:

> It stood on one of the traditional conqueror's routes to India, along which a hostile force could reach either of its two great gateways, the Khyber and Bolan Passes. Worse, in a region of vast deserts and impenetrable mountain ranges, it stood in a rich and fertile valley which — or so it was believed in India — was capable of provisioning and watering an entire army [Hopkirk 42].

Rawlinson argues just this point, stating that Herat would provide an ideal base of operations for an invasion of India:

> The earth-works which surround the town are of the most colossal character, and might be indefinitely strengthened. Water and supplies abound, and routes from all the great cities to the north, which would furnish the Russian supports, meet in this favoured spot. In fact, it is no exaggeration to say that if Russia were once established in full strength at Herat, and her communications were secured in one direction with Asterabad through Meshed, in another with Khiva and Mymeneh and the passage of the Oxus, all the native forces of Asia would be inadequate to expel her from the position [286–287].

The forces that Russia might potentially array against India should she occupy Herat would be formidable. From a base in Herat, Russia could fall upon India with

> a force of 50,000 Persian "Sirbaz," disciplined and commanded by Russian officers, and thus fully competent to cope with our best native troops; supporting such a force with 20,000 Turcoman and Afghan horse, than whom there is no better irregular cavalry in the world; and if she were in earnest, detaching also a small auxillary body of her own picked troops to give strength and consistency to the invading army [287–288].

In the event of such an attack, native Indian forces supplemented by British troops could very well stave off a general collapse, "but at any rate we should have to fight for our lives, and should be quite powerless to strike a blow against Russia in return"(288).

To prevent this tragedy from unfolding, Herat must be secured. Upon this point Rawlinson is adamant. He recognizes, however, that lingering memories of the disastrous First Afghan War may lead to an overcautious approach, playing into the hands of Backward School advocates. But so dramatic is the potential threat that Rawlinson merely brushes this objection aside:

> To some Indian statesmen, — especially those who have been bred up in the modern school of political puritanism, — the notion of occupying Herat with a British force, under any conceivable circumstances, may appear wild and extravagant. Visions will arise on their troubled imaginations of murdered envoys, of imprisoned ladies, of decimated legions, of England's honour

trailed in the dust, of defeat, of bankruptcy, of ruin. It is time that all this puerile absurdity, the stale refuse of a bygone period of panic, should cease. I am not insensible to the gravity of the step suggested, to the many weighty objections that may be urged against sending another British army above the passes, on the score of expense, and especially on account of the danger of reviving dormant enmities and bringing on political complications both with Persia and with Cabul; but, in a professional point of view, the movement on Herat would be a mere bagatelle [359].

A veteran of the "Great Game" and the struggle between Forward School and Backward School advocates in the government and the press, Rawlinson recognizes that his position will be criticized as jaundiced and parochial, admitting that as a longstanding Russophobe, he might "be supposed to incline rather to the side of suspicion." As justification for his claims, he argues that he and his Forward School colleagues

> have further been assured by sagacious foreign observers, free from all national prejudice, but who have, watched the progress of events, and have been more or less behind the scenes, that the continued advance of Russia in Central Asia is as certain as the movement of the sun in the heavens [339].

One of these "sagacious foreign observers" was none other than Arminius Vambery, a Hungarian scholar, and, significant to this study, an acquaintance of Bram Stoker, who in 1885 was the toast of England.

In the ten years between the publication of Rawlinson's *England and Russia in the East* and Vambery's triumphant tour of England, Russophobia grew as more and more accounts of Russian perfidy appeared in print. The year 1876 saw the publication of Captain Frederick Burnady's travelogue *A Ride to Khiva: Travels and Adventures in Central Asia*, a 487-page work containing extensive appendices listing Russian military strengths and charting Russia's likely movements toward India. Striking a sympathetic chord with the Russophic and jingoistic mood of the day, the book was an immediate best seller, running through eleven reprintings in its first year in publication. With war looming between Russia and Turkey that same year, Burnaby was given a 2,500 pound advance by his publisher to cover the unfolding dispute in eastern Turkey. The book that grew out of his experiences in the Russo-Turkish War, *On Horseback through Asia Minor*, published in 1877, was almost as successful as his previous book and was reprinted seven times (Hopkirk 377–379).

The Russian advance on the city of Merv in eastern Turkmenistan, a likely staging area for an attack on Herat, in 1880 further inflamed anti–Russian passions in England. Leading the assault was General Mikhail Skobelev, an outstanding field commander who had been nicknamed the "White General" by his troops because of his penchant for riding into battle in white dress upon a white mount. His savagery earned him another sobriquet, "Old Bloody Eyes." Having devised a plan to attack India in retaliation for British intercession on the part of Turkey during the Russo-Turkish War, Skobelev's presence in Merv set off alarms in British India. The conduct of the troops under his command at Geok-Tepe, a Turcoman stronghold astride the approach to Merv, would raise Russophobia to a fever pitch in England. This was so because of the work of one Edmund O'Donovan, a reporter for the *London Daily News*, who witnessed the massacre that unfolded (Hopkirk 402–404).

As O'Donovan recounted in his 1881 book *The Merv Oasis: Travels and Adventures East of the Caspian*, the battle pitched 7,000 Russian cavalry and infantry forces against 10,000 Turcoman troops protecting a population of some 40,000 civilians. At first the Russians were repelled by the town's strong fortifications. However, after repeated bombardment by over sixty artillery pieces and rocket launchers, the walls were breached. The slaughter that ensued was horrific:

> No one was spared, not even young children or the elderly. All were mercilessly cut down by Russian sabres. In all, 8,000 of the fugitives are said to have perished, while a further 6,500 bodies were counted inside the fortress itself. "The whole country was covered with corpses," an Armenian interpreter with the force later confided to a British friend. "I myself saw babies bayoneted or slashed to pieces. Many women were ravished before being killed." For three days, he said, Skobelev had allowed his troops, many of whom were drunk, to rape, plunder and slaughter [406–407].

When confronted with the barbarity of his actions, Skobelev remonstrated, "I hold it as a principle that the duration of peace is in direct proportion to the slaughter you inflict upon the enemy" (qtd. in Hopkirk 407).

Russian skullduggery and the threat of a fate similar to that of Geok-Tepe eventually led the Turkomans of Merv to accept annexation by Russia in 1884 (Hopkirk 411–414). Shortly thereafter, in 1885, Russian and Afghan troops skirmished along the contested frontier between Turkmenistan and Afghanistan at the oasis of Pandjeh, which lay half-way between Merv and Herat. The fight, which left several hundred dead, alarmed the Gladstone government, which obtained 11,000,000 pounds of war credits from Parliament, moved 25,000 troops to Quetta along the Indian-Afghanistan border, instructed the navy to occupy Port Hamilton in Korea for an assault on the Siberian stronghold of Vladivostok, and considered attacking Russia's Caucasian territories in conjunction with Turkish troops.[19] The cabinet even went so far as to agree that an attack on Herat would demand open war with Russia (Gillard 144 and Hopkirk 429). Compounding matters, at about the same time news reached England that General Gordon and his men had been slaughtered in Khartoum. These events struck a bellicose chord in the English public and ushered in a wave of Russophobic literature:

> In 1885, that *annus mirabilis* for all who addressed themselves to the Russian menace, [Charles] Marvin published no fewer than three books on various aspects of the subject, including one on the threat posed to India by the new Transcaspian Railway. Another, *The Russian at the Gates of Herat*, was written and published in the space of one week [...] it was to become a bestseller, 65,000 copies being sold in all [...]. Other Great Game works appearing that year included Demetrius Boulger's *Central Asian Questions*, Colonel G. B. Malleson's *The Russo-Afghan Question and the Invasion of India*, and H. Sutherland Edward's *Russian Projects against India*—to name just three. In addition there were innumerable pamphlets, articles, reviews and letters to the editor by these and other commentators, mostly backing the Russophobe cause [Hopkirk 419–420].

Of these voices raised in alarm about Russia in 1885, the best known was the Hungarian Russophobe Arminius Vambery.

In 1861, disguised as a Muslim holy man, Vambery commenced a series of extensive travels in Central Asia to seek the origins of the Magyars, the ancestral inhabitants of Hungary. An adroit student of languages,[20] Vambery garnered considerable evidence from the indigenous Khanates, among whom he sojourned, of Russian incursions in the region. Certain that evidence of the Russian threat would be of interest to the British government, he traveled to London in 1864 where he was greeted warmly by such notables as the Prince of Wales, Palmerston, and Disraeli. Although he was championed by jingoistic elements in the government and military, Vambery did not attract widespread public attention. The fall of Merv changed all that (Hopkirk 420).

When he returned to England in 1885, Vambery attracted a much greater audience:

> Once again he was lionised, but this time people listened to his warnings at a series of packed meetings which he addressed up and down the country. He received so many invitations that he was forced to turn most of them down. One admirer placed at his disposal, during his stay in London, a luxurious apartment, complete with cook, servants and wine cellar. More than once during his travels in the provinces luncheon baskets filled with expensive delicacies were thrust into his railway carriage, their donors signing themselves simply "an admirer" or "a grateful Englishman" [Hopkirk 421].

Upon his return to Budapest, Vambery recorded his warnings about Russia in a book entitled *The Coming Struggle for India*. It was to become, alongside Charles Marvin's *The Russians at the Gates of Herat*, an instant bestseller. The book, which bears the subtitle *Being an account of the Encroachments of Russia in Central Asia, and of the Difficulties Sure to Arise*

*Therefore to England*, is essentially a polemical travelogue, a work which both recounts Vambery's travels through Central Asia and describes the nature of Russia's presence in the area. Moreover, the book is a vehicle for Vambery to call attention to the threat posed by Russia to India, denigrate the liberal governments in England who have embraced the policies of the Backward School, and explain why India is important to England and must be defended. It ends with a chapter in which Vambery explains the basis for his staunch allegiance to England and western civilization.

Vambery makes his Anglophilic sentiments obvious at the very outset:

> The conquest of India was and is undoubtedly the glory of our western civilization; it is the best mark of the superiority of our indomitable European spirit, and of the strength of young Europe compared with old and crumbling Asia [2].

After establishing his pro–English credentials, Vambery proceeds to attack liberal governments for failing to take a more aggressive approach to Russia. Thus he contends that even in the face of intense public distrust of Russia and the Russophobia aroused by the Crimean War, which he terms "a costly and quite objectless undertaking," government reaction to Russian expansion in Central Asia has been marked by "leniency, indecision, and irresolution" (64). This is especially so of the Gladstone administration and Sir John Lawrence, Viceroy of India, who believed that the physical barriers of India's frontier would stymy a Russian attack. Gladstone comes in for particular derision:

> Having succeeded in undoing entirely the work of their predecessors, the party in power in England since 1880 have been afforded ample opportunity to become convinced of the gross mistakes into which they had rushed. But, alas! Blindness, a great misfortune with single individuals, is certainly far more disastrous in the case of a large body, and, particularly if that body is entrusted with the conduct of affairs of a powerful state such as Great Britain [73].[21]

The fall of Merv and the Pandjeh incident, which took place while British attention was diverted by events in the Sudan, proved the folly of the Backward School, forcing Gladstone, "the author and upholder of Russian sympathies in England," to reevaluate the relationship between the two powers and "to bitterly expiate his Russian proclivities" (86). Unfortunately, liberal molly-coddling has allowed Russia to assume a position in Central Asia perilous to India. For effect and emphasis, Vambery italicizes this point:

> we may now well consider the results which Russia has obtained in this protracted contest, by stating at once that *the unheard of short-sightedness of British statesmen has handed over to her the very keys with which she can now open, at her leisure, the gate of India; for she is in full possession of all the ways*

*which can bring her to Herat in a comparatively short time and without any difficulty whatever* [99].

Echoing Rawlinson, Vambery then goes on to discuss the strategic significance of Herat. In 1885 the threat is particularly acute because of the progress of the Transcaucasian Railway, which was then approaching the Afghan border. The railway, Vambery contends, will allow the reinforcement of the Russian garrison in the vicinity of Pandjeh "from the Caucasus at the rate of a division a week" (101). A march on Herat would be precipitous, reaching it "from the nearest point of what will probably be the new Russian frontier in eight days, and that the cavalry and Cossack batteries could so in four days" (102). Herat, "the gate of India" (103), is supremely important for Vambery for reason of its "agricultural, commercial, ethnic, and strategic advantages" (104).

In Vambery's estimation, Herat is a veritable Eden. Clearly, it is a place of plenty:

> The pears and apples are better than those so highly prized in Asia, known as Nathenzians, and the mutton more savoury than that of Shiraz and Karaman, which is saying a good deal. The inhabitants of Herat have good wool in abundance for the textiles required for raiment, wood for their buildings, and a great variety of minerals which are only awaiting development [105–106].

Of special significance in Central Asia is water, "that most essential element," of which "there is an abundance" in Herat (107). As a commercial center, it is surpassed by but a few cities in Asia, an "emporium for tea and indigo, on the one hand, and American and English wares, such as cotton, fabrics, cloth, trinkets, etc., on the other hand" (113). Strategically, Herat is *nonpareil*, having served as a jumping off point for incursions into India for ages:

> you are well aware of the fact, gentlemen, that all the conquerors of India in bygone days have passed through Herat, have marshaled their armies there, and allowed them to rest at Herat in order to prepare them for the change of temperature in the southern latitudes. To this very day, this traditional highway to India is preferred to the route over the Hindoo Koosh and Kabul, not only by armies and caravans, but by solitary travelers, such as pilgrims to Mecca [114].

Having established that Russia has placed herself in a position to move on Herat, Vambery launches into an impassioned plea for immediate action on the part of Britain.

He is most vehement in his rejection of the argument for a diplomatic solution advanced by the Backward School and continental powers wishing to avoid another war between European nations:

> To imagine that ambitious Russia will pursue a policy, for centuries, through the dreary steppes of Central Asia, without any palpable results other

than the possession of the three Khanates and of the Turkoman country—a possession which will never pay the heavy sacrifices of blood and money—is really more than political shortsightedness, for it's suggested by intentional malice and black envy. Do people really fancy, after Russia has spent over one hundred millions of pounds during only the present century, upon carrying out her old and favourite scheme, that she will stop, at the very gate of India, and will resist all temptation coming from the sunny land of the Ganges and on the Indus? No, I cannot believe in the sincerity of such an idea; its adoption would simply lull the English into the sleep of false security, and encourage Russia in her approach to the Achilles heel of the rival [163–164].

La mission civilatrice of imperialism must needs be the work of Englishmen, for, as Vambery argues, Russians have proven themselves wholly unfit for the task.

As evidence of this proposition, Vambery analyzes the results of "nearly four hundred years [of] the Russian process of civilization" among the native peoples of Central Asia. He hopes to show that they are, inevitably, "losers morally and materially, and are as far from any notion of our western culture as any of their brethren living under fanatical Mohammedan rule" (168). First, the Russians have failed to educate the people under their occupation. For example, among the Kazan-Tartars, a "mentally gifted" and cultured Moslem people, aside from a "familiarity with modern European beverages, there is not the slightest trace of the world of the nineteenth century to be remarked in the social and political life of those stubborn Asiatics." Moreover, other than supplying schools with very primitive books about Russian geography, history, and some translations of Russian fables, "they are left in moral stupor" (168). What instruction there is in the school system is crafted so as "to turn the Tartar into Christians and Muscovites, in order that they may become much more easily engulfed into the already gigantic body of Muscovitism" (169).

Russian administration has also failed to protect these native peoples from the "destructive work of the Russian Cossack, popa, and merchant" (169). Russian settlers have displaced the indigenous population, whom they have "exploited in the most unscrupulous manner." They have fallen victim to "usury," and their health has been compromised "by the use of the deadly poison vodki" (170). Such is the state of Russian rule, that the conquered people of Central Asia "have undergone little or no change since they came under the fatherly care of the Czar" (172). Undoubtedly, Russia is incapable of spreading western values and civilization because it is, to Vambery, a morally bankrupt nation:

> In accordance with the saying, that the river cannot rise higher than the source, it would be preposterous to expect from the Russian Government any degree of culture higher than she was able to confer on her own subjects. A

society where the main principles of administration are wanting; where bribery, embezzlement, and corruption are the order of the day; and where every official, either civil or military, is looking after his own personal interest, and has not the faintest idea of duty, honesty, and patriotism; there it is almost an impossible thing to get the beneficent rule based upon right and legality, so indispensable to the welfare of the masses [173–174].

England, on the other hand, has proven during its long rule in India to be the paragon of all imperial powers, a wise and beneficent presence that has brought the rule of law and prosperity to the people of Asia.

Any European, asserts Vambery, would "swell with pride" at Britain's accomplishments in India. Such are the astonishing gifts of English imperial rule that in a land where they are vastly outnumbered, "the shadow of a single Briton suffices to overawe the vast multitude, and to ensure obedience and respect for the doctrines of civilization" (175). For the taxes they pay to Britain, Indians have been saved "from the tyranny and despotism they had formerly to endure under the rule of their native princes," they have been enlightened "in schools supported by the Government," and their lives have been improved by the building of roads, railways, and telegraph lines (179). Under the fair guidance of British law, the crime of Sati, "whereby Hindoo widows were burned alive on the funeral pyres of their husbands," has been eliminated; the practice of female infanticide has ceased; the internecine strife occasioned by fanatical sects and creeds curtailed; and the incidence of "kidnapping, forgery, adultery, and perjury" reduced (179–180). British engineering and science have further improved agriculture. Some 20,350 miles of canals have been dug, irrigating approximately 6,310,000 acres (181–182).

Advances in education have been equally dramatic under British occupation. Over 65,000 schools of all types have been established, serving almost 2,000,000 students, 72,000 of whom are girls, at an annual cost of 800,000 pounds (184–185). The graduates of this system emerge proficient in the English language and English literature as well as the sciences. Finding "a swarthy-looking Asiatic quoting Shakespeare, Virgil, and Homer, is an extraordinary, but not unusual spectale" (185). But, unlike those educated in Russian areas of conquest, students in the Indian school system also receive training in their native culture and languages. Thus, out of the 4,900 works on history and literature published in a recent year, 550 are in English, 3,050 in the vernacular, 7,730 in the classical languages of India, and 570 in more than one language. Moreover, native-language newspapers and periodicals are proliferating; in their criticism of the government, they "almost begin to vie, in their free and unrestrained language, with the press of the English mother-country" (185–186).

Finally, transportation and commerce have flourished under British stewardship. By 1883, 10,317 miles of track had been laid at the cost of upward of 200,000,000 pounds. Although the rail system works most to English advantage by "developing the trade of India" and by providing the means for the "strategical" transit of military assets, it also benefits the natives, who "travel at fares that [...] are the cheapest in the whole world" (186). British investments in India similarly accrue to the advantage of occupier and occupied alike. Of the 24,000,000 pounds in goods exported from Britain annually, more than an eighth, 32,000,000 pounds, is destined for India, more than the exports to America and Australia. Especially significant is the trade in fabricated goods. Cotton, grown in India and spun into cloth in England, accounts for 25,000,000 pounds sterling. Machinery stands next in importance, with India receiving some 3,250,000 pounds in British exports (192–193). Pensions and salaries further contribute to the financial significance to Britain of its Indian colony. Englishmen in service in India, as well as those on pension, draw funds from the Exchequer of India which is more often than not "spent in the insular home," adding to the national wealth of England. This wealth, in turn, then flows back to India in the "immensely large sums of English capital invested in railways, irrigation canals, and other concerns" (194–195).

But, above all, Vambery emphasizes the "moral standing Great Britain enjoys through her Indian possession" (195). So well has Britain's civilizing mission been accomplished that the "name of Ferenghi, i.e. European, by which Englishmen are known in India [...] has obtained a luster unparalleled, hitherto, in the history of mankind" (195). Should Britain withdraw or fail to keep Russia at bay, disaster would be sure to follow:

> It is, therefore, in consideration of the strictly and purely humanitarian part which England plays in India, that every European must feel a lively interest in the maintenance of British rule in India. He must be convinced of the indisputable fact that, with the retreat of the English from that peninsula, either the most horrible anarchy will ensue, and raping, bloodshed, and murder take the place of the present settled, and peaceful condition of the country—for India was never able to govern herself—or that the barbarous despotism of Russia will inaugurate a new era of Asiatic disorders, and sweep away every trace of that glorious building erected through the skill, perseverance, and heroism of England [197].

But, as Vambery states in the last chapter, the English, once properly warned of the looming threat, are up to the task of not only guaranteeing the ongoing development of India but also of bringing civilization to all the people of Central Asia, for their "superior manhood, fearlessness and self-respect, enable them to carry through the regeneration of Asia more successfully than any of the European nations extant" (203).

In closing, Vambery expresses his appreciation for the warm reception he received during his 1885 lecture tour through England. He is especially heartened to note that government officials and the English public paid heed to his warnings about "the excessive increase of the power of barbarous and despotic Russia" (208). He ends with a nod of gratitude to "the solid rock of Anglo-Saxon character," the only conceivable barrier to Russian domination in Central Asia. As a writer, he contends, his goal has been "to animate the English to maintain their position in Asia, which is inseparably connected with their power in Europe" (208). Vambery would repeat this call to arms many times in the years to follow.

In 1890, five years after the publication of *The Coming Struggle for India*, Vambery was again in England spreading the message. On this visit, he was an honored guest of Henry Irving, the famous actor and owner-operator of the Lyceum Theatre, for a performance of the play *The Dead Heart* and, as was usually the case with special guests, an intimate private dinner in the Beefsteak Room located above the stage. On this occasion he met Bram Stoker, the manager of the Lyceum, who recorded his observations of Vambery in his biography of Irving, *Reminiscences of Henry Irving*. When they met again two years later during the celebration surrounding the Tercentenary of Dublin University, Vambery was still sounding the alarm, a warning that very much impressed Stoker, a Trinity graduate himself:

> On the day on which the delegates from the various Universities of the world spoke, he shone out as a star. He soared above all the speakers, making one of the finest speeches I have ever heard. Be sure that he spoke loudly against Russian aggression — a subject to which he had largely devoted himself [*Reminiscences* 1: 372].

So taken with Vambery was Stoker that he included him as a character in the novel *Dracula*, a work he began in 1890, the year he first met Vambery, and returned to in earnest in 1892, the year of Vambery's Dublin University address.

Clive Leatherdale, who has written extensively about *Dracula*, has remarked that Stoker "had a habit of dropping names of acquaintances into his fiction usually as a private joke or simple tribute" (*Dracula Unearthed* 337). Vambery's name appears in chapter eighteen, when Dr. Van Helsing confides to his fellow vampire hunters that he has "asked my friend Arminius of Buda-Pesth University, to make his record; and, from all the means that are he tell me what he [Dracula] has been" (*D* 291). Mention of Vambery here has led to a lively scholarly debate about the polemicist's role in the creation of the novel. Harry Ludlam, Stoker's first biographer, asserts in 1962 that "Count Dracula began to stir in his tomb" (80) when Stoker initially conversed with Vambery over dinner in the Beefsteak Room in

1890. Stoker, as Ludlam tells it, eventually "sought the help of Arminius Vambery in Budapest" for information about Voivoide Drakula, a figure Stoker had come across in his research for the novel. Vambery, in Ludlam's account, provided a host of details:

> Vambery was able to report that "the Impaler," who had won this name for obvious reasons, was spoken of for centuries after as the cleverest and the most cunning, as well as the bravest of the sons of the "land beyond the forest." He was a soldier, statesman and alchemist, who took his mighty brain and iron resolution with him to the grave. The Dracula's [sic] were also held by their contemporaries to have had dealings with "the Evil One"; the old records, besides labelling Dracula a "wampyr" using such words as "stregoica" — witch; "ordog" and "pokol" — Satan and Hell [100].

Stoker's next biographer, his great-nephew Daniel Farson, in 1975 reiterates and expands Ludlam's claims regarding Vambery.

Farson demands that Stoker "had the personal advantage of help from another source with undoubted authority: a Hungarian professor with the Stokerish name of Professor Arminius Vambery." Proposing that "there is a touch of Vambery in the character of Van Helsing" (124), Farson goes into quite some detail about Vambery's adventures in Central Asia and his reception in England, highlighting Vambery's efforts to warn England of the Russian menace in Asia. Noting that Vambery was widely praised for playing "an active part in the defence of British interests in Asia" (124), Farson writes,

> Vambery had the percipience to point out that the British would insist on treating Eastern problems in European terms and that the Russians achieved greater results with smaller use of men but more skillful diplomacy. For his advice he was awarded with the Commander of the Royal Victorian Order and was received by Edward, Prince of Wales, on 29 September 1888 during the Prince's visit to Pesth [125].

Farson ends with the suggestion that "it was the Hungarian professor who told Bram, for the first time, of the name of Dracula" (126). Radu Florescu and Raymond McNally make much the same claim in their seminal 1972 study *In Search of Dracula*. Asserting that "Stoker learned of 'Dracula' from this Hungarian friend" (13), Florescu and McNally proceed to state that after their dinner conversation in 1890, "Bram wrote to him, requesting more details about the notorious 15th century prince and the land he lived in" (178).

Such generous claims about Vambery's role in the creation of the novel have been called into question of late. The discovery of Stoker's working notes for the novel at the Rosenbach Museum and Library in Philadelphia in the 1970s led to a wholesale reevaluation of earlier arguments advanced about Stoker's sources, particularly the contention that Dracula was based on Vlad the Impaler, but also the contributions of Vambery. Leatherdale, writing in 1985, refutes suggestions that Vambery gave Stoker the name and background of Dracula. The working notes, Leatherdale contends, disprove the excessive credit attributed to Vambery:

> What is, finally, the most persuasive argument against the primacy of the Vambery connection is that all the important information in the novel concerning Dracula, or vampires in general, and which is attributed in *Dracula* to Arminius, can be found in the books and articles listed in Stoker's notes. These notes do not mention Arminius Vambery [*Dracula: The Novel and the Legend* 88].

Elizabeth Miller, a colleague of Leatherdale and long-time Stoker scholar herself, agrees categorically, stating in her 2000 review of *Dracula* scholarship, *Dracula: Sense and Nonsense*, that "Speculating about Stoker's sources without consulting his notes is asking for trouble" (19). The claim that Vambery imparted knowledge of Vlad or vampires in general to Stoker is bogus because "Arminius Vambery published nothing about vampires" and "no records of conversations that even remotely touch on the subject of vampires" between Stoker and Vambery exist (30–31). These facts lead Miller to insist that "[t]here is no reason to believe that Arminius Vambery was the source of any of Stoker's knowledge about vampire lore" (31). Reflecting the impact of the working notes on recent Stoker scholarship, Barbara Belford in her 1996 biography of Stoker gives Vambery but passing mention. She terms him at best an "ambiguous influence" on Stoker, observing that "there is no evidence that Vambery initiated the vampire myth" (260).

Undoubtedly, early biographers and scholars placed undue emphasis on the mention of Vambery in the novel. Even Florescu and McNally toned down their assertion about Vambery's role in the 1994 revised edition of *In Search of Dracula*, stipulating only that during their dinner conversation, "Stoker became impressed by the professor's stories about his homeland" (150). Still, although it is no longer accepted in academic circles that Vambery is the source of the vampire myth and the character Dracula himself, it is certain that Stoker and Vambery were acquaintances and that Stoker lent a sympathetic ear to Vambery's warnings about Russia. Another chance meeting at the Beefsteak Room must undoubtedly have reinforced Vambery's charges against Russia in Stoker's mind. This occurred on July 8, 1892, the same year as the Dublin University Tercentenary celebrations where Vambery spoke so eloquently about the Russian threat and the year when Stoker returned to writing the novel. In this instance, the guest was one Sergius Stepniak, a Russian émigré, who was brought to Stoker's attention by his friend Hall Caine, to whom Stoker eventually dedicated *Dracula*.[22]

Stoker records in *Reminiscences of Henry Irving* that "I sat next to him at supper and we had a great deal of conversation together, chiefly about the state of affairs in Russia generally and the Revolutionary party in especial" (2: 53). During their conversation, Stoker learned from Stepniak of the fate of Russian scholars and dissidents swept up in recent government raids:

> In our conversation at supper that night he told me of the letters which they were receiving from the far-off northern shores of Siberia. It was a most sad and pitiful tale. Men of learning and culture, mostly University professors, men of blameless life and takers of no active part in revolution or conspiracy — simply theorists of freedom, patriots at heart — sent away to the terrible muddy shores of the Arctic sea, ill housed, ill fed, over worked — where life was one long, sordid, degrading struggle for bare life in that inhospitable region [2:55].

Stepniak's remarks, which call to mind similar accounts in Alexander I. Solzhenitsyn's *Gulag Archipelago*, "interested and moved" Stoker, who readily agreed to read Stepniak's writings on the subject (2: 55). It seems quite clear, then, that between 1890 and 1892, Vambery and Stepniak had impressed on Stoker the dangers posed by Russia and the corruption and immorality of her government. Another of Stoker's circle of friends and acquaintances, someone certainly familiar with Vambery and who shared his views on Russia, would further reinforce these lessons. This was none other than the writer Rudyard Kipling, another of those London writers with whom Stoker interacted.

Rudyard Kipling came to literary fame in the late 1880s with the publication of the verse collection *Departmental Ditties* in 1886 and the short story collection *Plain Tales from the Hills* in 1888. Based on the author's experiences as a child and later as a journalist in India, these works reflect both Kipling's masterful style and command of the language and, notably, his profound understanding and sympathy for the common English soldier, the Tommy. They and later pieces also demonstrate Kipling's allegiance to the English cause in the Great Game, an expression that, according to Meyer and Brysac, was "given universal currency in *Kim*," Kipling's novel "about Kimball O'Hara, the ophaned son of an Irish soldier, who frustrates a Russian plot in British India" (xxiii).

Kipling and Stoker were undeniably personally acquainted with each other. At least two sources, Martin Seymour-Smith's *Rudyard Kipling* of 1989 and Stuart Murray's *Rudyard Kipling in Vermont* of 1997, state that when Kipling and his new bride, the American Caroline Balestier, departed Liverpool for the United States, they were seen off by Henry James, Kipling's best man, and Bram Stoker (Seymour-Smith 226 and Murray 7). Ludlam, Farson, and Belford describe a more tenuous connection between the two.

Ludlam notes that a Stoker short story, "The Man from Shorrox," debuted in 1893 in the *Pall Mall Magazine* along with a story by Kipling (90). Farson and Belford draw attention to the fact that Kipling published the poem "The Vampire" in 1897, the year *Dracula* was published, to commemorate the exhibition of a painting of the same name painted by his cousin, Phillip Burne-Jones (Farson 216 and Belford 275). Though no mention is made about an interchange between Stoker and Kipling occasioned by the exhibit and the poem, which was displayed with the painting, the Burne-Jones family does suggest an additional link between the two authors.

At age five, Kipling was left for some five years in the care of a Southsea family by the name of Holloway. Separated from his parents, who returned to India, and constantly berated by the puritanical Mrs. Holloway, Kipling came to think of the Holloway home, known as Lorne Lodge, as the "House of Desolation" (Gilmour 8). His only respite from this hell on earth was his annual Christmas sojourn to The Grange in Fulham, the residence of his Aunt Georgy and her husband, the Pre-Raphaelite painter Sir Edward Burne-Jones. The Grange, as David Gilmour records in his recent biography of Kipling, was a heaven on earth for the virtual orphan:

> On arrival he had to jump to reach its bell-pull, "a sort of 'open sesame' into a House Beautiful," a world of cousins and rocking-horses and "wonderful smells of paints and turpentine" wafting down from his uncle's studio. He climbed the mulberry tree with his cousins, he listened to his aunt reading Scott or *The Arabian Nights*, he encountered poets and artists all willing to talk to him and play except an "elderly person called 'Browning,' who took no proper interest" in the children skirmishing in the hall [9].

The young Kipling developed a lasting affection for his Uncle Edward, whom he affectionately called Uncle Ned, recounting after his death that Edward "had been a god to him" (10). It is through Uncle Ned that Kipling may very well have come to form a more direct relationship with Stoker.

In *Reminiscences of Henry Irving*, Stoker relates the participation of Edward Burne-Jones in the 1894 production of the play *King Arthur*, which ran for over a hundred performances. Sir Edward Burne-Jones was given the task of designing "scenes and dresses, armour and appointments" (1: 253). Stoker describes the relationship between Burne-Jones and Irving in glowing terms. He writes that for Irving it was "an intense pleasure to work with Sir Edward Burne-Jones" (2: 73) and that "To work with such an artist was to Irving a real joy" (2: 74). Stoker even suggests that "I veritably believe that Irving was sorry when the production of the play was complete." Possessing "a mind tuned to the same key" as Irving's, the actor found "fresh stimulation" in every encounter with the artist (2: 74). As was often the case at the Lyceum, artistic collaboration eventuated in lasting friendships and celebrations in the Beefsteak Room. During their after-hour gatherings, Stoker records that Burne-Jones regaled Irving with stories, especially stories about children, which

> seemed closest to his heart. In our meetings on the stage or at supper in the Beefsteak Room, or on those delightful Sunday afternoons when he allowed a friend to stroll with him round his studio, there was always some little tale breathing the very essence of human nature [2:75].

Tales of the precocious, rambunctious Kipling, whom Gilmour describes as the "pampered little sahib with his blues eyes and dark, podgy, strong-jawed face" who "was loud, aggressive and prone to tantrums" (7), may well have been among those Burne-Jones shared with Irving. Whatever the case, Stoker, the committed devotee of Irving, usually shared Irving's passions and through his association with Burne-Jones would certainly have had ample opportunity to engage in blandishments about the elder artist's famous nephew.

Clearly, then, Stoker and Kipling, who returned to England from America in 1896, were acquaintances. More importantly, however, they were both staunchly dedicated to the British empire and the professionals who oversaw England's vast global network of colonies. Rawlinson and Vambery had argued that the crown jewel of empire lay under the dire threat of Russian invasion. Kipling would piquantly illuminate this threat in his prose and verse. Gilmour asserts that Kipling "identified a number of threats, both external and internal, to the imperial project." Among these was the danger posed by "the Russian across the frontier in central Asia because of their talent 'only second to ours of turning all sorts of clans and races into loyal supporters.'" Nevertheless, Gilmour argues that the "Great Game" "occupies little space in his work" and that "the real enemies of British India were British: zealous and misguided missionaries (secular as well as religious) and interfering politicians in England" (80).[23] Gilmour's position here is at odds with that expressed about Kipling by none other than W. H. Auden, who in a 1943 review of Kipling's career wrote,

> while virtually every other European writer since the fall of the Roman empire has felt that the dangers threatening civilization came from *inside* that civilization [...] Kipling is obsessed by a sense of danger threatening from *outside* [qtd. in Howe xv].

Gilmour may well be correct when he asserts that in Kipling's *ouvre* accounts of Russian perfidy and intrigue occupy but a "little space"; nonetheless, it is irrefutable that between 1888 and 1891, Kipling often returns to this theme, one that occupies much of the action of his most famous novel, *Kim*. A travelogue published in 1889 by an Englishman soon to be identified with India and the Forward School, someone Kipling would come to know well, might be said to illustrate the thinking of Anglo-Indians of the day, such as Kipling.

George Curzon, who became Viceroy of India in 1899, published an account of his journeys in eastern Russia and Central Asia in 1889 under the title of *Central Asia and the Anglo-Russian Question*. Kipling and Curzon shared imperialistic, conservative, jingoistic political beliefs[24]; Kipling admired Curzon's intellect and political savvy, labeling him a "machine of necessary industry" (qtd. in Gilmour 292). The future viceroy's book, which ran to some 478 pages, offered a detailed account of the author's observations gathered along the length of the Transcaspian Railway and struck a sympathetic note with Russophobes. One stop that was sure to grab readers' attention was at Geok-Tepe, the scene of the Russian massacre of Turcomans described almost a decade earlier by O'Donovan. Noting that "it was impossible to ride over the plain without one's horse-hooves crushing into human skulls," Curzon was alarmed by how quickly the Turcomans had been assimilated into the service of Russia in such a relatively short time:

> I do not think that any sight could have impressed me more profoundly with the completeness of Russia's conquest than the spectacle of these men, only eight years ago the bitter and determined enemies of Russia on the battlefield, but now wearing her uniform, standing high in her service, and crossing to Europe to salute as their sovereign the Great White Czar. [qtd. in Hopkirk 442].

Later at Tashkent, which had been converted to a military garrison under Russian occupation, Curzon learned from conversations with Russian officers of their overriding antipathy toward England. He further came to discover that when the two hundred miles between Samarkand and Tashkent had been bridged, the railway would put Russia in a position to lodge some 100,000 troops on the border of Persia and Afghanistan (Hopkirk 444–446). Curzon's investigations convinced him that Russia's ultimate goal was the conquest of all of Asia and that Britain must oppose Russian expansion in Central Asia (Hopkirk 504). Adopting a Forward School stance, he wrote that

> Whatever be Russia's designs upon India, whether they be serious and inimical or imaginary and fantastic, I hold that the first duty of English statesmen is to render any hostile intentions futile, to see that our own position is secure, and our frontier impregnable, and so to guard what is without a doubt the noblest trophy of British genius, and the most splendid appanage of the Imperial Crown [qtd. in Hopkirk 293].

The British soldiers in India whom Kipling immortalized in print were prepared for just such an eventuality and were eager to take on the Russian bear.

Kipling manifested Russophobic tendencies from an early age.[25] Angus Wilson, in the 1978 biography *The Strange Ride of Rudyard Kipling*, offers an illustrative incident that occurred during Kipling's tenure at the United Services College at Westward Ho!, a school for the sons of military officers and civil servants who could not afford the cost of an education at England's more prestigious public schools. At age sixteen, in the fourth year of his studies, Kipling debated the headmaster over the proposition that "the advance of the Russians in central Asia is hostile to British Power," a debating point put forward by the young Russophobe himself. Kipling, whose father living in India kept him up to date on "Great Game" goings on,[26] argued in the affirmative and carried the motion twenty-one to nine (43).

That same year, 1882, offered another example of Kipling's concern with the Russian threat. A failed attempt on Queen Victoria's life that March prompted Kipling to write a poem espousing his schoolmates' joy at Her Majesty's survival. It also communicates their willingness to serve in her employ as imperial guardians. Titled "Ave Imperatrix!" it reads in part

> Such greetings as should come from those
> Whose fathers faced the Sepoy hordes,
> Or served you in the Russian snows,
> And, dying, left their sons their swords.

Incorporating obvious allusions to the Crimean War and the Mutiny of 1857, the poem goes on to state that "some of us have fought for you / Already in the Afghan pass," a reference to the first and second Afghan War. These expeditions had proven conclusively the difficulty of military operations on the northern frontier of India. Moreover, these wars demonstrated for all to see the tenacity, cunning, and deadliness of Afghan warriors and how important it was to deny them to Russia. When Kipling returned to India later that year, he assumed a position as an assistant editor of the *Civil and Military Gazette*, where he worked in an atmosphere of "recurrent fears about Russia's intentions" (Rutherford xiv), fears that would shortly find expression in his art.[27]

Two poems published soon after his return to England in 1889 indicate that Kipling had Russia on his mind. "The Ballad of the King's Jest," 1890, very much anticipates Kipling's "Great Game" classic *Kim*. Narrated by a British spy, either a native in the employ of the British government or a Briton in native guise, the poem is set in the bivouac of a caravan traveling south from Afghanistan through the Khyber Pass. The narrator informs his host, the "muleteer" Mahbub Ali, a character who appears again in *Kim*, that he is seeking "a word of a Russian post / Of a shifty promise, an unsheathed sword, / And of a grey-coat guard on the Helmund ford." This is the usual laundry list of grievances advanced against Russia by Forward School advocates. In the phrase "shifty promise," the speaker alludes to Russia's duplicity in her dealings with Central Asian nationalities. Rawlinson and Vambery offer countless examples of how Russian expansion in Central Asia followed a series of treaties signed and then ignored by Russian military commanders. Next, the "unsheathed sword" suggests both Russia's brutal conquests in Central Asia, such as the assault on Geok-Tepe, and the bellicose posture of her soldiers, much like those interviewed at Taskent by Curzon. Lastly, the "grey-coat guard on the Helmund ford" references Russia's designs on Afghanistan. The Helmand River almost perfectly bisects Afghanistan, flowing southwest from its headwaters near Kabul. Russian command of a ford on this important waterway would indicate a deep penetration of the Afghan buffer state, one that could be accomplished only after the fall of Herat, the great dread of Rawlinson and Vambery.

Further exemplifying Kipling's ongoing interest in the Crimean War is "The Last of the Light Brigade," 1891. The poem is both an indictment of the government for its failure to adequately care for her veterans and of the English people for turning their backs on the misery of their Crimean heroes. As in the *Punch* illustration "GRAND MILITARY SPECTACLE," a group of non-commissioned veterans, led by "an old Troop-Sergeant," display character traits usually associated with their social betters. Although "thirty million English" boast "of England's might," a reference to the jingoistic saber rattling common in the press of the day, few Englishmen, if any, had concern or care for the "twenty broken troopers who lacked a bed for the night." Despite the fact that "Russian sabres" had injured them, "want was keener than they," so "dying of famine" they turn for help and relief to "the Master-singer who had crowned them all in his song," Alfred Lord Tennyson. The subsequent verses he writes[28] to chronicle their plight "swept the land like flame," chastising the British government and public "with the thing called shame."

"The Last of the Light Brigade" reiterates a project underpinning Kipling's second major poetry collection, *Barracks Room Ballads*, which appeared in 1892. Kipling was committed to rehabilitating the reputation of the common soldier, whom he came to know so intimately during his years in India that the sergeant-major of the 5th Northhumberland Fusiliers said Kipling "knew more of the psychology of the private soldier of his day than any civilian ever had, or could have known [...]." (qtd. in Gilmour 50). Following in the footsteps of Florence Nightingale and William Russell, Kipling helps to elevate the social status of the common soldier. As Gilmour concludes, Kipling broke with the romantic, heroic tradition of military writing:

> Here was a poet not writing about impossible love, improbable valour, wine and roses, or the Middle Ages, but a bard using the dialect of the London working class in traditional ballad form to depict the personal much neglected feelings of the British soldier [91].

The poem "Tommy" best illustrates Kipling's method. Tommy Atkins is a typical soldier of the day. His lot is to be abused and disparaged at almost every turn. When he enters a tavern, the owner greets him rudely with the words "We serve no red-coats here." At the theatre he fares no better. While "a drunk civilian" is allowed to enter, Tommy must make do with "the music-'alls." Amongst the general public, he is ridiculed as a "brute." But, when the clouds of war gather, Tommy finds himself hailed as the "Saviour of 'is country," and provisions are made for a "Special train for Atkins." People then beckon him "to walk in front, sir." But, as in "The Last of the Light Brigade," when the storm has passed, Tommy knows it will not be long before the public will once again be "makin' mock o' uniforms that guard you while you sleep."

Such fondness and sympathy for the Tommy Atkins of the world is a salient feature of Kipling's short fiction as well. Tales of the lives of the common Tommy preponderate in his short story collections *Plain Tales from the Hills* and *Soldiers Three*, 1888, and *Life's Handicap*, 1891. The protagonists of "The Man Who Would Be King," considered by many to be Kipling's finest story (Gilmour 37), fit the mold perfectly. Daniel Dravot and Peachy Carnehan, who come to India as soldiers, have decided "that India isn't big enough for such" as they and have chosen to seek their fortune in Kafiristan, a mountainous region in the "top-right corner of Afghanistan, not more than three hundred miles from Peshawar" (37). Their plan is simple enough, as Dravot explains:

> "We shall go to those parts and say to any King we find — 'D'you want to vanquish your foes?' and we will show him how to drill men; for that we know better than anything else. Then we will subvert that King and seize his Throne and establish a Dy-nasty" [38].

Once they have ensconced themselves in Kafiristan, Dravot and Carnehan set about forming an army, a force they hope will win them an "Empire" (56) and, in turn, lead Queen Victoria to knight them. This last accomplishment will eventuate from their raising an army and setting it against Her Majesty's mortal enemy in Central Asia:

> "There must be a fair two million of 'em in these hills. The villages are full o' little children. Two million people — two hundred and fifty thousand fighting men — and all English! They only want the rifles and a little drilling. Two hundred and fifty thousand men ready to cut in on Russia's right flank when she tries for India!" [56].

Admittedly, the Russian menace hovers in the background in "The Man Who Would Be King," but in "The Man Who Was," what J. I. M. Steward has dubbed "a companion piece" to "The Man Who Would Be King" (64), the Russian foe stands center stage.

"The Man Who Was" reflects the "Great Game" realities of the day. According to Stewart, readers of the tale must keep in mind that "at the end of the nineteenth century, every British soldier in India believed that it was his destiny, at some early date, to confront and repel the invading armies of Russia" (66). The story recounts an evening in the regimental mess of the White Hussars, an Irish unit stationed in Peshawar, "which stands at the mouth of that narrow swordcut in the hills men call the Khyber pass," who had gathered to celebrate their triumph in polo over the Lushkar Light Horse, a native detachment. A most unusual guest has joined the White Hussars in their revelries, one Dirkovitch, an officer in a Cossack regiment and, unmistakably, a spy who "arrived in India from nowhere in particular." Although the Hussars are openly distrustful of him, the Indian government, "being in an unusually affable mood, gave orders that he was to be civilly treated and shown everything to be seen" (79). Dirkovitch's presence under these circumstances is meant as a slap at the Backward School proponents in India and England, as is Dirkovitch's suggestion that a "glorious future awaited the combined arms of England and Russia when their hearts and their territories should run side by side and the great mission of civilising Asia should begin" (80). The Hussars, like Rawlinson, and the narrator himself, are highly dubious of such a claim. The arrival of Hira Singh, the captain of the Lushkar team, and shortly thereafter the entry of what appears to be a beggar and thief dispel the pretty fiction of Anglo-Russian amity, however.

After expressing his admiration for the Hussars' extraordinary play and exchanging the typical sporting blandishments with the regimental commander, Hira Singh spies Durkovitch. In a sudden his mood and tone change. Employing the metaphors of sport, Hira Singh makes his enmity for Russia obvious:

> "But if by the will of God there arises any other game which is not the polo game, then be assured, Colonel Sahib and officers, that we will play it out side by side, though *they*," again his eye sought Dirkovitch, "though *they* I say have fifty ponies to our one horse" [86].

Hira Singh's speech is met with "a deep-mouthed *Rung-ho!* that sounded like a musket-butt on flagstones." The Hussars' cheering is presently halted by the sound of a shot fired and the appearance of a woeful figure "turbanless, shoeless, caked with dirt, and all but dead" (87). Eventually they pry from this pitiful creature that he is Lieutenant Austin Limmanson, missing in action since the Crimean War, having been captured before Sebastopol and kept in bondage for thirty years. Bearing the scars of a brutal imprisonment and reduced to a groveling, almost subhuman existence by his jailers, Limmanson arouses the Hussars' ire. Dirkovitch apologizes for Limmanson's fate, but his words fall on deaf ears. The narrator states that the "next time they have no engagements on hand the White Hussars intend to go to St. Petersburgh" and that to Dirkovitch's remarks the Hussars "exhibited un–Christian delight and other emotions hardly restrained by their sense of hospitality" (95–97).

The Hussars repeat their hostile intentions at the story's end when Dirkovitch is being shown off at the train station. Dirkovitch comments that he "will come again," indicating a return route "where the North star burned over the Khyber Pass" (99–100). As the "tail-lights" of Dirkovitch's train fade into the darkness on its journey north, one of the Hussars breaks out in a refrain from a popular "burlesque" in response to Dirkovitch's parting remarks:

> I'm sorry for Mister Bluebeard,
> I'm sorry to cause him pain;
> But a terrible spree there's sure to be
> When he comes back again [100].

Just beneath this passage, the story concludes with an illustration. It is of a Cossack standing against a mountainous background, a sabre clutched in his left hand. Above him shines a star, undoubtedly the North Star referred to in the song.

Such notions find expression in a number of other stories Kipling wrote in the late 1880's and early 1890's. "The Taking of Lungtungpen," for example, ends with another Irish soldier, a private Mulvaney, saying

> "Catch thim young, feed thim high, an' by the honor av that great, little man Bobs, behind a good orficer 'tisn't only dacoits they'd smash wid their clo'es off—'tis Con-ti-nental Ar-r-r-mies! They tuk Lungtungpen nakid; an' they'd take St. Petersburg in their dhrawers! Begad, they would that!" [190].

Moreover, in "The Swelling of Jordan," Captain Mafflin encourages his colleague Captain Gadsby to not retire because the "Russian shindy ready to come to a head at five minutes' notice, and you, the best of us all, backing out of it all!" (216). Likewise, "The Mutiny of the Mavericks" belittles Dhulip Singh, the last ruler of an independent Punjab, who sought out Russia as a potential ally against England (72). Later in the story, readers learn that the Mavericks have served with distinction at "Inkerman, The Alma, Sebastopol" (77). They also discover "the Sacred Song of the Mavericks":

> Listen in the North, my boys, there's trouble on the wind;
> Tramp o' Cossack hooves in front, grey great-coats behind;
> Trouble on the Frontier of a most amazin' kind,
> Trouble on the waters o' the Oxus!
> Hurrah! hurrah! it's north by west we go;
> Hurrah! hurrah! the chance we wanted so;

Let 'em hear the chorus from Umballa to Moscow,
As we go marchin' to the Kremlin [79].

Echoing the desires of the White Hussars, the narrator states that "nothing in the world will persuade one of our soldiers when he is ordered to the North on the smallest of affairs, that he is not immediately going gloriously to slay Cossacks and cook his kettles in the palace of the Czar" (80).

Some ten years after the publication of "The Mutiny of the Mavericks," 1901, Kipling was still beating the drum about Russia and the "Great Game." In *Kim*, his most famous and still popular novel, a book deemed "a master work of imperialism" by the late Edward Said (45), Kipling concludes the action with an act of "Great Game" subterfuge and espionage aimed specifically at a Russian agent and his French compatriot. Although the events are at times farcical, the mood is serious, for, as Hurree Babu says, they are to be feared because "They are Russians, and highly unscrupulous people" (272). Clearly, then, Kipling helped to popularize Russophobia in his verse and fiction produced at a time when Bram Stoker was setting about crafting his novel *Dracula*. The authors knew each other, moved in the same artistic and literary circles, and were both staunch imperialists, concerned about the health and maintenance of the British empire. Both, also, were cognizant of a very real Eastern invasion of sorts that had already established itself on their very doorsteps.

Exacerbating Russophobia and fears of the East during this time were the thousands of Eastern European and Russian immigrants who descended on England in the 1880s and 1890s. By far the majority of these were Jews from Russia, Austria-Hungary, and Romania. Between 1881 and 1905, of the more than one million Jews who emigrated from Eastern Europe, more than 100,000 took up residence in England, mostly in the East End of London (Holmes 3–6). Although a small number of Jews had lived peacefully in England since the 1600s, this new wave of immigrants engendered a pronounced anti–Semitism in their new homeland. Over the next two decades, they would be associated with images of sloth, decay, disease, crime, and sexual deviancy in the popular imagination, eventually coming to be viewed as a threat to the English nation itself.

Lloyd Gartner has shown that as a community, new Jewish arrivals tended to crowd in cities, especially in sections of "old residences growing increasingly shabby [...] houses of sunken eminence, once inhabited by well-paid skilled workers or even by the merchant classes, who had moved elsewhere as the neighborhood slowly declined" (142–143). In the Whitechapel district of London alone, the average population density rose from 286 persons per acre to over 600 an acre (147). With overcrowding came problems of sanitation. The notoriously inefficient water system in the East End often resulted in "water famines and highly irregular supply" (151). Compounding matters even further, new Jewish immigrants were apparently indifferent to "foul water closets, leaking ceilings, untrapped sinks, and cracked, moist walls" (152). The impression formed by many Londoners was that these new immigrants were almost a subhuman race.

According to Colin Holmes, author of *Anti-Semitism in British Society, 1876–1939*, anti–Semitism became increasingly more vocal among the middle class in the later years of the nineteenth century. Respected writers such as Robert Sherard and Joseph Banister typified middle-class prejudices. In one article for the *Standard*, Sherard described the physical characteristics of the ghetto Jews making their way to England:

> The faces that, under matted and verminous locks, peer out into the streets are scarcely human. They are the faces of imbeciles, of idiots, ape-faces, dog faces— all that is hideous and most profoundly pitiful. These people are clad in rags and live in kennels, where they ply their trades. In the doorways and the mire of the thoroughfare little children are moving about. Their half naked bodies are black with filth and red with sores [qtd. in Holmes 38].

Readers would certainly have drawn parallels with the inhabitants of the Jewish quarter in London's East End. An even more petulant attack on Jews appeared in Banister's *England under the Jews*, where the author vilified Jews for their foul odor and their "propensity to carry and spread disease" (40).

Later Banister joined other writers in emphasizing "a specifically Jewish contribution to the country's social problems and to decay and decline in England" (47).[29] One of those sharing these sentiments was Sir Richard Burton, a diplomat and translator of *The Arabian Nights* who, while stationed in Damascus, developed a bitter hatred for Jews. The culmination of his anti–Semitism was his polemical pamphlet *Lord Beaconfield, A Sketch* and his later book *The Jew, the Gypsy, and El Islam*. In the pamphlet, Burton accused Disraeli of belonging to a Jewish conspiracy seeking to dominate England, and thence the world, through interbreeding with titled families and by controlling international finances. He stated that hardly a noble family existed in England that was not "leavened with Jewish blood" and that the most stable throne in Europe was "the office stool of the house of Rothschild" (qtd. in Holmes 56). His book accused Jews, on the other hand, of a centuries-old conspiracy to commit ritual murders of Christians (Holmes 54).

As a corollary, the serialized killings of prostitutes by Jack the Ripper raised fears of a dangerous Jewish population intent on ritual murder in the East End. Sander Gilman has shown that the image of Jack that developed "is the caricature of the Eastern Jew," especially the shochet, or kosher butcher (156–160). Moreover, press reports in *The Times* and the illustrated journals gave substance to charges of ritual murder. The sketch *Jewish Jack* that appeared in the *Illustrated Police News* depicts the killer as an Eastern European Jew. The pronounced proboscis and other facial features in the sketch dovetail with conventional portrayals of the disheveled Jewish male frequenting the streets of London's slums. It was further assumed that Jack was seeking revenge on prostitutes who had infected him with syphilis; in this manner, fears of contamination merge with fears of murder at the hand of Jews. Stoker was very familiar with the Jack the Ripper saga and even intimates that it inspired his image of Dracula to some degree. In the preface to the 1901 Icelandic edition of *Dracula*, Stoker describes the events in the novel "as a series of crimes [...] which at the time created as much repugnance in people everywhere as the notorious murders of Jacob the disemboweller, which came into the story a little later." "Jacob the disemboweller," according to Leatherdale, is a rough translation of "Jack the Ripper" (*Dracula Unearthed* 25).

Stoker was well aware of the constellation of attitudes forming around the Eastern European Jewish community in London. It is easy to infer that he probably held the prejudices of his time. But his account of what he discussed with Hall Caine before his meeting with the Russian émigré Stepniak in 1892 suggests that he may well have shared the prejudicial view of the immigrant Jews of England enunciated by Banister and Sherard. The Russian "moujik," writes Stoker,

> was illiterate and as a rule a drunkard when he got the chance [...]. The moujik with his load of corn would take his way to the nearest market centre and there stay in the tavern till he had drunk up all he had received for his crop. The Jew tavern keeper was also the local usurer, and would make a certain advance on the man's labour for the coming year. When that credit had ended, since he never could get even, he would pledge the labour of his children. Thus after a time the children, practically sold to labour, would be taken away to the cities there to be put to work without remuneration. It was practically slavery. Then the Russian Government, recognising the impossibility of dealing with such a state of affairs, undertook to drive out the Jews altogether [*Reminiscences*, 2: 54].

The image of the rapacious, conniving Jewish financier here not only hints at possible anti–Semitism, but also comes strikingly close to the same language, as will be shown later, used by George Stoker in *With the Unspeakables* to describe the Jewish merchants of Bulgaria who likewise prey on the ignorant peasantry.

However, a more probable influence exists in Stoker's connection to Sir Richard Burton, author of *The Jew, the Gypsy, and El Islam*. Devendar Varma documents an ongoing contact between Burton and Stoker between 1878 and 1886. So intimate was their affiliation that Varma credits Burton's translations of Hindu vampire legends as the inspiration for Stoker's novel ("The Genesis of *Dracula*: A Re-Visit" 47). Furthermore, Barbara Belford contends that Stoker modeled Dracula in part on Burton. She argues that Dracula's teeth belong to the description of Burton in *Reminiscences of Henry Irving*, where Stoker writes that as Burton spoke after dinner "the upper lip rose and his canine tooth showed its full length like the gleam of a dagger" (1. 359). Kipling, too, presumably used Burton as a literary model of sorts. Gilmour contends that Strickland, a police officer in *Plain Tales from the Hills* "owes something to the figure of Sir Richard Burton," who like Strickland, "was a master of disguise" (55).

It goes without saying, then, that Bram Stoker matured in an atmosphere of unequivocal antipathy toward Eastern Europe and Russia. What he heard, read, and saw as a child was later reinforced by what he experienced as an adult. He was, therefore, very much a product of his times and culture, and his literary productions were reflections of his culture's beliefs and prejudices. His culture's special fear and hatred of all things Slavic, Eastern European, and Russian converged in the Balkans and the Crimean Peninsula in 1854. In 1878, George Stoker would show in *With the Unspeakables* that anti–Russian feelings still animated English anxieties about Eastern Europe. Later, the consequences of the war and a long-standing Russophobia fueled by the ongoing "Great Game" and Jewish immigration bore fruit in the form of his novels *Dracula* and *The Lady of the Shroud*.

# THREE

# *George Stoker's* With the Unspeakables: *A Family Portrait of Russophobia*

Toward the end of *The Coming Struggle for India*, Arminius Vambery writes

> The traveler lives and breathes for long time, if not during his whole life, *with* the peoples and nations he came across in his journeys and whom he has made the special subject of his inquiries. He likes to indulge in speculations about their future; he is eagerly bent upon ameliorating their condition; and as the future of such notions is intimately connected with the daily question of European politics, the traveler is, so to say, dropped into the field of political speculation, and cannot help becoming a politician himself [201–202].

This passage illustrates a position taken by European travel writers vis-à-vis the lands they visit, which Mary Louise Pratt has labeled the "monarch-of-all-I-survey" (201). Essentially, European travel writers converted "local knowledges (discourses) into European national and continental knowledges associated with European forms and relations of power" (202). In this rhetorical paradigm, the thing seen does not acquire value or meaning until "after the traveler [...] returns home, and brings it into being through texts: a name on a map, a report to the Royal Geographical Society, the Foreign Office, the London Mission Society, a diary, a lecture, a travel book" (204).

Pratt singles out as a most apt practitioner of the "monarch-of-all-I-survey" genre none other than Sir Richard Burton, Stoker's compatriot and at least a partial model for the character of Dracula. Focusing on Burton's 1860 travelogue *Lake Regions of Central Africa*, Pratt describes how Burton and his fellow travel writers convert the indigenous topography into a consumable replication of England for Victorian readers. Salient to the process

101

is that the "landscape is *estheticized*"; in other words, the scene must be ordered as would a "painting," with a "background, foreground, symmetries between foam-flecked water and mist-flecked hills, and so forth," lending the object of representation an "esthetic pleasure" that invests it with "value and significance" (204).

Once ordered in such a way as to appeal to the expectations of the European viewer, the scene must also be rendered with a "density of meaning," something the writer achieves by employing "a large number of adjectival modifiers," which present the landscape "as extremely rich in material and semantic substance." The use of "nominal color expressions" by Burton is quite revealing:

> "emerald green," "snowy foam," "steel-colored mountain," "pearly mist," "plum-colour." Unlike plain color adjectives, these terms add material referents into the landscape, referents which all, from steel to snow, tie the landscape explicitly to the explorer's home culture, sprinkling it with some little bits of England [Pratt 204].

Next in the process is "the relation of *mastery* predicated between the seer and the seen" (204). Pratt contends that by describing landscapes as he would a painting, "Burton is both the viewer there to judge and appreciate it, and the verbal painter who produces it for others." The outcome is absolute appropriation, for "what Burton sees is all there is" (205).

For Pratt such travel writing as this is akin to colonization. When the European traveler views the object of travel, "an interventionist fantasy completely displaces the reality of the landscape before him and becomes the content of the vision" (209).[1] This helps to explain what Vambery is getting at when he writes that the traveler's observations are "intimately connected with the daily questions of European politics." When Vambery sees a Samarkand or a Tashkent, his initial reaction is to visualize him as he might be under European rule, his desire to "eagerly" set about "ameliorating their condition" a natural tendency to remake them, as the British have attempted to do to their Indian subjects, into Europeans or, at least, approximations thereof — thus Vambery's prideful assertion that finding "a swarthy-looking Asiatic quoting Shakespeare, Virgil, and Homer, is an extraordinary, but not unusual spectacle" (185). And, as a corollary, through the ostensible good graces of *la mission civilatrice*, he hopes to convert them into allies of England, useful laborers in the fields, and wars, of empire.

In his study of the discourse of colonialism in imperial travel writing, David Spurr makes much the same argument as Pratt. He suggests that the "very process by which one culture subordinates another begins in the act of naming and leaving unnamed, of marking on an unknown territory the lines of division and uniformity" (4). Spurr further posits that in the establishment of colonies, the "abjection of the savage has always served as a pretext for imperial conquest and domination" (80). Imperial incursions, operating under the cover of spreading civilization to the primitives of the world, go forth under the assumption that the suffering of the individual savage is a consequence of the "corruption, xenophobia, tribalism, and the inability to govern themselves" (76) endemic to the societies in which they live, that the "disease, famine, superstition, and barbarous custom all have their origins in the dark precolonial chaos" (78). An equally compelling causal factor in the "debasement of the primitive" is "the fear that the white race could lose itself in the darker one" (82), much the same argument advanced by Arata's reading of *Dracula* as an imperial travelogue, of Count Dracula as an "Occidental tourist." The "constant reproduction of these images" of the debased other, at once an object of imperial desire and trep-idation, serves "both as a justification for European intervention and as the necessary iteration of a fundamental difference between colonizer and col-onized" (78).

At the narrative core of *Dracula* a struggle rages between an accept-able self and a detestable other. The self in question here is unmistakably an English one, possessing such associated attributes as honesty, courage, charity, magnanimity, and native intelligence. The other is Slavic, Eastern European, and, I contend, Russian, earmarked by the antithetical qualities of duplicity, self-absorption, disease, and corruption. Thus far I have main-tained that Stoker inhabited a political and social milieu which equated Russians with savagery, tyranny, treachery, and oriental autocracy. In this chapter, however, I will demonstrate that Bram Stoker had much more than just a casual contact with the generalized Russophobia permeating English society. Rather, I will show that he assimilated first hand racial stereotypes of Russians and other Eastern European Slavs, particularly Bulgarians, through a close working relationship with his younger brother George.

George Stoker, a physician, had served two years as a volunteer first with the Turkish army and later as Chef de l'Ambulance du Croissant Rouge, the Turkish version of the Red Cross, during the Russo-Turkish war of 1877–1878. Upon his return to England in 1878, George recorded his expe-riences traveling through Bulgaria and Turkey in a travelogue entitled *With the Unspeakables; or Two Years' Campaigning in European and Asiatic Turkey.* In this book George is very much the embodiment of Pratt's "monarch-of-all-I-survey." Traveling through the battle zone in Bulgaria and later Turkey, he paints a picture of the war and the Balkans that meets both the aesthetic and political expectations of his audience, a view of the event and the place refracted through the prism of Russophobia. Moreover, following the formula for colonial travel writings theorized by Pratt, George treats the Turks, Britain's long standing allies, as heroic or sympathetic beings, while the Bulgarians, Russia's Slavic brethren and imperial clients, come across as virtually subhuman savages, loathsome figures prone to corruption, ignorance, and wantonness. Thus, European intervention, in the form of Turkish colonization, is projected as a necessary means for civilizing the Bulgarian. George, not surprisingly, fails to mention that the problems plaguing Bulgaria are the result of the corrupt and ruthless colonization of Bulgaria by a succession of Ottoman rulers.

All three of Bram Stoker's biographers state that Bram gave George some assistance with the book. Harry Ludlam contends that after having heard George's grisly tales of the fighting in Bulgaria and Turkey, Bram urged his "brother to put his experiences into a revealing book," helped him organize, write, and edit it, and even suggested the title (49). Daniel Farson also believes that Bram "encouraged George to write down his experiences in the Turkish war" (156). Finally, Barbara Belford goes so far as to state that "George's book [...] provided background for *Dracula's* opening chapters, which so admirably evoke the geography, customs, and ethnic complexities of Transylvania, the 'land beyond the forest'" (128).[2] Bram Stoker makes no specific mention of his assisting George with the book, but he does record in *Reminiscences of Henry Irving* that George

> had been Chief of Ambulance of the Red Crescent and had been in the last convoy into Plevna and had brought to Philippoplis all the Turkish wounded from the battle at the Schipka Pass, and had had about as much experience in the handling of dead bodies as any man wants [1: 97].

Certainly, his conversations with George and his assistance with the book, whatever it may have been, would have left Bram Stoker with vivid impressions of Russian cruelty and would have reinforced the anti–Russian bias he shared with the British public at the time.

In the following chapters I hope to show just how extensively Bram Stoker incorporates his brother's descriptions of the Balkans and Asia Minor into the setting of both *Dracula* and *The Lady of the Shroud*. However, Bram garnered much more than just geographical and topographical details from *With the Unspeakables*. Working with George on the project, he helped to enunciate beliefs about and stereotypes of Russians and Bulgarians that reinforced racial prejudices he would have assimilated in his youth. Moreover, he helped to put into writing accounts of Jews that confirmed anti–Semitic notions he held in common with the English public. Thus I contend that his experiences involving *With the Unspeakables* gave him a very real set of enemies on which to model his evil count and a locale in which to situate him. The book, therefore, influenced Stoker to associate that "secret, stealthy, creeping mass, slowly dragging its enormous bulk like some reptile" (qtd. in Martin 199) that threatened England during the Crimean War in his youth with Russia and its Slavic allies in his maturity.

*With the Unspeakables* certainly reiterates Russophobic fears and stereotypes prevalent during the Crimean War. Because of the "Eastern Crisis" of 1875–1878, England was once again at odds with Russia. Openly violating the provisions of the Treaty of Paris that had ended the Crimean War, Russia declared war on Turkey in 1877, ostensibly to protect Christian Slavs in the Balkans. The latest troubles started when Serbian peasants in Bosnia and Herzegovina had revolted against Turkish rule in 1875. They were soon joined by the Bulgarians, who shared ethnic and religious ties with both the Serbs and the Russians (Seaman 210–211). Turkish forces quickly crushed the revolt, in the process committing horrific atrocities among Orthodox Christians. These were most pronounced in Bulgaria, where "about 60 villages were destroyed and 12–15,000 people massacred" (M. S. Anderson 184). Initially, news of the Turkish killings evoked a harsh anti–Turkish backlash throughout the West.

In England, matters came to a head in September 1876 when Gladstone, then out of office, published *The Bulgarian Horrors and the Question of the East*,[3] a pamphlet bitterly scornful of Turkey. So popular was its appeal that the pamphlet sold 200,000 copies in three weeks (Seaman 212). However, Gladstone's polemic did little to change the pro–Turkey policies of the Disraeli government then in power. Very much in the mold of Palmerston, Disraeli saw Turkey as an agent of English power in Asia and a buttress against Russian expansion in the Black Sea and Mediterranean. He had even conferred the crown of India on Victoria because he believed that the "Indians [...] might be less open to subversion by the agents of a Russian emperor if they had an empress of their own" (Seaman 209). Thus, even in the face of public opinion to the contrary, England did little more officially than join the other European powers in demanding reforms of Turkey. Shortly after Russia declared war on Turkey in 1877, however, popular English support shifted back to Turkey.

Early victories by combined Russian and Romanian forces set off alarms in England, where it was feared that Russia would quickly "set up puppet Slav states in the Balkans and seize Constantinople" (Seaman 216) and thereby threaten "the main artery of [...] communications with India" (M. S. Anderson 208). The English public changed its opinion of the Turks when under the command of Osman Pasha, they stopped the Russian advance for six months at Plevna in Bulgaria. By this act the Turks transformed "themselves in the eyes of the British public from bloody butchers of Bulgarian Christians into heroic fighters resisting the onslaught of the gruesome Russian bear" (Seaman 213). Facilitating this abrupt reversal in public opinion were English racial prejudices. Because of notions of Asia popularized by Urquhart, Fitzgerald, and Burton, many, including Disraeli, believed that "the Turks were splendid fellows" (Seaman 217). On the other hand, the English shared with most other western Europeans a virulent prejudice against Slavs. These anti–Slav feelings had been most acute in England since the Crimean War and were principally directed at Russia and her Slavic colleagues, the Bulgarians, Romanians, and Serbians. Of particular relevance here, William Russell's dispatches chronicling the suffering of the troops at Varna had forever linked Bulgaria with bitter memories of British failings in the persecution of the war and the care of the injured.

The press thus helped the public to see the Slavs of Bulgaria, Romania (i.e. Moldavia and Wallachia) and Serbia as Russian cognates and co-conspirators. In an article entitled *Turkey*, published in the *New York Times* in 1853, Karl Marx described the racial alliances existing in Eastern Europe. "Moldavia, Wallachia, and Servia," he writes, are aligned ethnically and politically with Russia (4). The first two "have princes of their own under the nominal suzerainty of the Porte and the real dominion of Russia" (6). Among these regions the dominant race is

> the Slavonic race, and more particularly that branch of it which is resumed under the name of Illyrian (Ilirski) or South Slavonian (Yugoslavyanski). After the Western Slavonia (Polish and Bohemian), and Eastern Slavonian (Russian), it forms the third branch of that numerous Slavonic family which for the last twelve hundred years has occupied the East of Europe [7].

In terms of religion, these peoples are, for the most part, members of the Greek Orthodox Church and "write their language in the Cyrillian character, which is also used in the Russian and Old Slavonic or Church language" (Marx 8). This shared language, more than anything else, ties the slavs closest to Russia:

> A man in Belgrade may not be able to read a book printed in his own language at Agram or Petch, he may object even to take it up, on account of the "heterodox" alphabet and orthography used therein; while he will have little difficulty in reading and understanding a book printed at Moscow in the Russian language [...]. The mass of the Greek Slavonians will not even have their Bible, liturgies, and prayer-books printed in their own country, because they are convinced that there is a peculiar correctness and orthodoxy and odour about anything printed in holy Moscow or in the imperial printing establishment of St. Petersburg [8].

Thus the various Slavonic peoples of the Balkans— the Bulgarians, Serbians, and Romanians— look to Russia for religious authority and guidance. George Stoker's book intimates that because of these close ties between the Slavs of Bulgaria, Romania, Serbia, and Russia, the Balkan states are dark places where the sinister power of Russia prevails.

Britain and Russia were to come perilously close to open warfare when, toward the end of the conflict in 1878, Russia had conquered Bulgaria and threatened Constantinople.[4] At this point Disraeli dispatched the fleet to the Dardanelles, reinforced the garrison at Malta with Indian troops, and informed the Czar that the Queen was determined to prevent Russia's entry into Constantinople "even if this led to war" (M. S. Anderson 200–201). Disraeli even dreamed of invading Russian Armenia and of driving the Russian armies into the Caspian Sea (M. S. Anderson 196). However, Russia accepted Austrian, English, French, and German intercession in working out a suitable treaty with Turkey. Nevertheless, direct Russian influence in the Balkans would remain unchecked until 1917, for out of the conflict arose an independent Bulgaria with substantial ties to Russia. Solidifying its place as an agent of Russia, Bulgaria endorsed its constitution in St. Petersburg, the Bulgarians acknowledged Alexander of Battenburg, who was related to the Russian royal family, as their new ruler, and they invited Russian officers to command their military (M. S. Anderson 227).

It is in this period of heightened Anglo-Russian tensions that George Stoker sets down his impressions about the war, the people, and the places he encountered. To the book, as will be evident, he brought all of the aforementioned political and racial prejudices of his era and culture. They find a prominent place in the book's most distinctive feature, its copious attention to descriptions of the different peoples the author meets in the course of his travels. Stoker makes his intention clear at the very outset:

> I can fairly state that I have had ample opportunities of judging of the various nationalities who inhabit European and Asiatic Turkey, of ascertaining, from personal observation and experience, their leading characteristics; and I now propose giving my readers a slight sketch of what the conclusions are which I have arrived at with regard to these people with whom I have come in contact — especially Turks, Greeks, Armenians, and Bulgarians [3].

By far the Bulgarians and the Russians, whom he does not specify here, receive his fullest attention and harshest criticism. It should come as no surprise, however, that the Turks, England's allies in the region, earn his highest praise. What most draws him to the Turks, as will become evident, is their allegiance to the West, to superior "white Anglo-Saxon races and civilisation" (Paul Rich 18).

From the very beginning of his account, Stoker has the warmest praise for his Turkish hosts. His description of the Turkish soldiery, for instance, verges on idolatry:

> One is struck with the splendid physique of the soldiers. They are strong looking, broad-shouldered, big-limbed fellows, with an air of perfect freedom and independence, but, withal, essentially polite and gentlemanlike in their bearing. There is no pushing and jostling the public, as is too common with

soldiers, while they saunter leisurely along in knots of five or six. There is no
rude laughter or shouting—all are quiet and dignified in their behaviour [2].

Befitting their dignified bearing, they also maintain a proper spiritual conduct, for they are "most regular in the exercise of their religion" (29). Even
under the most adverse circumstances, they prove themselves to be nonpareil comrades.

During one of his many excursions to the front, George sails on "a
small post-boat with accommodation for about ten first-class passengers";
however, over 2,000 Turkish soldiers have been packed on deck. In the face
of overcrowding, tempestuous seas, and general sea sickness, they remain
stoic and comradely throughout:

> The only rations served to the soldiers during the voyage were bread and
> water [...]. One, luckier than his fellows, had secured a box of figs, which he
> began dividing among his comrades. At last there was only one left; this he
> broke in two, and gave one-half away. He then looked round to see if all were
> served, and seeing a soldier eying the morsel somewhat longingly, handed it to
> him, having only for himself the satisfaction of having done a generous deed
> [50–51].

Despite their "miserable plight [...] not a grumble was to be heard" (50).

Turkish courage is no less evident than is Turkish dignity. The following description of one action typifies Stoker's general accounts of Turkish
arms:

> On the 27th of June the Russians completely surrounded the position by
> land, and left only the sea for the Turks to retreat by. For seventeen hours
> they continued to attack the camp, but gained no advantage whatever. Our
> troops numbered between 6,000 and 7,000, while theirs were estimated at
> 12,000. Our fellows fought splendidly, one battalion especially distinguishing
> itself—i.e. the Yildiz Tabur [...]. The great danger was lest the ammunition
> should run out; that did happen at one period of the fight, but the Yildiz
> refused to go back for more, and when urged to do so by their officers,
> declared it should be brought to them where they fought [58–59].

For Stoker, the common soldier derives his dignity and devotion to duty
from his peasant origins. An appropriate object for veneration, the Turkish peasant "is truthful and honest, sober and hospitable; his word requires
no written contract to confirm it; his hospitality extends to those of all
classes and religions" (4).

Stoker's characterizations of the generally corrupt "educated ruling
class" of Turkey reveal an important attribute of British racial ideology, that
the only good alien is one who accepts British cultural and political hegemony and even a British identity. Corruption, therefore, results from the
wrong kind of education. Stoker argues that the corrupt members of the

governing class "have been educated in the Levant" and have acquired their "views of civilisation and honesty [...] from their intercourse with oriental Christians," members of the Orthodox faith practiced in Moscow. Opposed to these officials are those few "perfectly honest and reliable" types "who have received their education in England and France." These are to be found mainly "amongst the officers of the army and navy, especially the latter" (4). Thus, "the best specimen of a Turkish officer" Stoker encounters in the war is a navy captain who "had served seven years in the English navy, and [...] spoke English perfectly" (53).

Stoker's British prejudices suffer no diminution even after Turkey's eventual defeat. To protect British prestige in the area, he makes it quite clear at the end of the narrative that though beaten, "All the Turks expressed their confidence in England." Moreover, they "desired to fight the Russians again if English officers were given them" (124). The obvious implication Stoker makes here is that no amount of imitation can substitute for a real British presence at the head of a native army. Bram Stoker will employ this very same idea in *The Lady of the Shroud.* In that work, a backward yet valiant Balkan people fail to gain their independence from Turkey until they have a British leader and British weaponry.

Stoker's treatment of Turkey's opponents, the Bulgarians and Russians, on the other hand, demonstrates an unmistakable Russophobic and anti–Slav prejudice. Before he could condemn Bulgarian and Russian injustices, however, Stoker had to clear away the objections to Turkish rule in the Balkans raised by Gladstone and others calling for reforms. He accomplishes this feat in three ways. First, he argues that Turkey had already begun to institute reforms in her administration of the region before the Bulgarian revolt. Yet her efforts to "mature the scheme of reformation" had been cut short by the Russian invasion (3). Next, he attempts to place the blame for the Bulgarian massacres onto what he considers "lesser" races living under Turkish rule, such as Circassians drafted from Turkey's Caucasian colonies.[5] According to Stoker, English writers, namely Gladstone, had erroneously ascribed the "horrors that were perpetrated during the late war" to "regular Turkish soldiers" when "in almost all cases" they were the work irregulars and colonial conscripts (4).

Finally, to diminish the impact of the purported massacres, Stoker contends that the reported killings either had been fabricated by the press or exaggerated by them. Thus, at one point he recounts a conversation he had overheard between two journalists in Constantinople:

> "How is it, old fellow," said A to B, "that you are so 'flush'?"
> "Oh," said B, "it's easy enough; the British public want atrocities, so I collect six or seven Turkish ones, and sell them to a philo–Russian paper at a pound a head. But," he remarked, "Russian atrocities are better

still; they fetch thirty shillings if sold to a paper with philo–Turkish tendencies" [12].

Such sensationalizing of events, according to Stoker, injures "the prestige of journalism" (12). He further ameliorates the gravity of the reported massacres by arguing that the press has intentionally bloated the numbers for shock value. The number of victims in one particular incident in the town of Batak, for example,

> was greatly exaggerated. It was, I believe, 5,000; but this was afterwards, by careful investigation, reduced to 1,800. The first computation was made much too soon after the massacre to be accurate; for this reason — that many persons had escaped, and as their whereabouts was unknown they were supposed to be dead. These persons either afterwards returned to Batak or were found settled in other places [40].

Oddly enough, 1,800 dead Bulgarians does not strike Stoker as an excessive number.[6]

Having ostensibly cleared Turkey of the charge of barbarity, Stoker turns his attention to describing the Bulgarians and the Russians. By far, the Bulgarians come in for the most truculent condemnation. Stoker begins by demanding that the Bulgarians themselves are to blame for whatever ills they suffer as a people. Although he admits that they "have been oppressed for centuries" under Turkish rule, they have nonetheless "prospered and become rich" at the same time (6), so they have no grounds for complaint. Those among them who have apparently suffered as a result of Turkish taxation have only their "own fellow-countrymen" to condemn, for Bulgarian tax collectors show much "more energy and persistence than it was usual or probable for the naturally lazy Turk to exert" (6). Such venality springs from an utter lack of morality, the latter "an unknown quality to a Bulgarian," whose own village priest will "offer his daughter to the highest bidder" (7). On the whole, Stoker finds the average Bulgarian to be little more than an amoral lout:

> We have, then, in the typical Bulgarian, who is found among the village labouring class, a slow, dogged, persevering, industrious agriculturist, capable of being educated to a high standard, given to strong drink, and, as a rule, a liar and a cheat. It is unfair to say he has been taught these vices by the Turks, because the Mussulman villagers, with whom he chiefly comes in contact, are addicted to neither lying, nor cheating, nor drunkenness [8].

Of such people one can apparently only expect the most dreadful behavior, and Stoker takes delight in enumerating Bulgarian vices. One of the first to appear is thievery. When one of the principal benefactors of England's aid mission to the region, Lady Strangford, pays a visit, "One of the drivers [...] (doubtless a true patriot) stole a bag belonging to one of the gentlemen, containing geometric instruments" (39). The Bulgarians are also for the most part a greedy and dishonest bunch as well. Thus he learns while setting up a residence that their merchants are not to be trusted:

> With the assistance of this same Bey, who was a kind of lord of the manor, I obtained a large house, and set to work to furnish it. The Bulgarian community came forward and offered me beds which they had in their possession. Of course I accepted their offer at once; but when on the morrow I sent for the articles in question, I was informed that they were twenty-two piastres each. I afterwards found a better article for eleven, so I declined the offer of the community, and learned a lesson about Bulgarian charity. Everything I wanted it was the same story; and at last I was forced to give up going to Bulgarian shops, and to buy what I wanted from Turkish merchants [41].

In another instance, he ridicules the Bulgarians for allowing their greed to undermine relief efforts intended for them:

> After a short time I went to the village of Perustitza before mentioned, to arrange an hospital there which had been constructed out of some wooden huts that came from Marseilles. Some of the villagers were jealous at not being employed on the construction of this hospital, and one morning we discovered that the supports and framework of one of the huts had been sawn close to the ground, and the whole thing had to be made over again [47].

Stoker further denigrates Bulgarian manners and customs by stressing how inferior they are to those of their Turkish lords. When describing "the reception one meets with in a Bulgarian village as contrasted with Turkish ones," Stoker downplays Turkish affronts to English sensibilities; he likewise conveniently ignores any Turkish responsibility for the impoverishment of Bulgarian life. In the Turkish village,

> the stranger and Christian cannot be received in the private dwellings, on account of the "harem;" but in each village a room is set apart for visitors— the "mustafir odasi" (i.e. strangers' room)—and to this you are shown. Then each one, in accordance with his wealth, brings you something to refresh the inner man [...] you have a comfortable bed to sleep on; and when you depart in the morning, if anything at all is accepted, it is in strict accordance with the marketable value of what you have received, and no attempt whatever is made to defraud you [42].

Bulgarian courtesy and hospitality, on the other hand, pale in comparison. For Stoker, their lack of social graces offers clear evidence of their cultural inferiority:

> When [...] you enter a Bulgarian village, you wander about in the mud and dirt looking for the "kayah" (the person appointed by Government to look after strangers) and he finds you a share of a dirty room, where you are obliged to lie with the family (not to sleep — there are too many vermin for that). You get bad, dirty food to eat; and in the morning when you leave,

hungry and unrefreshed, your fast-waning patience is irritated by being asked three prices for everything [42–43].

Stoker makes no mention of the economic disadvantages that the Bulgarians suffer as a colonized people and that account for the lifestyle differences between the colonizer and the colonized. Nor does he consider that a Turkish ally and agent should expect generosity and kindness from them. To admit the obvious would only undermine his polemic.

Finally, Stoker demeans Bulgarian military prowess. Unwilling to acknowledge the justification of their 1876 revolt against Turkish domination, Stoker ridicules the insurrection as "foolish and futile." His account of the fighting at the Bulgarian village of Panagurista, therefore, emphasizes the apparent imbecility of the Bulgarian warrior. To defend the town from Turkish attack, the villagers

> had thrown up entrenchments (with the ditch on the wrong side) on three of the four roads leading into the valley in which the village is situated, but, *mirabile dictu*, the troops came by the fourth one [45].

Stoker finds their choice of weapons equally amusing:

> The Bulgarians were, of course, very rudely armed, and some of their attempts to supply weapons of defence or offence were at least original. One ingenious smith constructed two cannons, instruments of wood surrounded by rings of iron. One of these was discharged twice; the first discharge wounded a Turk, but the second burst the weapon, killing seven Bulgarians [45–46].

At no time does Stoker show the slightest pity for this "rude" people struggling to throw off centuries of political, racial, and economic oppression. To him the Bulgarians are at best a suspect race whose ties to Russia make them a very real danger to English interests in the region. It is important, then, that they and their Russian protectors be shown in the harshest possible light, that they be described for the Victorian reader as inhuman creatures capable of any horror and injustice. Stoker's narrative, therefore, falls very much under David Spurr's rubric of "colonial discourse," in which the "moral and intellectual degradation" of the racial other "as a justification for European intervention and as a necessary iteration of a fundamental difference between colonizer and colonized" (78).

Not surprisingly, Stoker's revelations concerning the conduct of the Russians and their Bulgarian colleagues in the areas freed from Turkish rule stress the Eastern savagery and amorality of these Slavic brethren. In describing the finale of the battle of Plevna, for example, he points out that the Russians do not honor a flag of truce and other forms of war time protocol observed by Western armies, a charge that calls to mind the *Punch* illustration from the Crimean War "RUSSIAN SAVAGES PREPARING TO RECEIVE A FLAG OF TRUCE":

There was one of the Turkish forts that the enemy had attacked many times, but failed to take, and between it and the, so to speak, opposing Russian redoubt many of the latter's dead were lying. They sent a flag of truce to demand permission to bury these bodies. Of course Osman Pasha did not wish them to approach his fortification near enough to see into it, lest they should learn the disposition of his guns, &c., so he offered to draw a line midway between the forts to bury the Russian dead on his side of the line; but this offer they refused, showing clearly what their designs were [87].

Nor do the Russians treat civilian refugees fleeing the battle zones with the decorum afforded refugees by Western troops. Stoker records that bands of mounted Cossacks often roamed behind the lines attacking fleeing civilians. His description of the refugees' suffering evokes pity and outrage:

It was easy to see that many of their number were sick; and the newly-made graves that marked their halting places and were scattered along the roadside, showed too plainly that the busy hand of death had been among them. Here and there you saw a full-sized grave, and beside it two little ones, telling plainly of a mother and her children resting side by side — victims of the merciless hand of war [82].

As Stoker implies, only an evil, inhuman enemy could show such disregard for life.

Toward the end of the war, Stoker receives permission to treat the injured in the occupied Turkish city of Erezeroum.[7] The record of his days spent there are replete with examples of Russian degradation and immorality. First, as soon as they entered the city, the Russians introduced into a Muslim community the evils of strong drink:

Cafes and liquor shops were opened with most amazing rapidity, and drunkenness amongst the Christian inhabitants became very prevalent. I heard one lucky Armenian who was the happy possessor of two barrels of rum, whose daughters, that before were considered ugly, suddenly sprang into notice as beauties, and were married immediately [109].

Soon thereafter, they also imported other vices, for

two or three days after their occupation, several Russian ladies of the *demi-monde* arrived in Erzeroum. In fact the town became demoralised; and the American missionary commented to me, on several occasions, on the increasing immoralities of the people [109].

Moreover, unlike the native Turk who "is by nature cleanly in his person," the invading Russians proved to be as squalid in body as in mind. With a certain relish, Stoker records that the Russians "seemed [...] never to have washed since natal ablutions had first been performed" (111).

After the war Stoker returned to Bulgaria for a short time before his return to England. What stand out most in his record of this period are outrages committed upon the remaining Turkish colonists by the Russians and the "Bulgarians, who have, at all events, the moral support of their Slavic brethren" (114). Around Andrianople, Stoker reports that "twenty-one Turkish villages were burnt and sacked, and the women violated"; in other instances "young Turkish girls were carried off and confined in houses for the Russian officers, who visited them in relays, sometimes for a period lasting over two days" (116). Often conducting these "abductions" was a "native Bulgarian police [...] organised by the Russians" and "recruited from the greatest ruffians in the town" (117).

At other sites similar horrors take place. When the Russians captured the village of Kara Ach, they imprisoned the male population in a house "while the women were violated and the village sacked" (124). At Bourgas, Stoker reports that the "Russians [...] behaved scandalously after the occupation of the town, breaking into and pillaging the shops in every direction" (120). While at the villages of Daoulty, Yenige, and Tartar Kawi, the mounted Cossacks "turned their horses to graze on the young crops [...] selecting such fields as were the property of Turks, and leaving those of the Bulgarians untouched" (124).

In lesser acts of barbarism, the Russians forced Turks to perform unpaid labor, and while forced to work, these "unfortunate people received a very meagre supply of bread from the Russian authorities" (117). Also, Russians and Bulgarians swindled departing Turks out of their possessions, for example, compelling one man "to sell a yoke of bullocks worth eighteen or nineteen lesas for three." Another scene relates how "one poor fellow [...] gave his horse to a Bulgarian to try it before concluding the bargain, but that the trier had ridden off and never returned" (122). As a final touch, Stoker presents a scene of Turks gathered at the Bulgarian port of Varna awaiting repatriation to Turkey, a scene that is certainly meant to capture the sympathies of English readers, who might well remember Russell's accounts of the suffering of British troops at Varna during the Crimean War:

> The men sat silent and gloomy, with contracted brow. What their thoughts were I almost fear to surmise; but ideas of revenge must have been very near their hearts, though their tongues were silent. The women looked the picture of sorrow, with their heads, covered with their "yashmaks," bent forward in the attitude of grief, sobbing and thinking, doubtless, of happy days gone by that they should never know again [122].

For Stoker, these Turks may be "unspeakable" practitioners of an alien religion and may be corrupt and lazy. They may commit an occasional atrocity on Orthodox Christians as well. Yet, because they protect England's commercial and military interests in the region, they deserve England's pity and unequivocal support. Stoker drives this point home in a series of pointed questions at the very end of his narrative:

What is to become of these refugees in the future? Will Europe, especially England, permit that these hundreds of thousands of unfortunate people shall be prevented from returning to their homes? Are the massacres and atrocities now being committed by the Bulgarians to go on unchecked? Will England do anything to help these poor of God's great family, and put them in the way of winning their daily bread? — to put down by her moral force, or, if necessary, by force of arms, such proceedings as are a disgrace to humanity, and, even more, to Christianity? — to maintain the reputation which her sons have everywhere gained for her of being foremost in the noble work of charity — a very sister to suffering humanity? [124–125].

Although they are not as thoroughly excoriated as the Russians and Bulgarians, one other race receives derisive treatment in Stoker's text. These are the Jews of Turkey and Bulgaria. It should be remembered that from 1861, the number of Eastern European and Russian Jews immigrating to England had been steadily increasing. Still Jewish immigration had not yet reached the levels that would so alarm the English populace during the Russian and Polish pogroms of the 1880s and 1890s. Anti-Semitic discourse was on the rise, however. It was not as virulent as the language of the last two decades of the nineteenth century, but it was derogatory, nonetheless. Thus, in Stoker's travelogue Jews appear as either crafty Shylocks or lazy peasants rather than as ritual murderers, disease carriers, and sinister aristocratic financiers.

George Stoker's characterizations of Bulgarian and Turkish Jews have interesting parallels with those of William Russell, the correspondent for the *Times* posted to the same area during the Crimean War. Russell, for example, took pleasure in describing the cupidity of the local Jews:

Among the most amusing specimens of the race must be reckoned some Jew and Armenian money-changers— squalid, lean, and hungry-looking fellows— whose turbans and ragged gabardines were ostentatiously dirty and poverty-stricken — who prowled about the camp with an eternal raven-croak of, "I say, John, change de monnish —change de monnish," relieved occasionally by a sly tinkle of a leathern purse well filled with dollars and small Turkish coin [41].

Stoker likewise targeted Jewish bankers and money lenders for derision. In every instance, he portrays them as rapacious men more concerned with their accumulated wealth than the fate of their families or homes, much as his brother Bram described the Jewish merchants and usurers of Russia some years later in *Reminiscences of Henry Irving*. Thus at one stop in Sofia, George remarks upon the impossibility of obtaining funds from a Jewish agent of the Ottoman Bank:

The Jews, it appears, fearing the approach of the Russians, had sent all their valuables and money away to Kemia; and for this reason all the plunder that had been taken by the Bashi-bazouks at Carlovo, Calofar, Eski Zaghra, Kezanlik, &c., had been brought to Sofia and sold to the Hebrew bankers; and this the Bulgarians were perfectly aware of, so the Jews came to the conclusion that, when the Russians arrived, there would be more or less confusion, and they would lose all their ill-gotten gains [81].

Here Stoker has derogatorily identified the Jews as the accomplices— fences— of the Bashi-bazouks, "the very lowest dregs of the population [...] [who] hang about the rear of an army, pillaging whenever they get a chance, never going into battle till the fight is over, and then only to rob and mutilate the dead" (32).

In a story about a "rich Jew" in the village of Eski Zaghra, Stoker describes someone who is cannily similar to a group of Russian Jews Russell describes as "truly Shylock-like [...] cringing, wily and spiteful, as though they had just been kicked across the Rialto" (200). Stoker's Jew had sewn all his valuables in a coat and fled to Adrianople before the Russians arrived. Unfortunately, he took the wrong coat with him, and discovering his error, he "wandered about the streets very low-spirited indeed." After a few days he sees a Circassian wearing his other coat, follows him home, and tries to buy the coat back without divulging its worth. When the Circassian refuses his offer, the Jew summons him before a judge, but the judge rules against the Jew who does not tell anyone about the contents of the coat "lest the authorities should seize the valuables." The Jew is left "more disconsolate than ever," but after three more weeks the Circassian offers to sell the coat to him for a substantial price. The Jew agrees, retrieves the coat at "five times its original value ... but, alas! not a piastre was left. The wily Circassian's suspicions had been aroused, and he had searched and found, and the Hebrew was clearly sold" (90–91). Stoker and his colleagues must have certainly shared a hearty laugh over this fellow's folly.

Stoker gives other examples of Jewish greed, such as that of the Jewish rentier who makes double profits by charging twice the price for the use of his abandoned home as a hospital (33). But the well-to-do in the Jewish community are not the only objects of Stoker's contumely. His most biting sarcasm is directed at a poor "Jew, who, although very stupid, was useful as being a butt for others, and a continual source of amusement" (65). The following incident involving this poor man must have provided Stoker and company with hours of entertainment:

> Just outside the town is a marsh of black mud, which the road traverses on a causeway built with rough stones. Crossing this the Jew went to sleep, and the horse, left unguided, walked off it into the mud, upsetting the cart and burying the Hebrew up to his neck. He presented a most ludicrous figure when he got out — his red hair absolutely standing on end, his cheeks streaming with tears of penitence and fear, and his body encased in a well-fitting suit of the aforesaid black mud [66].

Bram Stoker will reiterate many of these attitudes about Russians, Balkan Slavs, and Jews some twenty years later in *Dracula* and almost thirty years later in *The Lady of the Shroud*. For *Dracula*, he will consolidate in the image of the count the manifold impressions of these peoples he learned from his brother George so as to construct a foreboding Eastern presence with tangible analogues in the English imagination. In the later novel, however, he will adapt his impressions of the Balkan Slavs to support contemporary English foreign policy. Moreover, he will demonstrate the belief, one confirmed for him by his brother's experiences in the Balkans, that such primitive peoples as the Bulgarians or Turks require English command to be successful in modern warfare. And, as stated earlier, he will take his descriptions for the physical features of both the count's homeland and the "Land of the Blue Mountains" in the later novel from his brother's firsthand accounts of the Balkans.

# FOUR

# Dracula: *Righting Old Wrongs and Displacing New Fears*

In 1897, the year of *Dracula*'s publication, Karl Marx's daughter, Eleanor Marx Aveling, and her husband Edward brought out a collection of Marx's letters and articles featured in the *New York Tribune* during the Crimean War. The Avelings' stated purpose for publishing at this particular time was a renewed interest in the "ever-recurring Eastern Question." Although the Eastern Question had "entered upon another phase" with the growth of "Social Democracy" in the Balkans,

> One thing [...] remained constant and persistent: the Russian Government's policy of aggrandizement. The methods may vary — the policy remains the same. To-day the Russian Government [...] is, as it was in the "fifties," the greatest enemy of all advance, the greatest stronghold of reaction [viii–ix].

Two years earlier, in 1895, Russia and England were once again at loggerheads over Turkey. The cause, in this instance, was Turkish atrocities among the Armenians, a people residing on the border of the Ottoman and Russian empires. Salisbury, then Prime Minister, suggested in 1896 that the European great powers finally resolve the Eastern Question by partitioning the Ottoman Empire amongst themselves. Russia, however, bitterly opposed the plan, for it stymied her ambition to control the Black Sea and Dardanelles. Although Salisbury threatened to send the fleet back to the Black Sea to thwart any possible Russian incursions, nothing more than a diplomatic flap between Russia and England ensued. By 1897 the Turks had ceased their attacks on the Armenians, and war was averted. Nevertheless, the crisis revealed that the "old rivalries and antagonisms" between England and Russia lived on (M. S. Anderson 256–259).

At the very time, then, when Bram Stoker was finishing the novel *Drac-*

118

*ula*, anti–Russian sentiments were again running high in England. It is important to place the novel in this context, for as Daniel Pick suggests, *Dracula* "must be read in relation to a whole set of late nineteenth- and early twentieth-century concerns, images and problems" (83). Of special concern in *Dracula* is what Rhys Garnett generally terms "a fear of the emergence of a superior and necessarily antagonistic rival" (30). That rival, I argue, is Russia and her Slavic client states in the Balkans, who posed political, social, military, economic, and racial threats to Victorian middle class stability. For the most part, the middle-class fears articulated in *Dracula* had their source in the social and political changes evolving in England subsequent to the Crimean War of 1854–1856. The novel, therefore, serves both to allay these anxieties and to assuage the national embarrassment over the abysmally flawed conduct and frustrating outcome of the Crimean War by re-enacting the conflict in a manner wholly favorable to England.

So far this study has shown that Stoker matured in a culture hostile toward Russia and her Slavic kin. In 1854 at age seven, the invalided Stoker heard and saw jingoistic accounts of Russian savagery and bestiality in his parents' daily conversations and readings from the popular press. Later as a young adult he listened to first-hand reports of the fighting in the Crimea from his father-in-law. In his early years as acting manager of the Lyceum Theatre, Stoker learned of the political and foreign policy aims of the war from Gladstone during their many meals at the Beefsteak Room. From his work with George Stoker on *With the Unspeakables*, Stoker participated in the crafting of a derogatory polemic aimed at Russians and other Slavic peoples, notably the Bulgarians. These attitudes were reinforced through his association with Arminius Vambery, Stepniak, and, to some degree, Rudyard Kipling. Therefore, by 1890 when he began work on *Dracula*, Stoker had lived for thirty-six years in an environment rich in negative impressions of Russia and Slavs in general. His research for the novel would certainly have rekindled these impressions.

## Vampirism, Russia, and the Slavs

In preparing to write *Dracula*, Stoker consulted a number of relatively contemporaneous documents about the geography, peoples, and customs of Eastern Europe.[1] Excerpts from most of these sources are available in Clive Leatherdale's *The Origins of Dracula: The Background to Bram Stoker's Gothic Masterpiece*. Among the books "written by British official servants — soldiers, administrators, or their wives" (97) that Stoker consulted, William Wilkinson's *An Account of the Principalities of Wallachia and Moldavia: with various Political Observations Relating to Them* of 1820 gave Stoker the material for Dracula's racial and ethnic identity, an identity with pronounced

Russian and Slavic antecedents. Wilkinson writes that toward the end of the seventh century,

> a nation, known under the names of Slaves and Bulgarians, came from the interior of Russia to that part of Maesia, which has since been called Bulgaria. Soon after a great number of Slaves [...] crossed the Danube and settled in Dacia, where they have since been known under the name of Wallachs. [...] The modern Wallachians, however, exclude it altogether from their language, and call themselves "Rummunn" or Romans, giving to their country the name Roman-land, "Tsara-Rumaneska" [92].

Thus Stoker learned that in their inception, the Wallachians,[2] and by association the Moldavians, the predecessors of the modern Romanians, descended from Slavic peoples immigrating to the region from Russia and sharing close blood relations with the Bulgarians.

Dracula's genealogy reveals marked vestiges of Wilkinson's text. But more importantly, Dracula's heritage suggests clear Russian and Slavic antecedents. According to the count, in his "veins flows the blood of many brave races," especially that of the "Ugric tribe," who "bore down from Iceland the fighting spirit which Thor and Wodin gave them, which their Berserkers displayed to such fell intent on the seaboards of Europe [...] Asia and Africa." So fierce were they that their victims believed "that the were-wolves themselves had come." In an explanatory footnote to this passage, Leonard Wolf points out that in the "early stages of the superstition in Eastern Europe, werewolves and vampires were closely akin." But more importantly, he comments that the Ugric tribe "denotes an ethnological group that included [...] related people of western Siberia" (D 40), a region conquered by Russia during Stoker's life. Although critics have for the most part rejected his having educated Stoker in vampire lore, Arminius Vambery, Stoker's friend and arch Russophobe, may have contributed something to Stoker's vision of the count's heritage, as well. In the opening chapter to *The Coming Struggle for India*, he writes that the "Russians were at the beginning only a small number of Slavs, grafted upon Ugrian, Turko-Tartar, and Finnic elements" (2–3).

Among his progenitors Dracula also claims Attila the Hun, who descended from "those old witches [...] expelled from Scythia" (D 40). Once again in a note to this passage, Leonard Wolf indicates that Scythia refers to "a region in southeast Europe and Asia lying north of the Black and Caspian seas" (D 40), an area that included Russian Armenia and bordered on the Crimean peninsula, site of Russo-Turkish hostilities and British anxieties in 1895. Wolf does not investigate, however, the associations to Russia suggested by Dracula's Scandanavian heritage. The word Russia is derived from *Rus*, a corrupted form of *Ruotsi*, a Finnish term — Vambery's "Finnic" — describing the Varanger, the Vikings, the "Berserkers"[3] (D 40) who settled in conquered towns and villages along the Volga beginning in the ninth century (Pares 28). Furthermore, the Vikings have been credited with organizing the first Slavic state in Russia, and the first Russian Chronicle glorifies the exploits of the Viking prince of Novogrod, Rurik (Pares 19 and *Columbia History of the World* 470).

The Huns further connect him with the Slavs in general and Russia in particular. Bernard Pares, the noted Western scholar of Russian history, has shown that in the course of his conquests in the West, Attila subjugated much of the territory that comprises modern day Russia and the Balkans. Furthermore, Attila incorporated many Slavic people in the Hunnish Empire. When Attila's short-lived empire broke up in 453, the Slavs coalesced into a united group. Their original homeland occupied most of the arable lands from the Carpathian Mountains in the south to the Dnieper River in the north, extending west to the Elbe River and east to the Vistula River (*Columbia History* 461). From this central location, the Slavs would eventually spread their domain throughout what is now Eastern Europe, the Ukraine, and Russia, from the Baltic to the Balkans (Pares 11–12). Castle Dracula, it should be noted, sits, conspicuously, within this Slavic zone of expansion.

Stoker situates the castle "in the extreme east [...] just on the borders of three states, Transylvania, Moldavia, and Bukovina" (*D* 3) near the conjunction of the Pruth and Seret rivers (*D* 417). This specific location suggests further allusions to Russia. First, it describes a disputed area at the border of Wallachia, Moldavia, and Bessarabia,[4] a territory that Russia won from Turkey in 1812. After the Crimean War, England and France forced Russia to return the tract to Turkey. Russia subsequently recovered the territory from Turkey after the war of 1878 only to lose it later that same year when the Congress of Berlin — a great power conference dominated by England, France, and Germany — demanded that Russia cede the land to newly independent Romania (M. S. Anderson). Thus Castle Dracula rests not only on a site of many ancient "battles" (*D* 38), but also on a source of prolonged Russo-Turkish and Anglo-Russian hostility. As late as 1895, Vambery notes that by mid-century from "the Isker in Siberia to the banks of the Pruth, all became Russian," a position of strength that now allows Russia to focus her ambitions south, toward India (4–5).

Moreover, at the location of Castle Dracula a significant event in the career of Peter the Great occurred. Pares describes him as "a barbarian in his habits, direct and practical in his insistence on knowing everything that was to be learned, and with the kind of genius which consists in extraordinary quickness of thought" (198). What Peter most wanted to learn was the military and bureaucratic practices of the West. So in 1697 he began a "journey of education to Europe" (Pares 197), taking in the secrets of the

Swedish fortress at Riga and working incognito in the shipyards of Amsterdam and London so as to master modern shipbuilding theory, all the while trying to hire the best experts in the military and practical sciences each country could provide (Pares 198). Equipped with this new knowledge, he proceeded upon his return to prosecute successful wars of expansion on his neighbors to the north, west, and south. Fortunately for Europe, Peter was not always victorious, and one of his most famous defeats came at the hands of the Turks at the Pruth River, in the vicinity of Castle Dracula, in 1710 (Pares 206).

This defeat at the Pruth is but one parallel between Dracula and Peter, however. Dracula's reasons for sojourning to England are also very similar to Peter's, but much more sinister. According to Jennifer Wicke, Dracula journeys to "London to modernize the terms of his conquest, to master the new imperial forms and to learn how to supplement his considerable personal powers by the most contemporary understanding of the metropolis" (487). However, Dracula visits England not, as had Peter, to export innovation and expertise, but as an invader who plans to conquer and stay. Thus, as Stephen Arata suggests, Dracula educates himself to be "the most 'Western' character in the novel" before commencing on his trip:

> No one is more rational, more intelligent, more organized, or even more punctual than the Count. No one plans more carefully or researches more thoroughly. No one is more learned within his own spheres of expertise or more receptive to new knowledge [637].

Stoker, who at age twenty-five was elected auditor of the historical society at Trinity (Ludlam 24), was much too thoughtful a student of history to have been unaware of Peter's exploits in England, exploits that resonate in his evil Eastern count.

Since the 1970s, scholars have contended that in his research for *Dracula*, Stoker happened upon Vlad Dracula, a Wallachian prince whose cruelty in battle earned him the sobriquet Vlad the Impaler, and modeled Dracula after him. Although this assertion is now a matter of scholarly debate,[5] Stoker may well have drawn inspiration from another infamous impaler. In his first major study of the novel, *Dracula: The Novel and the Legend, A Study of Bram Stoker's Gothic Masterpiece*, Clive Leatherdale suggests that Stoker could have drawn a connection between the historical Vlad Dracula and Ivan the Terrible. According to Leatherdale, after reading of Vlad Dracula's penchant for impaling his victims, both domestic and foreign, Stoker added staking to the list of measures for killing vampires. Further investigations of the subject would have shown that within a century of Vlad's death,

> his impaling exploits [were] seized upon by Ivan the Terrible in Russia.
> Vlad had shown himself to be a hero of the Orthodox faith and a model of the

harsh, autocratic ruler. As such he was taken to justify Ivan's supposed divine right to tyranny and sadism [216].

Felix Oinas, a student of Slavic folklore, lends support to Leatherdale's argument, for he reports that tales of Vlad Dracula's cruelties "were especially popular in Russia, since the Russians associated him with the person of Ivan the Terrible" (115). Oinas goes one step further in establishing a correspondence between vampires and Russia by arguing that vampires are a predominantly Slavic and Russian phenomenon:

> There are clear indications that the beliefs in vampires have deep roots among the Slavs and obviously go back to the Proto-Slavic period. These beliefs are also well documented among the early Russians. The term "vampire" (*upyr*) appears as the name of a Novgordian prince (Upir Likhyi) as early as 1407 and resurfaces in 1495 as a peasant name. This term has also been recorded in western Russia as both a personal and place name. The previous existence in Russia of a vampire cult is illustrated by the fight clerics waged in encyclicals against sacrifices made to them [113].

Furthermore, Oinas shows that the vampire's ability to assume the form of a bat appears first "among the Slavs" (109).[6] It is well within the realm of possibility, then, that Stoker would have uncovered much of this information about the vampire tradition among the Slavs and in Russia during his research and incorporated it into his novel.[7]

Stoker's inherited antipathy to Russia combined with the links he very possibly discovered between Eastern vampire myths and Russia could account for the prominent allusions to Russia and to Slavic vampire folklore that the author placed in or considered for what some scholars believe to be the original opening chapter of *Dracula*.[8] Although eventually excised from the novel, the chapter was published separately by his wife after his death under the title "Dracula's Guest." The chapter contains close parallels with the vampire legends among the Russians, Bulgarians, Romanian, and Serbians enumerated by Oinas. For example, Oinas records that among the Slavs, vampires

> are believed to lie in their graves as undecayed corpses, leaving at mignight [sic] to go to houses and have sexual relations with or suck the blood of those sleeping, or to devour their flesh, sometimes causing the death of the victims. If the grave is opened, the presence of a vampire can be recognized by finding the body in a state of disorder, with red cheeks, tense skin, charged blood vessels, warm blood and growing hair and nails; in some cases the grave itself is bespattered with blood, doubtless from the latest victim [109].

Similarly, in "Dracula's Guest" Jonathan Harker learns from a carriage driver that in a deserted village near their route

> that long ago, hundreds of years, men had died there and been buried in their graves; and sounds were heard under the clay, and when the graves were

opened, men and women were found rosy with life, and their mouths red with blood [448].

Later in the novel after Lucy Westenra has become a vampire — a "*nosferatu*, as they call it in Eastern Europe" (D 261), says Van Helsing — she is described in her coffin as "more beautiful than ever [...]. The lips were red, nay redder than before; and on the cheeks was a delicate bloom" (D 245). When he next encounters the vamped Lucy, Dr. Seward notes that her "lips were crimson with fresh blood, and [...] the stream had trickled over her chin and stained the purity of her lawn death-robe" (D 257).

Also like the Eastern European vampires described by Oinas, Lucy becomes sexually active after her vamping. Just before she is staked, the "undead" Lucy attempts to seduce her fiancé, Arthur Holmwood, later Lord Godalming, in language fraught with sexual allusions:

> "Come to me, Arthur. Leave these others and come to me. My arms are hungry for you. Come, and we can rest together. Come, my husband, come!" [D 257].

Such behavior violates Victorian sexual mores, characterized by "male-initiated and male-dominant genital intercourse" (Cranny-Francis 65). Lucy, therefore, elicited horror as a vampire victim and as a sexual predator, "the nymphomaniac or oversexed wife who [threatens] her husband's life with her insatiable erotic demands" (Showalter 180).

"Dracula's Guest" features a significant direct reference to Russia as well. Harker becomes intrigued with the driver's story and asks to be shown the village in question. When the driver refuses to accommodate his wishes, Harker sends the driver back to Munich and proceeds alone on foot. Once Harker reaches the deserted town, a sudden snow storm breaks, forcing him to seek refuge in the only available refuge, "a great massive tomb of marble" (451). As he enters the structure, a sudden flash of lightening reveals "a beautiful woman, with rounded cheeks and red lips, seemingly sleeping on a bier" (452). Before he can investigate further, however, an unseen force hurls him back out into the storm, he loses consciousness, and when he awakes, he discovers a giant wolf gnawing at his throat. Fortunately, he is saved by a group of mounted troopers. What makes this scene significant, other than the obvious allusions to Slavic vampire myths, is that before entering the tomb Harker notices a most unusual inscription on its back, "'The dead travel fast,'" a message "graven in great Russian letters" (451).

The chapters with which Stoker eventually did open the novel feature similar references to Russia. Chapter one places the castle, as has already been shown, well within the Slavic realm and the sphere of Russian influence. Likewise, Dracula's description of his heritage, also examined above, occurs in chapter four. Chapter two provides another, perhaps more concrete connection with Russia. To explain his intense desire to master spoken English, Dracula says to Jonathan Harker,

> Well, I know that, did I move and speak in your London, none there are who would not know me for a stranger. That is not enough for me. Here I am noble; I am *boyar*; the common people know me, and I am master. But a stranger in a strange land, he is no one; men know him not — and to know not is to care not for [28].

In a note to the passage, Wolf comments that *boyar* originally signified "a member of the old Russian nobility" with estates in Russia or conquered territories (28); Leatherdale further elucidates, stating that "In Russia, *boyar* referred to the higher Russian nobility, below the rank of prince" (*Dracula Unearthed* 55). According to Pares, the boyars had a long history "in the service of Moscow and had contributed to build up her power" (96) from the twelfth century on.

Unquestionably, then, Stoker uncovered a great deal in his studies for *Dracula* that would have made him particularly conscious of the role of the Slavs and the place of Russia in the myths and folklore surrounding vampirism. I further believe that his choice of a setting for the Count's fortress had as much to do with his perceptions of Russia and the Balkans as with the tradition of Eastern European vampires. Certainly, the references to Russia and the Balkan Slavs already mentioned are more than just coincidental. However, more conclusive proof of specific, intentional references to Russia and the Balkans can be found if the novel is interpreted as a fictional narrative that attempts to resolve, if only in the popular imagination, a host of fears and anxieties that entered the English consciousness as a direct result or indirect consequence of long standing Russophobia, England's participation in the Crimean War, and the ongoing imperial struggle known as the "Great Game" in Central Asia.

## *Dracula and Late Victorian Anxieties*

The Crimean War, it should be remembered, precipitated a number of far-reaching changes in English society and left indelible scars on the English psyche. Unlike the forces of the glorious Wellington and Nelson, English arms faltered miserably in the Crimea. Perhaps even more galling to the English public, the long distrusted French saved British forces from utter destruction and finally defeated the Russians at Sebastopol. Aside from those bloodied in combat, the great losers were the British aristocracy. Once the dominant force in the government and the military, the aristocracy after the war were reviled as superannuated, impractical, self-absorbed. The professionals of the middle class had shown that they were better equipped to manage the government, the army, and the emerging *laissez faire* economy that had steadily replaced the aristocratic-controlled agrarian economy of England since the late eighteenth century.

Also called into question after the war was the tradition of English patriarchy. Florence Nightingale, among others, challenged the authority of the male-dominated medical community and army command. Her efforts before, during, and after the war at reforming military health care practices and at professionalizing nursing assured her widespread public acclaim and, conversely, resentment until her death in 1910. Because of her exploits she stood for many as a prominent symbol of what came to be known as the New Woman, an appellation first enunciated by Sarah Grand in her 1894 essay "The New Aspect of the Woman Question" (Chothia x). A phenomenon of the 1880s and 1890s, the New Woman sought equal legal standing —female adultery was considered legally worse than male adultery at that time — greater economic opportunities "in professions such as nursing and in the civil service," political equality, and "sexual emancipation" (Altick 59 & 301). In the decade before the publication of *Dracula*, the image of the New Woman was the subject of popular controversy in England. Henrik Ibsen's *A Doll's House* and *Hedda Gabler* were performed in London, respectively, in 1889 and 1891. Conservative critics attacked them as "depraved works" (Chothia ix). In addition to Grand's essay, 1894 witnessed women gaining the right to vote in local elections in England and, ironically, the production of Sidney Grundy's play *The New Woman*, a work in which "Female education, interest in art, questions about the sexual double standard are all held up for mirth" (Chothia xiii–xiv). Although the press organs of the day reflected almost exclusively middle class male prejudices,[9] toward the end of the century, fewer and fewer Victorian women were content with the supposedly ideal life for women described in Coventry Patmore's "Angel in the House."

Psychologically and intellectually, the English public was forced by the war to recognize the limitations of English military power and to question the validity of the nation's foreign policy ambitions. Like America in the twenty years following her withdrawal from Vietnam, England maintained a similar period of relative isolationism, figuratively licking its wounds while putting its political and military houses in order. Moreover, just as "No more Vietnams" became the rallying cry for conservative elements in the American government and military bureaucracies during the regional wars of the late 1980s and early 1990s and the Iraqi incursions of 1991 and 2003, so too did the memory of failures in the Crimea motivate conservatives in England to institute military reforms that helped to secure colonial victories in Asia and Africa in the 1880s and 1890s.

The Crimean War also fixed in the English conscience the idea of the Balkans as a locus of disease, pestilence, and brutal death. The reporting of subsequent wars between Russia and Turkey would reinforce these notions. George Stoker's *With the Unspeakables*, for instance, confirmed the savagery and barbarism of the Balkan Slavs and their Russian brethren and refocused attention on the horrible diseases common to the Balkans. In the 1880s and 1890s, the waves of Jewish immigrants that descended on England from Russia, Romania, Bulgaria, and other Slavic countries would revive English fears of the East. Though not Slavs themselves, these new immigrants would incur the wrath usually reserved for Russia and her allies and suffer under an intensified anti–Semitism. Although her ambitions in the Balkans and Turkey were temporarily thwarted by the Crimean War, Russia emerged from the conflict a still virulent threat to English commercial interests in Asia and an obstacle to expansion of the empire. As such, Russia appeared to the public and those in power as England's primary enemy on the world stage. Until the Boer War of 1899 and the emergence of a unified, militaristic, and commercially ambitious German state, Russia would continue to fill the role of "enemy number one." She was the *raison d'etre* for increased naval spending, diplomatic legerdemain, and great power solidarity.

As a moderately successful, middle-class professional — both as a lawyer and a professional theater manager — Stoker benefited from the social changes eventuated by the war. But, he also lived with the residual fears and anxieties his society inherited from that conflict. These cares and concerns, I suggest, are at the very core of the narrative in *Dracula*, and Count Dracula should be seen to represent a multiplicity of social and political dangers to Stoker and his ilk. First, as a *boyar*, an Eastern European/Russian aristocrat, he threatens to replace English democracy with an oriental despotism and to undermine middle-class *laissez faire* capitalism, to return to power an aristocratic class humiliated and discredited during the Crimean War. Furthermore, like the ominous Russian menace dramatized in cinema and fiction in the 1950s and 1960s, Dracula insidiously invades England, following, in cold war terms, a plan for conquest laid out over many years and expedited with the help of "brainwashed" natives. In the course of his assault, he appropriates his enemy's women for his own needs, emulating the behavior attributed to Russians and Bulgarians by George Stoker. Once Dracula has had his fill of them, his female victims themselves threaten Victorian stability, for they have been contaminated, deracinated, and most opprobrious of all, liberated. Finally, as a wandering, pestilential Jew, he visits disease and degradation upon his Victorian hosts.

## Dracula as an Aristocratic Menac

For some time, many critics have viewed Dracula as an Old World aristocrat. Malcolm Smith writes that "*Dracula* pits Eastern Europe, tyranny and aristocracy against England, democracy and the middle class" (93). Clive Leatherdale agrees, arguing that "Dracula is the embodiment of the anachronistic land-owning class, seeking to sequestrate the newly-earned privileges of the *nouveaux riches* and reopen the historic struggle between the aristocracy and the bourgeoisie" (*Legend and the Novel* 217). Anne Cranny-Francis moreover deems the Count "an ancient, East European aristocrat" (76). Undoubtedly, then, Dracula is both socially and, as Burton Hatlen believes, "culturally" challenging to the Victorian middle class "values of technology, rationality, and progress" (125).

As a cultural alien, Dracula threatens the liberal, bourgeois democracy of England, which after the Reform Bill of 1832 allowed the middle class ever greater political and economic opportunities. Nicholas Daly attests to the rising influence of the middle class, noting that the dramatic growth of the empire in the latter part of the century "depended upon the existence of a new class of experts," the professional middle class (30). Jan Scandura goes so far as to acclaim that Stoker's working notes indicate that he "hoped to achieve some sort of occupational balance between characters, to create a 'working' portrait of the British middle classes" (1). Dracula militates against this emerging social and economic force, attempting to re-establish the political and economic power of the privileged landed gentry of the past. Even more frightening to Victorian readers, Dracula symbolized the formidable Russian aristocracy, whose hold over the populace was many times more brutal and comprehensive than any exercised by the English aristocracy since the Middle Ages.

As a *boyar*, Dracula has absolute command over his subjects, who live in mortal dread of him. One subject group, the Szgany, is sworn to do the Count's bidding and to protect his person, much like the Praetorian Guard of ancient Rome. Jonathan Harker describes them as

> gipsies [...] peculiar to this part of the world, though allied to the ordinary gipsies all the world over [...]. They attach themselves as a rule to some great noble or *boyar*, and call themselves by his name [*D* 56–57].

The Szgany, interestingly, have Russian cognates in the Streltsy and the Szlachta. The Streltsy served as the czar's "Palace Guard, officered and partly manned by Russian nobles," while the Szlachta were, in Peter the Great's time, "the gentry of Russia" who composed a "service class" for the czar (Pares 194 & 212). As did sitting Russian czars at the time, Dracula can likewise call on the aid and service of various "Slovaks" under his dominion (*D* 68 & 413).

Also like the Russian aristocracy, Dracula lives parasitically off the labors of his subjects. Thus Van Helsing appropriately describes him as having a "child-brain that lie in his tomb for centuries, that grow not yet to our stature, and that do only work selfish and therefore small" (*D* 401). David Glover has shown that Dracula's underdeveloped mental capacities reflect notions of degeneracy popularized at the time by Caesar Lombroso and Max Nordau. Glover cites the example of the Manchester economist W. R. Greg, who "bemoaned a civilization in which 'rank and wealth, however diseased, enfeebled or unintelligent,' triumphed over 'larger brains'" (*Vampires, Mummies, and Liberals* 68). Dracula is certainly, then, an anachronism, a type of the ancient aristocrat, a member of a class who consume the fruits of the labors of the dispossessed, who fritter away their lives in vain, childish pursuits while those in thrall to them, to borrow lines from E. A. Robinson, "worked, and waited for the light / And went without the meat, and cursed the bread" ("Richard Cory" 13–14). When Harker records in his journal the appearance of the Count sleeping off one of his nightly debauches, he strikes upon a most apposite metaphor for Dracula and his aristocratic kin, the leech:

> There lay the Count, but looking as if his youth had been half renewed, for the white hair and moustache were changed to iron-grey; the cheeks were fuller, and the white skin seemed ruby-red underneath; the mouth was redder than ever, for on the lips were gouts of fresh blood, which trickled from the corners of the mouth and ran over the chin and neck.[...] It seemed as if the whole awful creature were simply gorged with blood; he lay like a filthy leech, exhausted with his repletion [*D* 67].

Although Dracula goes to great lengths to disguise his origins and purpose once in England, he cannot hide his aristocratic origins. The keeper at the London Zoological Gardens recognizes him right away "as a lord" (*D* 178) and instantly dislikes him because of "the airs as he give 'isself" (*D* 177). When he purchases one of his many properties around London, Dracula vainly signs the deed as "Count de Ville,"[10] what Wolf describes as a "generic name for an aristocrat" (*D* 326). Dracula's choice of homes is equally demonstrative of his social pretensions. For example, as his primary base of operations, he acquires an estate founded at Carfax Abbey. Though dilapidated and sorely in need of repair, it still is distinctly aristocratic. Sitting on over twenty acres surrounded by a stone wall, the

> house is very large and of all periods back [...] to mediaeval times, for one part is of stone immensely thick, with only a few windows high up and heavily barred with iron. It looks like part of a keep, and is close to an old chapel or church [*D* 32].

Dracula maintains a smaller yet equally run-down lair in Piccadilly, the most fashionable part of Victorian London, an area where the nineteenth-century gentry kept residences for their stays in town (*D* 318). In whatever apparition, country squire or London dandy, Dracula manifests an aristocratic hauteur out of place in a thoroughly middle-class Victorian England.

Opposing the Count is a diverse group, what Christopher Craft calls the "Crew of Light" because of their struggle to save Lucy Westenra, the light of the West (169). Consisting of a Dutch physician and philosopher, Dr. Van Helsing[11]; an English aristocrat, Arthur Holmwood, later Lord Godalming; three middle-class English professionals— Dr. Seward, a physician; Jonathan Harker, a solicitor; and his wife Mina Harker, a teacher — and an American millionaire, Quincey Morris, the Crew fights to secure "the values of the English professional middle class" (Malcolm Smith 93).[12] Although Van Helsing and Quincey Morris are, strictly speaking, outsiders, they nonetheless serve English interests. Van Helsing, a native of "that other classic homeland of free trade" (Moretti 74), provides "an important ideological bridge," for he is at once a "Westerner [...] but enough of a European to be able to understand the exotic world of Dracula" (Malcolm Smith 92). Also as a religious outsider, a "superstitious/idolatrous Catholic," he possesses a knowledge unavailable to the scientific "Anglican Englishmen with their 'matter-of-fact' religion" (Garnett 49). On the other hand, Quincey Morris, who Seward notes "had always been the one to arrange the plan of action" in all their "hunting parties" (D 363), provides the know how of a "pragmatic campaigner," and as the supplier of "military aid in the form of Winchesters," he acts as England's "armorer" (Wasson 22).

The sole aristocrat in the group, Lord Godalming,[13] an outsider by reason of class, renounces his title so as to fit in with the others. This fact is apparent shortly after the death of his fiancée, Lucy. When Van Helsing starts to address him as "Lord," Godalming cuts him off, saying, "No, no, not that, for God's sake!" And he informs Van Helsing and the others that the only title he wishes to have is "the title of friend" (D 212). Godalming, therefore, is an acceptably "tamed" aristocrat (Leatherdale, Legend and the Novel 217), what Burton Hatlen sees as a "bourgeois aristocrat" who prefers the company of his middle-class confreres in the Crew "to that of his fellow peers" (121). When the Crew actually draft their plan of attack, the ascendancy of the middle class is evident. Recording the event, Mina writes that

> we unconsciously formed a sort of board or committee. Professor Van Helsing took the head of the table, to which Dr. Seward motioned him as he came into the room. He made me sit next to him on the right, and asked me to act as secretary; Jonathan sat next to me. Opposite us were Lord Godalming, Dr. Seward, and Mr. Morris— Lord Godalming being next the Professor, and Dr. Seward in the centre [D 286].

The Crew is thus headed by a man of science, and sitting to his right, a position of most favored status, sit a solicitor and a teacher. For Daly, this assemblage represents the emergence of a "corporate" hero, an "increasingly fraternal, or associationist, and in specific ways patriarchal, group" (46–47).[14] The marginalization of Quincey Morris and Lord Godalming signifies, Daly further contends, the elevation of the "idea of the heroic professional" over the "older idea of masculine heroism" (39).

Besides protecting female virtue and middle-class political prerogatives, the Crew fights to preserve unfettered *laissez faire* capitalism and free trade against "the vestiges of feudal ideology which continued to exist" (Cranny-Francis 76), especially in Russia. Franco Moretti contends that Dracula threatens to "subjugate [...] the liberal era and destroy all forms of economic independence" enjoyed by the middle class (74). As "the aristocrat, the figure of the past, the relic of distant lands and dark ages," Dracula consumes the labor of others but produces nothing in return (74). Judith Halberstam conceives of him as "an image of monstrous anti-capitalism" which interferes with the "natural ebb and flow of currency" (346).

While seeking an escape route from the castle, Harker uncovers evidence supporting these claims. Searching Dracula's bedroom for a key, Harker finds

> a great heap of gold in one corner — gold of all kinds, Roman, and British, and Austrian, and Hungarian, and Greek and Turkish money, covered with a film of dust, as though it had lain long in the ground [*D* 63].

Capitalism dictates that currency "should be used and circulated" (Halberstam 346) to stimulate economic growth and development. The Count, however, apparently refuses to allow his money "*to become capital*," preferring to treat it as an "end in itself," to delight "in its continuous accumulation" (Moretti 75). Dracula has also obviously been stockpiling the coin of the realms with which he has warred in the past and with whom he will engage in the future. Dracula cannot carry out his invasion of middle-class London without money, a fact best exemplified by his actions when surprised by the Crew at his Piccadilly lair. Harker lunges at the Count with a "Kukri knife,"[15] but "the point just cut the cloth of his coat, making a wide gap whence a bundle of bank-notes and a stream of gold fell out." When Harker strikes again, Dracula "swept under Harker's arm, ere his blow could fall, and, grasping a handful of the money from the floor, dashed across the room, threw himself at the window" (*D* 364). Ultimately, Dracula knows that he must have funds to further his ambitions in England. In terms of my argument, the monies that Dracula accumulates are further significant. Except for the Roman coins, the others have been taken from countries hostile to Russia at one time or another during Stoker's lifetime.

Money for the Crew of Light, conversely, must be put into circulation so as to expel the Count — i.e., the aristocratic Russian threat — from England and to track him down and to kill him in his homeland. Thus, money performs a "moral" service (Moretti 75). Mina makes this point clear when she writes "of the wonderful power of money! What can it not do when it is properly applied; and what might it do when basely used" (*D* 420). She is referring here specifically to money spent lavishly by Godalming and Morris to pay for travel and accommodations, to bribe foreign officials and natives, and to purchase the implements necessary to defeat the Count. Underlying the statement, however, is the middle-class notion, justified by social Darwinism, that wealth accrues to those who most deserve it by dint of personal effort and that it makes possible the ultimate expression of Victorian society, the middle-class home. It is only appropriate that both this home and England itself should be saved from destruction at the hands of a despotic, feudalistic Eastern European aristocrat by a group pledged to uphold the middle-class virtues of the day.[16]

## Dracula as a Russian Invader

In 1966, at the height of the Cold War, the first essay to treat *Dracula* as a political document appeared, Richard Wasson's "The Politics of *Dracula*."[17] Wasson argued that

> the novel represents those forces in Eastern Europe which seek to overthrow, through violence and subversion, the more progressive democratic civilization of the West [19].

A little over twenty years later, Rhys Garnett wrote that the "role" of the Count is that of an imperial "rival to and potential conqueror of Britain and its empire" (36). Although Wasson and Garnett refer only to some unspecified, generic Eastern menace, I suggest that Stoker envisioned Russia and her Slavic allies in the Balkans endangering English democracy and empire, thereby anticipating by almost fifty years cold war relations between England and Russia. A close examination of Dracula's invasion of England will, I contend, corroborate this assertion.

Much like Peter the Great, Dracula assimilates as much knowledge as he can about the language, people, government, and military of England before launching his invasion of the West. By conversing with Jonathan Harker, Dracula hopes not only to improve his English but also to learn the idioms of English law and customs, thus his request that Harker "shall stay with [him] a month" (*D* 45). Moreover, at Castle Dracula, Jonathan Harker stumbles across evidence of the Count's studies and well-laid plans. Looking for diversion in the library, Harker to his "delight" discovers "a vast number of English books." What appears on first sight to be merely the reading material of a conscientious tourist turns out to be the homework of a potential invader:

The books were of the most varied kind — history, geography, politics, political economy, botany, geology, law — all relating to England and English life and customs and manners. There were even such books of reference as the London Directory, the "Red" and "Blue" books, Whitaker's Almanack, the Army and Navy Lists, and — it somehow gladdened my heart to see it — the Law List [*D* 27–28].

A tourist would have no need to know the names of "all persons serving or pensioned by the state" contained in the Red Book or the parliamentary acts published in the Blue Book (Wolf 28). Someone planning a detailed invasion scheme, however, would wish to know the whereabouts of all those with government service as well as the list of personnel serving in the Army and Navy. A historical figure who closely resembles this description of the Count was none other than the arch Anglophobe Count Nikolai Ignatiev. While serving in London, the debonair count masked his anti–British sentiments behind a pleasant demeanor, but when a London map seller reported to the Foreign Office that "he had been discreetly buying up all available maps of Britain's ports and railways," he became the subject of constant surveillance (Hopkirk 295–296).

Later Harker comes across an atlas opened at a "much used" map of England. On closer inspection, he notices

in certain places little rings marked [...] one was near London on the east side, manifestly where his new estate was situated; the other two were Exeter, and Whitby on the Yorkshire coast [*D* 32–33].

Situated along the eastern seaboard, these are all ideal invasion sites. Whitby, where the count debouches on English soil, would provide a convenient staging area in northern England for forces descending out of the Baltic, whereas vessels sailing north out of the Mediterranean would find Exeter, where Jonathan Harker lives and works, suitable for debarking. The Count's estate at Carfax, in Purfleet, moreover, is not only well to the east of London near the more navigable entrance to the Thames, but it is also strategically located near a number of government arsenals, such as the one at Woolwich, and the important Royal Victoria, Royal Albert, and King George V docks.[18] Furthermore, Dracula arranges to have crates of his native soil, his war materiel, preshipped to Newcastle, Durham, Harwich, and Dover (*D* 44), all ports on the eastern seaboard or sites located on waterways with easy access to the North Sea.

When he launches his assault, Dracula sails from Varna, in Bulgaria. During the Crimean War, it should be remembered, Varna played an important strategic role as a staging area for British naval and army forces. Varna was also the site of the first epidemics[19] to lay waste the forces, prompting Russell's initial published condemnations of the government and high command. In her 1859 official, but unsigned, report to Parliament, *A Contribution to the Sanitary History of the British Army During the Late War with Russia*, Florence Nightingale describes the encampments in and around Varna as pestilential killing fields:

> In June, 1854, the army, as already mentioned, went to Bulgaria, an undrained uncultivated country, at all times suffering more or less from malaria, and consequently rendering its inhabitants, but especially strangers, remarkably susceptible to attacks of any epidemic disease which may happen to prevail, altogether apart from the occurrence of what are commonly called sanitary defects. Judging from the experience of the shipping, the influence of this malarial atmosphere extended out to sea. In such a region, part of the army was encamped in a district so unhealthy that it had attained the Turkish name of the Valley of Death. Cholera soon appeared... [8].

Later during the siege of Sebastopol, she reports that scorbutus, "a blood disease" that usually produced "diarrhoea, dysentery, and fever," contributed mightily to the decimation of British forces (8). George Stoker recorded similar scenes of pestilence and death in Varna and Bulgaria a generation later in *With the Unspeakables*. Plus, in George's account, Varna is the scene of many Russian and Bulgarian abuses of the Turks. Thus Varna's associations with cholera,[20] the Crimean War, and his brother's stories of Russian brutality might well have fixed the location in Stoker's mind as a particularly fertile image of the port of debarkation for an Eastern/Russian menace.

The vessel that carries Dracula to English shores is, appropriately, a Russian one, the *Demeter*. Devendra Varma interprets the ship's name as an allusion to the myth of Persephone:

> In *Dracula, Demeter* is a coherent choice for the name of the schooner that brings the vampire count from the Black Sea to the shores of England because of the goddess Demeter's connection, by her daughter's marriage, with the King of the Underworld ["Dracula's Voyage" 208].

Wolf's footnote about the ship echoes Varma's assumption. However, I would suggest that Stoker has a Russian allusion in mind as well. As Belford notes, Stoker took the name for the wrecked vessel from an actual ship washed ashore at Whitby in October 1885 during a terrible storm. The ship was the Russian schooner Dimitry, which sailed from Narva on the Baltic carrying a load of silver sand. Because "Stoker loved codes," Belford further contends that Varna, the port from which the Demeter sails, is really an "anagram of Narva" (223–224). If true, Belford's assertion is doubly significant. First, Stoker might quite consciously have associated Narva with Varna because both signify important places in Russian history. Varna, as I have already shown, is a significant site in the English experience of the

Crimean War and the Russo-Turkish War of 1877–1878. Narva, on the other hand, is the scene of another defeat, like that at the Pruth in 1710, suffered by Peter the Great, this time at the hands of Sweden under Charles XI. So thorough was Peter's failure that Charles had medals struck commemorating the battle, featuring on one side the image of "the flying Tsar" (Pares 200).

The name Dimitry is likewise infamous in Russian lore. In 1604, during the reign of Boris Godunov, Uyrey Otrepyev, the son of a retainer in the Romanov household, tried to take the throne of Russia by claiming to be Prince Dimitry, the rightful heir who had been murdered in 1591. With the assistance of Polish nobles like the Voevode of Sandomir,[21] the pretender raised an army, defeated the forces of Boris, who died at the height of the crisis, and proclaimed himself czar before the people on the Red Square of Moscow (Pares 138–141). Although he reigned only until unmasked and subsequently assassinated in 1606, his memory was immortalized in Pushkin's 1825 historical drama *Boris Godunov*. According to *The Oxford Companion to English Literature*, third edition, the first translation of Pushkin's works appeared in England in 1835. A one-time drama critic and lover of dramatic literature, Stoker could certainly have been familiar with the text. Quite possibly, then, the *Demeter* could quite easily be but an Anglicized version of Dimitry.

Once the vessel arrives in Whitby, the Russian allusions continue to proliferate. Her cargo of "silver sand and boxes of earth" (*D* 109) corresponds almost exactly with the actual cargo of the Dimitry, "silver sand from the Danube" (Belford 222). The Danube is fraught with significance. Not only does Dracula traverse the Danube going to and returning from England, but it was at the Danube that the historical Vlad was defeated by the Turks in 1462 (Wolf, *D* 42). Moreover, Russia and Turkey fought over control of the entrance to the Danube from the Black Sea from the seventeenth century on through the nineteenth, and the Danube figured large in peace negotiations after the Crimean War in 1856 and the Russo-Turkish War in 1878.

A clue to Stoker's having these wars in mind here is a passage recorded at Whitby by Mina Harker a week before the wreck. Lucy and she strike up a conversation with a retired sailor, Mr. Swales, a veteran of the Napoleonic Wars, during their daily walk through the cemetery overlooking the harbor. When they ask Mr. Swales if he knew any of the people buried about them, he specifically mentions "Edward Spencelagh, master mariner, murdered by pirates off the coast of Andres, April, 1854, aet. 30," "Andrew Woodhouse, drowned [...] in 1777," and "John Rawlings [...] drowned in the Gulf of Finland in '50" (89). The Crimean War started in 1854, and Wolf notes that "Andres" refers to "Cape Andreas, at the end of a long narrow peninsula of northeast Cyprus," an island just south of Turkey in the Mediterranean Sea. Wolf further remarks that the "1777" date given by Swales for the death of Andrew Woodhouse should read 1877, during the Russo-Turkish war in which George Stoker served, "since Swales claims to have known the man."[22] Finally, Wolf notes that the "Gulf of Finland" is an "arm of the Baltic Sea, south of Finland" (D 89). This last reference is noteworthy because before the Crimean War England and France had "probed the possibility of using their superior sea power to attack Russia in the Baltic" and eventually sent "a formidable naval force into the Baltic that in August 1854 succeeded in capturing Bomarsund, the principal fortress on the strategic Aaland Islands" (Norman Rich 124) located at the entrance to the Gulf of Finland.[23]

The form Dracula assumes to escape undetected from the Demeter also has Russian ties. A correspondent for "The Dailygraph" reports that "the very instant the shore was touched, an immense dog sprang up on deck from below, as if shot up by the concussion, and running forward, jumped from the bow on the sand" (D 105). The animal in question, however, proves to be a grey wolf. In the same guise, Dracula later entices from its den a large white wolf at the London Zoological Garden. There too a gardener had mistaken Dracula for "a big grey dog" whom he saw "a-gallopin' northward faster than a horse could go" (D 178). When Harker asks the head animal keeper about the incident, he tells Harker that the animal was a grey wolf, for dogs "don't gallop" (D 179). In a footnote to this passage, Wolf writes that grey wolves were virtually extinct in western Europe at this time and could only be found in "Russia, and parts of Asia" (D 179). Because a vampire can only enter a house if invited, Dracula uses the wolf from the London Zoological Gardens to gain entrance to Lucy Westenra's room. The "Russian consul" in Whitby provides a similar service, for the correspondent reports that he "took formal possession of the ship, and paid all the harbour dues, etc" (D 107) and thereby officially invited Dracula into England.[24]

In the course of reporting the story of the wreck of the Demeter, the "Dailygraph" correspondent also reveals native English hostility toward Russia. For example, of the first sighting of the Demeter out at sea, he writes

> The only sail noticeable was a foreign schooner with all sails set, which was seemingly going westwards. The foolhardiness or ignorance of her officers was a prolific theme for comment whilst she remained in sight, and efforts were made to signal her to reduce sail in face of her danger [D 102].

The foolhardy and ignorant officers are none other than a Russian captain and a Romanian first officer. Though it could be argued that the correspondent is unaware of the makeup of the ship's staff at this point and is not purposefully insulting, his later comment that the Russian clerk's translation of the captain's log "must be taken *cum grano*," or, as Wolf notes, with a grain of salt (*D* 109), makes his distrust and contempt for Russia clear.

Once he is safely ensconced on English soil, Dracula does what almost all invaders do, carry away his enemy's wives and daughters. Dracula thus recalls George Stoker's account of Russian and Bulgarian appropriations of Turkish colonial women in Bulgaria after the 1877–1878 Russo-Turkish War. Moreover, the Count threatens to undermine the entire Victorian social and political superstructure by destroying the very foundation of English life, the middle-class home. Citing Dracula's comment to the Crew of Light that "Your girls that you all love are mine, already; and through them you and others shall yet be mine" (*D* 365), John Allen Stevenson contends that the Count is "an imperialist whose invasion seeks a specifically sexual conquest," namely to "take other men's women away and make them his own." However, Dracula poses not just the danger of "miscegenation, the mixing of blood," but something even more sinister and pernicious to the security of England, the eventual deracination of his victims, the production of "new loyalties" in those he vamps (144). When he confronts the undead Lucy, Seward recognizes that she is no longer the ideal Victorian mate of his dreams. So, in an instant, his abject love for her "passed into hate and loathing," for she is now to him just a "thing" which he could kill "with savage delight" (*D* 257). Only when they have driven a stake through her heart, severed her head from her body, and stuffed her mouth with garlic is she "no longer the foul Thing" but once more the image "of unequalled sweetness and purity" (*D* 264).

Through the subversion of English women — the ostensible justification for the "power and privilege" of the middle-class male (Hatlen 121) — the Count both emasculates Englishmen and, more frightening still, inverts the gender roles underlying Victorian social stability. He performs the latter by creating, as in the case of Lucy Westenra, "sexually aggressive women" (Cranny-Francis 68). Lucy and her ilk thus come to represent the era's greatest challenge "to patriarchal bourgeois society," the New Woman (Cranny-Francis 64). The New Woman of the last two decades of the nineteenth century, writes Carol Senf, sought "financial independence and personal fulfillment as alternatives to marriage and motherhood."[25] The New Woman also "felt free to initiate sexual relationships" (35). As Linda Dowling suggests, for many men and women in Victorian England, the New Woman spelled the coming of social chaos and eventual collapse:

> The New Woman [...] was perceived to have ranged herself perversely with the forces of cultural anarchism and decay precisely because she wanted to reinterpret the sexual relationship. Like the decadent, the heroine of New Woman fiction expressed her quarrel with Victorian culture chiefly through

sexual means—by heightening sexual consciousness, candor, and expressiveness [qtd. in Senf, "New Woman" 37].

David Glover argues that Stoker "seldom missed an opportunity to excoriate the presumption of sexual equality" (*Vampires, Mummies, and Liberals* 106).

Dr. Van Helsing iterates Stoker's bias toward and fear of the New Woman when he explains that Dracula's strategy is to father "a new order of beings" (*D* 360), a progeny of racially and ideologically different beings who, left unchecked, will destroy from within male-dominated, middle-class Victorian society. Alexandra Warwick has shown that the "trope of infection"[26] became a component of the vampire myth in the nineteenth century only as the increasingly liberated woman came to be viewed as a "source of danger." Most alarming was the "disruption of gender identity" threatened by the vampire's bite, the inevitable consequence of which was the feminization of men and the masculinization of women (203–204). So powerful is this menace that even the staunchly traditional and self-effacing Mina Harker is not safe from infection (impregnation?) by the Count. It takes all of the energy and resources of the Crew of Light, a possible metaphor for England and her commonwealth and commercial allies, to save Mina, by extension English patriarchy itself.

Dracula's strategy is nothing less than genocide via rape, practiced by the Russians of Stoker's time among the Turks and by their Serbian brethren among the Bosnian Muslims in the early 1990s. Dracula symbolizes the possibility of deracination and racial contamination as well as gender inversion. These too may be seen as Eastern European/Russian threats posed by what must have been for many Victorians a disturbing figure. During the 1880s and 1890s, thousands of Bulgarian, Polish, Romanian, and especially Russian Jews immigrated to England either to escape the pogroms which followed the assassination of Alexander II or to avoid state-sponsored anti–Semitism carried out by Russia at home and in her sphere of influence (Colin Holmes 3 & Zanger 34). Undeservedly, they were perceived as an "'alien invasion' of Jews from the East, who in the view of many alarmists, were feeding off and 'poisoning'" the blood of the nation (Pick 80). *Dracula*, it will be seen, is to a large extent a projection of these alarmists' fears.

## Dracula as an Eastern European/Russian Jew

The word anti–Semitism first appeared in 1879 in a pamphlet written by Wilhelm Marr warning of "the Jewish domination of Germany" (Kushner 2). By the last decade of the nineteenth century, England too witnessed a profusion of anti–Semitic literature. In 1895 one of the most popular plays of the day featured a sinister Jew. Appearing shortly after the Dreyfus affair in Paris, this was none other than Svengali, the villain of Herbert Beerbohm Tree's stage adaptation of George Du Maurier's novel *Trilby*. Jules Zanger suggests that such works as *Trilby* "owed much of their vitality to the way in which they embodied and alluded to a number of popular apprehensions which clustered around the appearance in England of great numbers of Eastern European Jews at the end of the century" (33). In her introduction to *Trilby*, Elaine Showalter argues that Du Maurier capitalized on a deep-seated anti–Semitism in British society, asserting that "his portrait of Svengali as an 'Oriental Israelite Hebrew Jew' created a character who stands alongside Shylock and Fagan in the annals of anti–Semitic literature" (ix). Much as Dracula works his evil through a retinue of vamped female victims, "Svengali, the 'little foreign Jew,'" likewise employs Trilby's "body as a vehicle" to achieve his ends (Showalter xx).[27]

Foremost among the apprehensions surrounding the immigrant Jewish community in England was the belief that Jews spread disease and contamination. As noted earlier, Robert Sherard fomented the image of the new Jewish immigrants as a "brutalized race" whose bodies were "black with filth and red with sores" (qtd. in Colin Holmes 38). Joseph Banister, in like manner, attributed to the East End Jews of London an extraordinary lack of hygiene and a concomitant foul smell. He once wrote that Jews stood out for reason of their odor and

> their repulsive Asiatic physiognomy, their yellow oily skin, their flat feet, fat legs and loathsome skin and scalp diseases [qtd. in Colin Holmes 40].

Jews also posed a threat because of their "propensity to carry and spread disease and thereby infect and weaken other elements of the population" (Colin Holmes 40). Thus, Banister warned against mixing English and Jewish bloods:

> If the gentle reader desires to know what kind of blood it is that flows in the Chosen Peoples veins, he cannot do better than take a gentle stroll through Hatton Garden, Maida Vale, Petticoat Lane, or any other London "nosery." I do not hesitate to say that in the course of an hour's peregrinations he will see more cases of lupus, trachoma, favus, eczema, and scurvy than he would come across in a week's wanderings in any quarter of the Metropolis [qtd. in Colin Holmes 40].

A fellow anti–Semite, John Foster Fraser, lamented in the *Yorkshire Post* that England had no provisions for preventing the influx of "smallpox, scarlet fever, measles, diptheria" with the "unwashed verminous alien" from Eastern Europe and Russia (qtd. in Holmes 38).

*Dracula* has unmistakable similarities with Victorian accounts of the immigrant Jews crowding the dilapidated and poorly drained slums of the

East End.[28] The Count's residence at Carfax, in Purfleet, for example, is well to the east of downtown London, near the Whitechapel district, the epicenter of the London immigrant community. In addition to its dense Jewish population, Whitechapel was also noteworthy as the scene of the murders ascribed to Jack the Ripper, a figure often represented in newspaper stories and sketches as an Eastern Jew (Gilman 156–160). Further marking Carfax and Dracula's other lairs as Jewish residences is their foul smell. The laborer who delivers Dracula's boxes to Carfax tells Jonathan Harker that one "might 'ave smelled ole Jerusalem in it" (D 276). When the Crew subsequently enter the estate in search of the Count, they encounter a "malodorous air" (D 302). Even upon stepping into the Count's upscale digs in Piccadilly, Godalming remarks, "The place smells so vilely" (D 356).

The Count himself is also markedly Jewish in appearance. Stoker, it should be remembered, was a practitioner of the pseudo-science of physiognomy. According to David Glover, Stoker "regarded physiognomy as an eminently practical form of knowledge, and there are countless references to it scattered throughout his work." Stoker owned a rare five-volume quarto edition Johann Caspar Lavater's 1789 work *Essays on Physiognomy*, "the book which more than any other had been responsible for the modern revival of this age-old set of beliefs" (*Vampires, Mummies, and Liberals* 71–72). Furthermore, Glover suggests that Stoker was familiar with the nineteenth-century theory of "ethnological physiognomies," which posited that "social identities were [...] plainly readable from appearances" and that these "appearances could be used as data from which to extrapolate judgments as to a nation's social and moral well-being" ("Bram Stoker and the Crises of the Liberal Subject" 988–990).

Stoker's fascination with physiognomy appears early on in *Dracula* when Jonathan Harker first meets the Count. Describing Dracula's "very marked physiognomy," Harker records that his

> face was a strong — a very strong — aquiline, with high bridge of the thin nose and peculiarly arched nostrils; with lofty domed forehead, and hair growing scantily round the temples, but profusely elsewhere. His eyebrows were very massive, almost meeting over the nose, and with bushy hair that seemed to curl in its own profusion. The mouth [...] was fixed and rather cruel-looking, with peculiarly sharp white teeth; these protruded over the lips [...] [D 25].

Harker also cannot help but notice that the Count's "breath was rank" (D 26). Additionally, when Harker looks upon Dracula's hands, he is surprised to see that "there were hairs in the center of the palm" (D 25). Wolf, in a footnote to this passage, suggests that Dracula's hairy palms affiliate him "with the standard nineteenth-century image of the masturbator." This figure, argues George Mosse, was thought to be akin to "those infected with venereal disease," people who were "pale, hollow-eyed, weak of body and spirit," common stereotypes of the pestilential Jew in the popular imagination (*Nationalism and Sexuality* 11).

According to Judith Halberstam, the description of Dracula bears an unmistakable resemblance to "both other fictional Jews in the nineteenth century and to the Jew as described by the anti–Semitic literature of the time" (*Parasites and Perverts* 122). Corroborating Halberstam's contention, Zanger details a host of similarities occurring between Svengali and Dracula:

> Both figures are aliens among us, and both move from the East [...] to the innocent West on missions of corruption. Both are shown possessing supernatural powers of control. Both are physically very like one another [...]. In addition to their physical similarities, both are repeatedly linked literally or metaphorically to non-human creatures [...] [35].

Among their "supernatural powers of control" is the ability to manipulate the sexual appetites of women. Thus Sander Gilman sees Dracula as a "seducer" and his victims as the "embodiment of the degenerate and diseased female," the prostitute (160). Because it was assumed that Jack the Ripper was "the victim of the prostitute, the syphilitic male, so too were the Jews closely identified with sexually transmitted disease" (163). Not surprisingly, then, after she is assaulted (seduced?) by Dracula, Mina screams "Unclean, unclean! I must touch [Jonathan] or kiss him no more" (*D* 339). Later, when Van Helsing touches the Host to her forehead, she is left with a mark, similar to the syphilis victim's ulcerous skin eruptions, and screams again "Unclean! Unclean! Even the Almighty shuns my polluted flesh!" (*D* 353). The image of the Jew and the prostitute intertwine with respect to money as well as disease.

Gilman suggests that Victorians perceived a monetary relationship between the Jew and the prostitute, for the two "both seek money as a substitute for higher values, for love and beauty." Jews were further thought to treat "money as if it were alive, as if it were a sexual object" (163). Remarkably, here Gilman is describing Moretti and Halberstam's "anti-capitalist" aristocrat. Appropriately, Halberstam suggests that the Count "fits in with the popularly received image of the Jew as the friend to aristocracy" (*Parasites and Perverts* 122) while Zanger contends that to the Victorian conception of the "Jew as Ritual Murderer or as Anti-Christ" the image of "the Jew as Usurer, as Miser" should be added (40). The image of the Count is therefore also in keeping with the rapacious Jewish bankers and money lenders described by William Russell, George Stoker, and, it should be recalled, Bram Stoker himself in *Reminiscences of Henry Irving*. In Dracula, then, coalesces the multiple anti–Semitic notions of the Jew as a "bloodsucker [who] drains health and wealth, [and] feeds on lives and labor" (Halberstam, *Parasites and Perverts* 132).

In his 1908 essay "The Censorship of Fiction," which appeared in *The Nineteenth Century*, Stoker asks

> Are we or are we not ultimately to allow fiction to be put forth without any form of restraint whatsoever? The question is not merely a civic or a national one. It is racial, all-embracing, human [qtd. in Halberstam, *Parasites and Perverts* 115].

Although he was an author whose own fortunes rested on the discretion of the "blue pencils" of the Lord Chamberlains Office (Belford 271), Stoker nonetheless saw fit to encourage censorship as a safeguard of the nation's racial inheritance. Residing in a city home to "more Jews than Palestine" (Belford 91), Stoker was quite conscious of the anti–Semitic literature directed toward the new immigrants in London's East End. That he subscribed to the notions of Sherard, Foster, Banister, and others of the same ilk is likewise clear. In an introduction Stoker wrote for a 1901 Icelandic translation of *Dracula*, he "hints at a connection between the vampire killings and the Whitechapel murders of 1888" (Belford 227). Stoker writes,

> This series of crimes has not yet passed from the memory — a series of crimes which appear to have originated from the same source, and which at that time created as much repugnance in people everywhere as the notorious murders of Jacob the disemboweller [Jack the Ripper], which came into the story a little later [*Dracula Unearthed* 25].

Thus in the figure of Dracula, Stoker combines Victorian fears of the dangerous, pestilential Jewish immigrant, an image that also calls to mind the loathsome aristocrat of Eastern Europe and Russia. The novel does much more than just distill these anxieties in a fictional menace, however. Rather, it provides a mechanism for restoring "cultural order" (Croley 85) and of reasserting the "'natural' superiority of Englishmen over the 'lesser' races" (Spencer 218) of Eastern Europe. As I will next elaborate, one way in which the novel asserts this superiority is by transforming Britain's failures in the East in 1856 into signal victories.

## Crimea Redux: An English Triumph in the East

The 1890s marked the "zenith of European imperial expansion" (Schmitt 30). In England, leading voices in government and commerce promoted the "doctrine of unlimited expansionism as justified by racial superiority, manifest destiny and divine mission" (Garnett 33). Shortly after the publication of *Dracula* in 1897, an expedition under the command of General Horatio Kitchner invaded the Sudan to revenge the death of General Gordon at Khartoum (*Columbia History* 930). By 1898, Gordon's killer had been "finally and ruthlessly crushed by Kitchner," the Sudan fully incorporated into the empire, and the honor of the nation restored (H. C. G. Matthew 508). *Dracula* performs much the same feat. Although English forces failed to effectively blunt the imperial designs of its chief imperial rival with the ease they dispatched poorly armed primitives, the novel may be seen to restore the prestige lost during the Crimean War by wreaking, at least in fiction, the nation's revenge on Russia and her Balkan allies. The novel thus operates much like what Wolfgang Schivelbusch calls a loser's myth. These myths,

> arising from frustrated desires for revenge, are the psychological mechanisms for coming to terms with defeat. Moreover, they are not merely neurotic fictions of the imagination but also healthful protective shields or buffer zones—emotional fortresses—against a reality unbearable to the psyche. Their function can be compared to the coagulation of blood and formation of scabs necessary for wounds to heal, or to the convalescent world of the sanatorium, or lastly (Freud's analogy) to the "reservations" or "natural reserves" in the industrial landscape [26].

As does Sylvester Stallone in the *Rambo* franchise and Chuck Norris in *Missing in Action*, Jonathan Harker and his colleagues assuage national pride and exorcise the social anxieties troubling Victorian society by returning a British force to the Black Sea and Balkans. David Glover, employing the language of the Vietnam war, makes much the same point:

> With everyone armed to the teeth, the campaign against the vampire ends in true imperial style with a paramilitary raid, a search and destroy mission into the heart of Transylvania. Beneath the Gothic wrapping lies a tale of buccaneering, an adventure story to raise the cheer of civilians in which the *unheimlich* terrors of home are expelled and then quelled on foreign soil [97].

From the very beginning Jonathan Harker functions as an agent of England's commercial empire. His initial trip to Castle Dracula is, for me, something approximating a reconnaissance mission. What makes Jonathan ideal for this task is that like the famous Green Berets of Vietnam lore, he is one of the best and the brightest. As Troy Boone notes, Jonathan "represents rational English masculinity" (78) because he is at one and the same time "a good specimen of manhood" and a "business-like gentleman" (*D* 273), the perfect emissary of the middle class. As would any professional commando, he makes a "search among the books and maps" in the British Museum "regarding Transylvania" (*D* 2–3) before departing. However, to his unmistakable disappointment, no "Ordnance Survey" map—"a military map showing the topography of a terrain," according to Wolf— exists for the region (*D* 3). Like the colonial explorer of his time, he is forced to chart a dark region as he goes in preparation for future consolidation.

Alluding to the cultural theories of Edward Said, Canon Schmitt suggests that Harker "orientalizes eastern Europe" as he travels to Castle Dracula (27). Said argues that the Orient has, among other things, been "the place of Europe's greatest and richest and oldest colonies" and at the same time "one of its deepest and most recurring images of the Other" (*Orientalism* 1). As a place of difference, otherness, the Orient became in the European psyche a likely site "of domination, of varying degrees of a complex hegemony" (*Orientalism* 5).[29] Notions of empire, Said further demands, were popularized by "nearly every nineteenth-century writer" (*Orientalism* 14). I would add Stoker to that list, and I would argue, much as does David Seed, that as Jonathan Harker travels East, he "constantly tries to normalize the strange into the discourse of the nineteenth-century travelogue" (197) and thereby appropriate it for England. His observations during this first journey out to the East reveal his "Orientalist" (Arata 635), imperialist, tourist perspective, for they provide manifest proof of deeply-held ethnic and cultural prejudices, very much like those evidenced by George Stoker in *With the Unspeakables*.

According to Belford, Stoker never journeyed further east than Vienna (220). She further suggests that the background material for the opening chapters of *Dracula* comes almost exclusively from George Stoker's descriptions of Bulgaria and Turkey (128). David Glover agrees, asserting that "one of several sources for Stoker's descriptions of people and places in *Dracula*" is his brother's book, where Bram found

> the men with their enormous black moustaches and traditional peasant dress consisting of wide baggy trousers and white homespun shirts; the packs of wolves coming down from the hills to terrorize the villagers; and the difficult journeys across snow-clad mountains through precipitous gorges and dangerous ravines [*Vampires, Mummies, and Liberals* 33].

Manifesting his Orientalist attitude toward Eastern Europe, early in chapter one Harker remarks contemptuously "that the further East you go the more unpunctual are the trains. What ought they to be in China?" (*D* 4–5). George, in comparison, has this to say of the trains in Bulgaria:

> The journey by railway from Constantinople to Adrianople occupies about eleven hours, but it might easily be done in half the time; the train only goes about ten miles per hour. The line is badly constructed, and would fall a to bits if it was too much shaken [20].

The Slav natives Harker meets along the way to the castle likewise incur his disdain:

> The women looked pretty, except when you got near them, but they were very clumsy about the waist. They had full white sleeves of some kind or other, and the most of them had big belts with a lot of strips of something fluttering from them like the dresses in a ballet [...]. The strangest figures we

saw were the Slovaks, who are more barbarian than the rest [...]. They are very picturesque, but do not look prepossessing. On the stage they would be set down at once as some old Oriental band of brigands [*D* 5].

Moreover, among the unprepossessing Slovaks he notices, with requisite revulsion, that "goitre was painfully prevalent" (*D* 12). The Slavic peasant women here bear striking resemblances to the Bulgarian women described by George Stoker — the women wear "sukhman," highly embroidered dresses complete with "a silver waist-belt, white stockings, and coloured slippers" (*With the Unspeakables* 9). The Slovak men, on the other hand, virtually replicate George's description of the Zeibecks of Asia Minor, who "are great robbers and scoundrels, but are very finely built and extremely handsome men" (*With the Unspeakables* 67).

Most of the accounts Harker gives of the flora, fauna, and topography of the Carpathians are also strikingly similar to what George describes in *With the Unspeakables*. In his ascent to the castle, Harker passes through "an endless perspective of jagged rock and pointed crags"; the "mighty rifts" between the mountains afford a glimpse of "the white gleam of falling water"; and the roadside is dotted with "oak, beech, and pine" (*D* 12–13). On a journey to Bazardjick, a Bulgarian village "4,000 feet" up in the Balkan Mountains, George records a similar scene:

> The road or path that leads to it is a most picturesque but excessively difficult one. It follows the course of a mountain torrent which you are obliged to cross no less than seventeen times. Nothing can exceed the wildness of the scenery. The gorge through which the torrent rushes is shaded by overhanging trees, which grow out of the cliffs on either side, and on a hot day form a most agreeable shade [*With the Unspeakables* 40].

Only later does George reveal that the trees he mentions are none other than the beech and oak (58). Finally, whenever he draws near the Count's castle, Harker encounters ferocious wolves (*D* 17, 65, 439). George might well have supplied Bram with this idea as well, for he recounts an incident of wolves which "had been driven down from the higher mountains by the excessive cold, and were committing sad ravages amongst the scanty herds of the villagers" and amongst the inhabitants themselves in one Bulgarian village (*With the Unspeakables* 45).

As a "scientific, sceptical, matter-of-fact nineteenth-century" traveler (*D* 289), Harker dismisses his carriage mates' warnings about his destination and the strange behavior of the wolves as mere superstition and fancy. However, despite all of his apparent superiority, Harker still falls victim to the Count, the evil of the East. Dracula imprisons him, impersonates him, and eventually leaves him to be the plaything — dare I say blood bank — of three vampiric women. Nonetheless, through pluck, daring, and English determination, he escapes the castle and somehow makes his way to "Buda-Pesth" (*D* 131). After recuperating in a Catholic run hospital, he and Wilhelmina Murray are married there by "the chaplain of the English mission church" (*D* 139).

Harker's finding asylum in Hungary and his subsequent marriage are especially significant. First of all, in an illustration of English chauvinism, their marriage can be solemnized only in the presence of an English clergyman, not a European Catholic. Secondly, though not the equals of their English patient and spouse, the Hungarians are nonetheless acceptable, worthy hosts. In articles featured in the English press just before and during the Crimean War, Kossuth had substantiated Russian brutalities among the Hungarians in 1848 thereby attracting the sympathy of the public and the government. Hungary was therefore viewed as a potential ally against Russia, and by giving Harker asylum and nursing him back to health, the sisters exemplify Hungarian support of English aggression against Russia. The Hungarians even provide the necessary military intelligence required to defeat the Count. It is from Van Helsing's colleague, "Arminius of Buda-Pesth University," that the Crew learns of Dracula's past, habits, and abilities (*D* 291).

Armed with the intelligence supplied by Arminius and the scouting report of Jonathan Harker, the Crew sets out to capture and execute the Count, who, only appropriately, has retreated from English soil on a ship named the "Czarina Catherine," embarked for, where else, Varna (*D* 375). In strictly military fashion, the Crew formulates a "Plan of Campaign" and provisions themselves "with Winchesters," the most advanced weapon of its day, proven highly effective in subduing savages in the American West (*D* 383). Quincey Morris, who recommends the use of Winchesters, knows from experience the need for such weapons when confronting the Russians. He and Godalming, it turns out, had confronted a Russian foe previously in "Tobolsk," a city in western Siberia, without the benefit of modern weapons (*D* 383). The mention of Winchesters also brings to mind one of the few successes of the Crimean War, the Minie rifle carried by British and French troops. Unlike the highly inaccurate smooth-bore muskets of the Russians with an effective range of only 100 yards, the Minie rifle was deadly up to 1,000 yards (Norman Rich 126).

As the Crew follows the Count's route of retreat, they retrace in almost every particular the path taken by British forces in the advance on and withdrawal from the Crimea, a route that George Stoker also follows in 1877. As in the Crimea, then, their assault begins with an occupation of Varna,[30] where they take rooms at the hotel "Odessus," named after the Russian port of Odessa and, I believe, a symbol of Russian interests in Bulgaria[31] (*D* 393). By means of bribery — it seems that Bram's Bulgarians are no less corrupt than those described by George — they discover that Dracula has moved on in the night. But thanks to telegraphic surveillance provided by Lloyd's of London, they learn that the Count has disembarked at Galatz, modern day Galati, a Romanian Black Sea port located near the confluence of the Seret and Pruth rivers, in the disputed region of Bessarabia (*D* 398). It should be noted here that whereas such technological innovations as the telegraph, kodak, and steamship failed to insure an English victory in 1856, in *Dracula* they guarantee triumph.

At Galatz a group that evokes images of Russia comes to the Count's assistance. One Immanuel Hildesheim,[32] "a Hebrew of rather the Adelphi Theatre type," a Petrof Skinsky, and a party of "Slovaks" take possession of Dracula's box for transhipment up the Seret to the castle (*D* 412–413). Later, the Count's Szgany join the expedition. Realizing that they face a "strong and rough" though inferior opponent, the Crew adds to their "small arsenal" a steam launch and a team of horses (*D* 418–420). In the manner of combined naval and ground forces, Jonathan and Godalming pursue on water while Quincey and Dr. Seward follow the Count's entourage on horseback. Overseeing the operation as would a command staff, Mina and Van Helsing set up an observation point overlooking the battlefield (*D* 439–440).

As the Crew approaches the castle, a heavy snow commences to fall, prompting Seward to worry that they may be forced to find sledges and proceed "Russian fashion" (*D* 424). When the battle is finally joined, it is set against a frigid landscape resembling combat around Sebastopol in the winter of 1855 described by Russell. The four combatants advance on foot toward the Count's party, who have "formed round the cart in a sort of undisciplined" perimeter. Jonathan Harker boldly dashes into their midst, heedless of possible injury. However, no harm befalls him, for before a determined Englishman, the undisciplined Slavs "cowered aside and let him pass." While Godalming and Seward provide cover with their Winchesters, Jonathan severs the Count's head with his Kukri knife as Quincey plunges a bowie knife into his heart (*D* 442–443). Thus, Dracula dies from wounds inflicted by imperial warriors wielding what Arata terms "weapons of empire" (641).[33]

Though victory is theirs, the Crew's triumph is not without cost. While fighting his way through the ring of Szgany protecting Dracula, Quincey Morris is fatally wounded. Yet even in the midst of his death throes, Quincey musters the strength to utter, "I am only too happy to have been of service!" before expiring in Jonathan's arms, ever the "gallant gentleman," as Mina observes (*D* 444). Quincey's death removes, according to Glover, the "implicit dangers of interimperial rivalry," insuring that the fruits of imperial conquest accrue solely to England (*Vampires, Mummies, and Liberals* 94). Quincey's ultimate act of "service" also guarantees that credit for Dracula's defeat rests with the professional members of the Crew, demonstrating that their skills take precedence over what Daly terms the superannuated "heroic amateur values" of the wealthy American adventurer (39). Daly further opines that Quincey's death is necessary to maintain the "homosocial arrangement of the text," to obliterate any suggestion of sexual deviance, the penetration of man by man, that would call into question the professional, patriarchal, middle-class credentials of the Crew (40).[34]

With the Count's death, "his threat to the progress of Western civilization [is] brought to an end" (Wasson 23), and put back into the bottle with the genie are the anxieties he produced in Victorian society. Erased are the threats posed by the revenant aristocrat and his feudalistic economy; the pernicious, disease-ridden Yid; the tyrannical, despotic czar; and, closer to home, the independent, sexually assertive New Woman. Mina Harker is saved from the contagion which doomed Lucy Westenra because unlike Lucy—who in typically New Woman fashion once asked Mina "Why can't they let a girl marry three men, or as many as want her, and save all this trouble?" (D 78)—she renounces independence and fights against the Count's seduction. As Carol Senf has shown, Mina thus represents the "traditional kind of woman" ("Stoker's Response to the New Woman" 37) preferred by Victorian men.

Recognizing that she is but "a poor weak woman" (D 390), Mina puts her fate in the hands of men who are "so earnest, so true, and so brave" (D 420), the same men who ruthlessly killed an unrepentant Lucy. Because she has a practical "man's brain" (284) and thus knows her place in Victorian society,[35] Mina willing accepts a subservient position as the secretary for the Crew, helping her husband while remaining "supportively in the background,"[36] and after the battle, she assumes a "woman's traditional role as a mother" (Senf 46). Mina may also be seen to contrast markedly with Florence Nightingale, who waged a "war against medical men" (Poovey 192). Stoker could very well have had Florence Nightingale in mind when he created Mina. For some years, Stoker had endured a loveless relationship with his wife Florence, named after the Crimean heroine. Indifferent to the demands of decorum, Florence went about London with "any number of fascinating escorts" during her husband's frequent absences (Belford 121). Moreover, according to Farson, Florence's "frigidity" after the birth of their son Noel "drove [Stoker] to other women" (234). The dutiful, devoted Mina therefore provided an antidote to the New Woman encoded in the image of Florence Nightingale.

It seems fitting that the novel closes with a note from Jonathan Harker reporting a recent return visit to Transylvania and the birth of their son Quincey, named for all of the Crew.[37] Sounding very much like an old veteran reminiscing over the battlefields of his youth, Harker writes we made a journey to Transylvania, and went over the old ground which was, and is, to us so full of vivid and terrible memories. It was almost impossible to believe the things which we had seen with our own eyes and heard with our own ears were living truths. Every trace of all that had been was blotted out. The castle stood as before, reared high above a waste of desolation [*D* 444].

The old wrong has been redressed, and English pride has been restored at the expense of Russia and her Balkan allies. Moreover, the castle and its environs are now a safe haven for tourists because what Jonathan had once described as "a whole world of dark and dreadful things" (*D* 422) has been pacified. In terms of what Paul Rich identifies as the "ideology of racial improvement in colonies of white settlement," the Count's homeland is thus potentially a fit "rural and pastoral" site for the "regeneration of a race that was undergoing deterioration in the imperial metropolis itself as cities and industrial conglomerations destroyed the old idea of England as a green landscape" (14–15). Impressions of the countryside that Mina records shortly before the battle suggest just such an underlying intention:

The country is lovely, and most interesting; if only we were under different conditions, how delightful it would be to see it all. If Jonathan and I were driving through it alone what a pleasure it would be. To stop and see people, and learn something of their life, and to fill our minds and memories with all the colour and picturesqueness of the whole wild, beautiful country and the quaint people! [*D* 424].

Glover further asserts that the novel, published just as "Britain was moving into its last brief climactic imperialist phase," responds to theories of social and cultural degeneration popular at the time, to the concern that an advanced civilization is increasingly incapable of producing "the heroes it needs" to maintain the empire (97). In *Dracula*, at least, Stoker affirms that it can. And, twelve years after the publication of *Dracula*, in his next vampire novel, *The Lady of the Shroud*, Stoker will reiterate his vision of a vital empire when another set of indomitable British subjects once again defeat an Eastern menace and plant a British colony in the Balkans.

# FIVE

# The Lady of the Shroud:
## *John Bull in the Balkans*

In 1909, twelve years after the publication of *Dracula*, Bram Stoker published another vampire tale, *The Lady of the Shroud*. A contemporary reviewer in the *Bookman* dubbed it a "romantic melodrama" (W.F.P. 154). More recently, Victor Sage has described the book as a conflation of the "Gothic novel and the Empire adventure story" (116) while Lisa Hopkins reads the work as a "compelling adventure story, sustained experiment in narrative technique, travelogue, comedy of manners, heroic yarn and tale of suspense all in one" (145). Despite such praise, the novel unquestionably lacks the sophistication and appeal of its predecessor. Stoker scholar Barbara Belford dismisses the novel as a "boring book" (317). No matter the novel's reception, Carol Senf argues that *The Lady of the Shroud* should be read in conjunction with the *Dracula* because it "adapts the mythic figure of the vampire [...] to eliminate the uncanny and disturbing psychological characteristics so often associated with the figure" ("Stoker's Successor to *Dracula*" 82). Written nine years after the death of Stoker's mother Charlotte and four years after the death of Henry Irving, Stoker's surrogate father, the novel, Senf contends, "dilutes the intense personal feelings associated with the Oedipus complex and with men's ambivalence about women's sexuality" (92) expressed in the earlier novel.[1]

I agree with Senf that *The Lady of the Shroud* should be read in conjunction with *Dracula*, but for wholly different reasons. *The Lady of the Shroud*, regardless of its literary merits,[2] demands attention because it completes the British imperial project in the Balkans initiated in *Dracula*. Specifically, the rehabilitation and colonization of the Balkans imagined at the end of *Dracula* is enacted in *The Lady of the Shroud*. Sage suggests as much, positing that the novel fictionally performs this task by "redrawing the map [of the Balkans] once and for all,"[3] in the process restoring "Britain's Imperial presence in Europe through creating a buffer-state [...] which would deter German ambitions in the south and the east" (132). William Hughes, editor of the 2001 annotated edition of the novel, echoes Sage, deeming the novel, Stoker's "most political [...] of fictions" (Introduction 6), a "form of imaginative geography-a political hybrid whose cultural contours lie not in the hinterland of the declining Ottoman Empire but in the polemic and prejudice of British public opinion and Foreign Office rhetoric" (Introduction 10). Stoker thus reflects British foreign policy at the dawn of the twentieth century, which regarded Germany, not Russia, as England's greatest threat and which necessitated improved relations with Russia and her allies in the Balkans.[4] Nevertheless, although Stoker's narrative accommodates the new political alliances existing after the turn of the century, the author still manifests a long-held animosity toward Slavs in general and Russia in particular.

A series of events occurring at the end of the nineteenth and the beginning of the twentieth centuries radically altered the relations between the great powers in Europe and changed English public sentiment toward the Balkans.[5] First, in 1888 Turkey granted a German syndicate a contract to build a railway from Constantinople to Ankara. Known as the Baghdad Railway, the project made evident Germany's increasing economic influence in the Near East and raised apprehensions in England that the nation's commercial interests might suffer at the hands of German competition. When another German firm was given a new concession to extend the railway to the Persian Gulf, the threat to England's economic advantage in that region became more pronounced, and anti–German sentiments began to appear in the press and in parliament. Russia also took a dim view of the project, for she feared that the new railway would improve Turkey's ability to mobilize and conduct operations against her (M. S. Anderson 264–265). Russian antipathy to Germany was further heightened when Turkey next invited German military advisers to help reform her army and purchased German arms (Jelavich 2:81).

German actions in 1898 and 1899 substantiated English fears. As part of an overall strategy for imperial expansion, Germany initiated in 1898 a naval building program aimed at achieving parity with the Royal Navy (*Columbia History of the World* 978). The next year Germany once again revealed herself as a direct menace to England by supplying arms and diplomatic assistance to the Boer rebels fighting British troops in South Africa. Thus Germany, who once had seemed England's "most likely friend" in Europe, was now her most "potent threat" (Matthew 509). Furthermore, Germany's support of Austro-Hungarian incursions in the Balkans in the early 1900s eventuated in a great power realignment that would have seemed impossible twenty years earlier.

By 1900 the Slavic peoples of the Balkans had achieved a relative measure of independence from the Austro-Hungarian and Ottoman empires. Romania had gained its outright independence, and, with Russian support, Bulgaria had become an autonomous state within the Ottoman Empire. The Serbian Slavs in Serbia and Bosnia-Herzegovina, however, were to a large degree still under the dominion of Austria-Hungary. Matters came to a head when in 1903 the king of Serbia, Peter Karageorgevich, began to curtail economic ties with Austria-Hungary. Fearing that Serbia would become the nucleus of an independent south Slav state incorporating many groups presently under Habsburg rule, Austria-Hungary annexed Bosnia-Herzegovina in 1908 in an effort to effectively destroy Serbia (M. S. Anderson 278–279).

By this move Austria-Hungary undermined the international accord that had kept peace in the region since the Russo-Turkish War of 1877–1878. England, France, and Russia strongly protested while Germany defended the move. Although the Serbs pleaded for Russian military intervention, the Russo-Japanese war of 1905 had left Russia too weak to act on their behalf. Nevertheless, the incident created a bitter hostility in Russia to Austria-Hungary and especially Germany. It also spurred reforms and improvements in the Russian military and led to better diplomatic relations with England and France. Thus, after resolutions reached in 1904 and 1907, two alliances stood bitterly opposed over the fate of the Balkans: the Triple Alliance, composed of Austria-Hungary, Germany, and Italy; and the Triple Entente, consisting of England, France, and Russia (Jelavich 2:95–97).

Despite improvements in formal relations between London and Moscow, Russophobia and anti–Slavic sentiments like those manifested in George Stoker's *With the Unspeakables* still prevailed in early twentieth century England. Illustrating the vestigial presence of such long held animosity, an incident in October 1904 "raised Russophobia to fever pitch and very nearly led to war between the two powers" (Hopkirk 514). As the Russian Baltic Fleet steamed through the North Sea on its passage to relieve the garrison at Port Arthur in Korea, then under attack by Japanese forces, it fired on the English Dogger Bank fishing fleet, mistaking the trawlers for Japanese torpedo boats. Only a hastily arranged international arbitration prevented war (Clarkson 379). Later, in 1907, notable Russophobes Lord Curzon and the seemingly ever-present Arminius Vambery raised alarms about the recently concluded Anglo-Russian agreement over the disposition of Tibet, an arrangement which effectively endorsed Russian hegemony in Persia. Both were fearful that the pact would damage British prestige in

Asia and give Russia another base of operations from which to threaten India (Hopkirk 521–522).

However, with the emergence of German commercial and military power, which through ties with Turkey threatened English interests in the Persian Gulf, England was suddenly in need of a client in the region. Appropriately, then, Stoker's narrative valorizes a Slavic nation that has seen fit to align itself with imperial Britain. But, reflecting the existence of the bitter popular resentment toward Slavs manifested since the time of the Crimean War, Stoker chooses as a locus for his narrative a nondescript country identified only as the Land of the Blue Mountains, a place and a people with seemingly no connection to the Balkan Slavs aligned with Russia. However, the Slavs inhabiting this land are, notwithstanding, Serbians, who, though culturally, ethnically, and racially associated with Russia, were then the object of English sympathies. Sage makes just this point, contending that the novel "suggests to the reader the desirability of Serbian expansion against Austria-Hungary, in the wake of the latter's annexation of Bosnia in 1908" (116).

The geography of the novel provides ample proof that Stoker had a Serbian land[6] in mind when penning the novel. Set along the Dalmatian coast between Ragusa, now known as the Croatian seaport of Dubrovnik, and Durazzo, present day Durres in Albania, the majority of the action occurs near or on the "Spear of Ivan,"[7] a strip of land that resembles many of the headlands dotting the coastline. Once again, personal experiences could well have suggested this locale to Stoker. Although no record exists of his ever having visited the Adriatic coast of the Balkans, Stoker was in Cava di Terreni, Italy, in the province of Campania, between Naples and Salerno, in 1876 for his father's funeral (Belford 69). He may very well have crossed over to the Adriatic coast of Italy or even the Balkans during his sojourn, or he may have based the Spear of Ivan on the peninsula that separates the Gulf of Salerno from Naples.

No matter the source of inspiration, Stoker provides enough clues to make it fairly certain that he is describing a Serbian homeland. Situated on the "Adriatic"[8] (*L* 19), the Spear of Ivan harbors Castle Vissarion, home of Voivode Peter Vissarion, the ruler of the Land of the Blue Mountains. On his return from a diplomatic voyage to England, Peter sails southeast from Fiume, today known as Rijeka in Slovenia (*L* 237), docks temporarily at Ragusa, and disembarks at the port of Ilsin, where he takes up residence at the Hotel Reo (*L* 234). From here he is kidnapped by Turkish agents, who spirit him away to the Silent Tower, "a massive tower of immense strength, built as a memorial [...] after one of the massacres of the invading Turks," established on "a rocky knoll some ten miles inland from the Port of Ilsin" (*L* 238–239). Later, after Peter is rescued from the tower by means of an "aeroplane" no less, his party passes east of Ilsin "just as the sun was dropping down over the Calabrian Mountains" (293). In a footnote to this passage, Hughes contends that if this range in southern Italy is actually visible, "then the Land of the Blue Mountains would appear to lie somewhere in the region occupied by present-day northern Greece or Albania"; he goes on to state that the Calabrian Mountains may also be seen "from the coast of present-day Montenegro" (293). The text, I will demonstrate, more fully supports a Montenegrin setting than the other two suggested by Hughes. For example, the port of Ilsin, which does not appear on maps of the region, can be shown to be a thinly veiled analogue for the port of Ulcinji located on the coast of modern-day Montenegro.

This Montenegrin locale would have appealed to Stoker for a host of reasons.[9] First of all, Ulcinji sits astride the long contested boundary separating Montenegro and Albania, a centuries-old line of demarcation denoting the advance of the Ottoman Empire into southeast Europe. Although Montenegro was ceded to the Turks in 1499, the Empire could never establish effective political and military control of the region, a place Barbara Jelavich has described as "the most primitive area in the Balkans" (1: 84). Montenegrin highland tribes, the basic political and social units of the country, maintained autonomy from the Ottoman Empire, establishing a bulwark against incursions by Turkish forces garrisoned in nearby Albania. The threat of wholesale invasion and domination by Turkey ended in 1796 when an invading Turkish force was defeated at Krusi and the Ottoman pasha of Albania, Kara Mahmud, captured and beheaded (Jelavich 1:87). Still, the Ottoman Turks in Albania were to pose a constant source of trouble to Montenegro until the First World War.

Ulcinji, Ilsin in English, thus offered Stoker an ideal setting for Peter's kidnapping. The port, with almost equal Montenegrin and Albanian populations, had long been caught up in the tug of war between Orthodox Slavs and Muslim Turks and did not become a Montenegrin possession until 1878, when it was ceded to Montenegro in the Treaty of San Stefano that ended the 1877–1878 Turko-Russian war. A contested space, Ulcinji was certainly a site of political intrigue and espionage. Redoubts like the Silent Tower garrisoned with Ottoman troops would surely have dotted the border between Montenegro and Albania.[10] Stoker would have found the people of Montenegro equally useful as models for the inhabitants of the Land of the Blue Mountains. A primitive people ill equipped materially and politically to conduct modern warfare, the Montenegrins nevertheless held their own against larger, better equipped Turkish armies. Fighting in small units organized at the tribal level and operating in mountainous terrain that offered ideal natural barriers and sources of concealment, the Montenegrins mounted a tenacious and flexible defense of their homeland that denied larger Turkish forces freedom of movement and the ability to bring their formidable resources to bear.

The Montenegrins would have appealed to Stoker and his British audience for another reason as well. Although admittedly "Serb in nationality and Orthodox in religion" (Jelavich 1:85), the Montenegrins of Stoker's day had a long history of good relations with Italy and, to a lesser degree, Austria-Hungary. In the eighteenth century, the Kingdom of Venice, which occupied neighboring Dalmatia, sought Montenegro's assistance in its ongoing struggles with Turkey. To formalize the allegiance between the two realms, in 1717 the doge of Venice created "a political officer, called a *guvernadar* (civil governor), for Montenegro" (Jelavich 1:85). Out of necessity, Montenegro also sought an accord with the Habsburg empire, which had occupied Bosnia, Herzegovina, and the Sanjak of Novi Pazar, all bordering on Montenegro. When Kara Mahmud launched an attack on Montenegro in 1787, Austria-Hungary sent military advisors, weapons, and money to Montenegro (Jelavich 1:87). Later, at the time of the Treaty of Berlin, Austria was entrusted with the task of providing naval forces to protect the Montenegrin coast.

By the early twentieth century, Montenegro had, for all intents and purposes, secured its southern boundary against a large-scale invasion by the Turks in Albania. It recognized, however, that its erstwhile allies Italy and Austria-Hungary were not wholly trustworthy. The two powers had for some time looked upon Montenegro as "a possible area of exploitation" (Jelavich 2:37). Moreover, Montenegro's ethnic and cultural ties to the Serbs of Bosnia, Herzegovina, and Serbia worried Austria-Hungary, which feared the emergence of a greater Serbia aligned with Russia against the Habsburg Empire. Such fears were not unfounded, for since the early eighteenth century, Montenegro had been the willing recipient of Russian aid. By 1910, Russia was supplying Montenegro with wheat and, more importantly, financial support that accounted for over half of the country's national budget (Jelavich 2:36). Prince Nicholas, who had ruled Montenegro from 1860 onward, took steps to more firmly bond his country with Russia. He sought greater financial assistance, reorganized his army on the Russian model, and even married two of his daughters to Russian grand dukes (Jelavich 2:37).

Nonetheless, Nicholas well understood that Russia, for all her assistance to Montenegro, could not immediately intervene on her behalf in the event of invasion by Italy or Austria-Hungary. So as to maintain peaceful relations with these countries, Nicholas encouraged them to loan money to his government and to make investments in Montenegrin agriculture and industry. And, as he had with the Russian court, Nicholas married his fourth daughter to Victor Emmanuel III. She would eventually become queen of

Italy (Jelavich 2:37). All told, then, Montenegro could well have impressed Stoker as the ideal place to situate his Balkan narrative. Its geographical location, exotic history, and, perhaps more significantly, its ties with western Europe made Montenegro palatable to a British audience and an appropriate target for British foreign policy bent on establishing a client state in the Balkans to halt the expansion of German influence in the region.

Phyllis Roth has argued that in *The Lady of the Shroud* Stoker "once again employs Transylvania as the exotic land" (*Bram Stoker* 109) in which to situate the action. The setting of Stoker's narrative, however, offers little evidence to support such a claim. The Land of the Blue Mountains has much more in common with Montenegro, not landlocked Transylvania. Still, Roth is correct in assuming that many of the sites described in *The Lady of the Shroud* hearken back to similar descriptions in *Dracula*. I would account for this apparent discrepancy by arguing that Stoker, who, it must be remembered, never traveled in the Balkans, borrowed heavily from his brother George's accounts of Bulgaria and Asia Minor in *With the Unspeakables* for his depictions, first, of Transylvania and, later, the Land of the Blue Mountains. One proof of this second assertion can be found in the description of the Spear of Ivan given by Rupert Sent Leger, the protagonist of *The Lady of the Shroud*. The Spear of Ivan is

> a headland running well out into the sea. It is quite a peculiar place — a sort of headland on a headland, jutting out into a deep, wide bay, so that, though it is a promontory, it is as far away from the traffic of coast life as anything you can conceive. The main promontory is the end of a range of mountains, and looms up vast, towering over everything [...] [*L* 79].

This description of a descending series of mountains leading down to the sea reads a great deal like the setting of Soukoum on the Black Sea described by George:

> The situation of Soukoum is very beautiful. The town is built on a level plain close to the sea. Immediately behind the town the hills commence — low at first, but successively rising higher and higher, like the steps of an ampitheatre, and clothed to their very summits with virgin forests, whose verdure becomes less distinct as the hills recede in the distance, and at last become merged in the far-off snow-capped peaks of the Caucasus [*With the Unspeakables* 53].

Moreover, the actual promontory on which Castle Vissarion sits and the Castle itself are but slightly altered versions of scenes George records on first entering the Bosphorus and seeing Constantinople. The Castle,[11] "a huge pile of buildings of every style of architecture, from the twelfth century to where such things seemed to stop in this dear old-world land-about the time of Queen Elizabeth" (*L* 80), recalls the diverse architecture of

Constantinople, with its "magnificent palaces," "charming villas," and "Tall minarets and massive domes, stately towers and imposing ranges of military barracks" (*With the Unspeakables* 14).

The natives of the Land of the Blue Mountains, however, have nothing in common with the Bulgarians and other Slavs described by George Stoker. Unlike the cowardly, base, mendacious, and profligate Bulgarians of George Stoker's travelogue, the Slavs in *The Lady of the Shroud* are brave, honest, and fierce in battle. Nevertheless, as indicated above, these people are Slavs, in particular members of the majority Serbian populations of Montenegro, Bosnia, and Herzegovina, who like the Bulgarians, allied themselves with and sought protection from Russia. Ample textual evidence establishes a Serbian connection. For example, the people of the Land of the Blue Mountains belong to "the old Greek Church" (*L* 620) as do the Bulgarians, Romanians, Russians, and Serbians. Moreover, the "Head of the Eastern Church" in the country is "Archbishop Steven Palealogue" (*L* 211), a probable descendent of the Paleologue family which ruled the empire of Nicaea in Asia Minor in the thirteenth century (*Columbia History of the World* 457). Nicaea figures large in Serbian history as the seat of the Greek Orthodox Church after the Crusades. Furthermore, in the city of Nicaea, "the greatest of the Serbian national saints," St. Sava, was consecrated in 1219 (Ware 152). In the Land of the Blue Mountains, Archbishop Steven Palealogue performs his ecclesiastical duties from "the old church of St. Sava," a half-hour journey from Castle Vissarion (*L* 182). Here, also, Voivodin Teuta, Voivode Peter Vissarion's daughter and princess of the realm and "in her own person the glory of the old Serb race" (*L* 212), hides from national enemies in the guise of a vampire. Undoubtedly, then, the people of the Land of the Blue Mountains are Serbians by virtue of faith and heritage.

Although England and Russia had worked out a diplomatic rapprochement just two years prior to the publication of *The Lady of the Shroud*, Stoker, I contend, still shared with the majority of the English public a hostility toward Russia, and, as a result, he could not bring himself to treat Russia and her allies kindly.[12] Thus in the novel, the natives of the Land of the Blue Mountains have had to fight off invasions by Slavs from "Albania, Dalmatia, Herzegovina, Servia, Bulgaria" as well as incursions by "Greece, Turkey, Russia, Italy, France" (*L* 30). Russia, "often hurled back," always awaited "an opportunity to attack" (*L* 30). In this novel, Stoker's antipathy to Russia also has a very personal source. Stoker dedicated *The Lady of the Shroud* to Genevieve Ward, the Countess de Guerbel, someone with every reason to hate Russians. Stoker had discovered Ward in 1873 during a performance of *Adrienne Lecouvreur*. Although the play failed miserably, Stoker wrote glowingly of Ward, thus helping her to win better roles (Belford 57).

Later at the Lyceum, Stoker would once again save her career by suggesting she stage "*Forget-me-not* by Herman Merivale and F. C. Grove" (Belford 117). Stoker and Ward were to remain life-long friends, and at Stoker's funeral in 1912, she was among the small group of mourners in attendance (322).

Eighteen years prior to their meeting during a family vacation in Nice, Ward, who was but seventeen at the time, was engaged to the Count de Guerbel, a member of an old Swiss family that had emigrated to Russia at the time of Peter the Great. After marrying Ward in a civil ceremony there, the Count left to arrange a formal Russian Orthodox wedding in Paris (Belford 57–58). However, according to Ludlam, "the blackguardly Count [...] sneaked off with another woman, declaring that by Russian law, which did not acknowledge a marriage until it had been performed in a Russian church, his marriage with Genevieve was not legal" (36). Eventually, Ward's well-connected father, Colonel Samuel Ward, petitioned the czar, who ordered de Guerbel to marry Genevieve in Warsaw. Stoker recounts the events of the wedding in *Personal Reminiscences of Henry Irving*:

> The altar was set for marriage and before it stood the injured lady, her father, Colonel Ward, and her mother. Her father was armed, for the occasion was to them one of grim import. De Gerbel yielded to the mandate of his Czar, and the marriage — with all needful safeguards this time — was duly effected. Then the injured Countess bowed to him and moved away with her own kin. At the church door husband and wife parted, never to meet again [2: 171].

Count De Guerble,[13] then, might well be the inspiration not only for Count Dracula, but also another source of the bitterness Stoker evinces toward Russia in *The Lady of the Shroud*.

Russia is clearly a threat, if not the most immediate, to the people of the Land of the Blue Mountains and the Pan Balkan confederation, Balka, imagined at the end of the novel. The principal villains at this time, however, are Turkey, Britain's foe just then, who is "preparing for a war of offence" as the novel opens (*L* 62), and, to a lesser degree, Austria-Hungary. Still, the Russian menace is palpable as are the anti–Russian sentiments of the author. Illustrating the anti–Russian tone of the novel is the presence of a Japanese delegation at the coronation of the king of Balka in the finale of the novel. Among the throng of international delegations assembled to celebrate the event and to recognize the legitimacy of the new confederation, one is singled out by the narrator: "we could distinguish the cheers of the various nationalities, amongst which, more keen than the others, came the soft 'Ban Zai!' of the Japanese" (*L* 347). As Hughes notes, Japan at this time was enjoying a sense of "enhanced confidence [...] on the world stage following its military and naval success in the Russo-Japanese

War of 1904–05" (*L* 253).[14] The Russian threat is most fully portrayed, however, prior to the coronation during the deliberations leading up to the founding of Balka. At this point, the "Czar of Russia" is asked to be "the referee in the 'Balkan Settlement.'" But, he declines "on the ground that he was himself by inference an interested party" (*L* 335–336). The threat of continued interference in Balkan affairs by Russia, who "historically enjoyed imperial and diplomatic interests in the Balkans, and claimed racial connection with ethnic groups, particularly in Serbia" (Hughes 336), could not be more apparent.

Nevertheless, as noted earlier, the principal threats are Turkey, rearmed and emboldened by Germany, and Austria-Hungary, Germany's continental ally. Reflecting the new political realities of the day and England's desire for a base of operations in the Balkans to forestall "German expansionism to the south" (Sage 130), the Slavic people of the Land of the Blue Mountains turn to "mighty Britain" (*L* 120) in their "hour of need" (*L* 211), willingly accepting British intervention in their internal and external affairs. By doing so, the people of the Land of the Blue Mountain invite their eventual absorption into the empire itself as British colonists come to assume control of their military and government. Further cementing the ties that bind them to England, their crown princess, Voivodin Teuta, marries Britain's imperial representative, Rupert Sent Leger, a most fitting agent for England by virtue of birth, experience, and station.

Much as was the case with Stoker himself,[15] Rupert is an assimilated, appropriated English subject.[16] He is the scion of an Anglo-Irish marriage, having been born to an Irish father serving in Her Majesty's service and an English mother of affluent middle-class origins. Though poor, his father's family has a distinguished career in the British army in the imperial wars of the 1890s and 1900s. A "Captain in the Lancers," his father wins the "Victoria Cross" at the "Battle of Amoaful" during the Ashanti Revolt of 1900 in Uganda (*L* 25). Moreover, a paternal great uncle died in the "Indian Mutiny at Meerut in 1857" (*L* 25), while a paternal uncle, a "subaltern," was killed at "Maiwand"[17] during the Second Afghan War (*L* 27). On his maternal side, Rupert is related to another appropriated imperial warrior, the Scotsman "Major-General Sir Colin Alexander MacKelpie, Baronet, holder of the Victoria Cross, Knight Commander of the Order of the Bath" (*L* 46).[18] Whereas from his Irish father he inherits fighting skills, from his English mother he gains middle-class business acumen.

Rupert's presence in the Land of the Blue Mountains comes about as the result of an inheritance from his maternal uncle, Roger Melton. A self-made millionaire and thoroughly middle-class man of business, Roger made his money in "'the Eastern Trade'" (*L* 39). As an agent of Britain's commercial empire, he risked life and limb pursuing business in Turkey, Greece,

Morocco, Egypt, Russia, Persia, India, China, Japan, and the Pacific Islands (*L* 40). When he dies, Roger leaves the majority of his wealth to Rupert,[19] who made his way in the world as a seaman and psychical researcher.[20] Akin to Jonathan Harker, whom Dracula describes as "English and therefore adventurous" ("Dracula's Guest" 456), Rupert is "a man to whom no adventure is too wild or too daring,"[21] one whose "reckless bravery is a byword amongst many savage peoples and amongst many others not savages" (*L* 67). What Roger most desires is that Rupert will distinguish his "name" and "race"[22] (*L* 71).

Ostensibly, Roger provides Rupert with a wealthy inheritance to aid Peter Vissarion in defeating a Turkish invasion and to return to him Castle Vissarion, which Peter had given as security for a loan to purchase defensive weapons. However, Roger's real hope is that Rupert will "carve out for himself a name and a place in history" (*L* 58). For this purpose the Land of the Blue Mountains is ideal because, in the thinking of Roger Melton, "It is only in a small nation that great ambitions can be achieved." Thus the Land of the Blue Mountain's "is [Rupert's] ground" where one day he might fulfill his uncle's dream and "yet become a Voivode," a prince of the realm (*L* 69). Should Rupert's adventure in the Land of the Blue Mountains prove successful, Roger further stipulates that Rupert must still maintain allegiance to his race and above all else his "British nationality" (*L* 70).[23] This idea is repeated again later in the novel after Rupert has married into the royal family when his paternal aunt, Janet MacKelpie, informs Voivodin Teuta that by marriage she has become "Mrs. Rupert Sent Leger. For he is still an Englishman and a good subject of our noble King"[24] (*L* 190). This insistence on allegiance to England reveals an underlying imperial agenda, the desire to assimilate and absorb the people of the Land of the Blue Mountains into the empire racially, militarily, and politically.

The issue of race appears early in the novel when Major-General MacKelpie, who is raising a Scots army for service in the Land of the Blue Mountains, remarks in a letter to his sister Janet, then residing in Castle Vissarion, that

> I think you are quite wise about waiting to bring out the lassies, and wiser still about the marrying. I dare say there will be more marrying when they all get settled in a foreign country [*L* 101].

This passage reveals, writes Hughes, a "eugenic sub-text" at work in the novel:

> Effectively, the implication is that a Scots husband is likely to be more suitable than one from Vissarion stock — one who is likely to be a member of the Orthodox church as well as of a supposedly Slavic or Eastern race [*L* 101].

Stoker, as discussed earlier, was intimately familiar with the pseudo-science of physiognomy and would very likely have been attracted to the theories Karl Pearson, a leading English eugenicist, and Robert Knox, a Scottish anatomist and anthropologist, who in 1850 published *Races of Men*. The last half of the nineteenth century gave rise in England to what George Mosse has described as a fascination with notions of "national origin." Writers, such as Sir Walter Scott, were especially keen to illustrate that "virtues like honesty, loyalty, and love of freedom" were inherent in the nation's Anglo-Saxon heritage. Endowed with this genetic inheritance, "Englishmen exemplified the qualities of the race wherever they went." So endowed, English colonizers, as exemplified by "the United States of America as colonized by Englishmen," through interbreeding with native populations, could remake those people, literally, in their image (*Toward the Final Solution* 66). Intermarriage with British subjects, therefore, will dilute and, perhaps, eventually eradicate the inferior Slavic traits of the people of the Land of the Blue Mountains.

Rupert begins the process of Anglicization by winning the respect and admiration of the native populace, especially the militia. Although they are "an indomitable, proud people to whom pride is more than victuals" (*L* 94), Rupert, who is "well accustomed to all sorts of people, from cannibals to Mahatmas,"[25] is not deterred from his mission. Thus he tells his Aunt MacKelpie that

> I'm sure of one thing: that in the end we shall get on capitally together. But it will be a slow job, and will need a lot of patience. I have a feeling in my bones that when they know me better, they will be very loyal and true; and I am not a hair's-breadth afraid of them or anything they shall or might do [*L* 94].

Determined to pursue his course, Rupert spies out their meeting place and boldly walks "straight into the midst" of two to three hundred armed men (*L* 96). Even though he is virtually unknown to them, they drop their rifles and gather about him, "regular and quick and simultaneous as a salute at St. Jame's Place" (*L* 97).[26] Just as the Szgany part to allow Jonathan Harker to get at Dracula, these Slavs also become "amazingly civil, almost deferential" (*L* 97) before a superior English specimen possessed of unshakable *sang-froid* and a seven-foot frame (*L* 120).

Like Lawrence among the tribes of Arabia, Rupert wins the militia over by apparently throwing in with their lot, convincing them that their cause is also his, telling them that his only interest is

> "the security and consolidation of your country-of *our* country, for I have come to live amongst you. Here is my home whilst I live. I am with you heart and soul. I shall live with you, fight shoulder to shoulder with you, and, if need be, shall die with you!" [*L* 125].

The tribal militiamen[27] are soon "quite willing to drill" when and how Rupert wishes them to (*L* 148). Later, when he leads them in rescuing both

Peter and Teuta Vissarion from Turkish kidnappers, they prove just as intractable at times as Lawrence's Arab troops. Yet, they eventually obey all of Rupert's commands, for he shows himself to be their physical and intellectual superior.

Rupert first proves himself a better mountain tracker. Because as a well traveled imperial colonizer he has "larger and more varied experience than any of them" (L 150), Rupert is able to call on a "West African experience" to determine the kidnappers' route where the Blue Mountain men have failed (L 151). Once on the scent, he also keeps "ahead of them" even though they are as "keen as leopards, and as swift" (L 221). Here in the narrative, the point of view shifts from Rupert's first-hand journal accounts to second-hand reports of Rupert's daring and leadership written by various religious authorities and dispatched to Janet MacKelpie. Roth sees this shift in point of view as merely "an awkward mechanism for getting the tale told" (Bram Stoker 77). What Roth fails to recognize, however, is that this narrative technique foregrounds Rupert's actions to the virtual exclusion of all others. Moreover, the native writers' praise for Rupert and England Rupent clearly suggest that has won their devotion and acquired an inestimable influence in the affairs of the Land of the Blue Mountains.

The letters, meant to explain Rupert's long absence from Castle Vissarion, begin by extolling the strength and courage of "Gospodar Rupert" who, like King Richard of the Crusades, has "a lion's heart meet for his giant body" (L 221).[28] The designation of gospodar, indicating the rank of provincial governor and similar to the title of hospodar in Romania, reveals that he has been given a royal title. Furthermore, the letters document that in pursuit of the Turks, Rupert exhibits energy and endurance[29] in excess of the native militia (L 235). He also proves to be more decisive and collected in battle. When those about him want to strike out blindly in a fit of passion and anger, Rupert provides "direction" and "guidance"[30] without "hesitation," earning himself their "strict obedience" (L 224). And, though the men of the Blue Mountains "have good eyes," Rupert's sight is better, like that of an "eagle" (L 227). When he finally effects Teuta's rescue, Rupert is described as having seemingly been sent "straight down from Heaven itself" (L 230), performing a feat "worthy of any hero of old romance" (L 231). The diction and tone of these letters proves beyond a doubt that Rupert has gained the undying respect and, better yet, subservience of the people of the Land of the Blue Mountains by rescuing their voivodin and by proving himself a nonpareil warrior.

To rescue Voivode Peter Vassarion, secure the land from invasion, and, as a corollary, solidify England's hold over the nation, Rupert introduces into the country British military expertise and a phalanx of professional British soldiers as well as the most advanced weapons to be had.[31] In terms of technology, with his inheritance from Roger Melton,[32] Rupert acquires "a torpedo yacht. A small cruiser, with turbines up to date, oil-fuelled, and fully armed with the latest and most perfect weapons and explosives of all kinds" (*L* 170). She is a marvel of English business and technology, the "fastest boat afloat," the product of such English firms as Thorneycroft, Parsons, and Armstrong (*L* 171).[33] For the troops afield, he acquires "fifty thousand of the newest-pattern rifles, the French Ingis-Malbron" (*L* 127) and "a whole park of artillery of the very latest patterns" (*L* 171). But the jewel of the arsenal Rupert assembles is an "aeroplane," a machine apparently combining features of both a fixed-wing aircraft and a dirigible (*L* 204).[34]

Rupert next sets about creating a professional military force for the Land of the Blue Mountains, one commanded by and supplemented with British personnel. Overseeing the creation and training of an army is Rupert's Scottish uncle, Major-General MacKelpie, whom Rupert charges with the task of bringing "to perfection as a fighting-machine" the native militia (*L* 149). As was the case with the British colonial army in India, this force will be led by officers recruited from England (*L* 289) and organized around a core of two hundred Scots troops hand picked and trained by General MacKelpie himself (*L* 235). The newly formed and "expanding navy" will likewise be manned by "nearly all man-of-warsmen; of various nationalities, but mostly British" (*L* 204) under the command of Rooke, an English seaman and long time friend of Roger Melton, whom Rupert appoints as "Lord High Admiral of the Land of the Blue Mountains" (*L* 287). Rupert himself comes to command what Ludlam calls the "royal air force" of the Land of the Blue Mountains (142). Although such moves are ostensibly meant to insure the independence and sovereignty of the Land of the Blue Mountains, Major-General Mackelpie articulates an underlying foreign policy/military agenda when, in an aside to Rupert, he says that his ultimate goal is to help form "a new 'nation' — an ally of Britain, who will stand at least as an outpost of our own nation, and a guardian of our eastern road" (*L* 288).[35]

Once Peter is returned home, Rupert assumes ultimate political control, participating in the complete restructuring of the government of the Land of the Blue Mountains, with the willing assistance of Peter Vissarion, to reflect that of Great Britain. Peter first convinces the members of the National Council to adopt "Constitutional Monarchy, such as that holding in Great Britain" to replace the "present form of ruling by an Irregular Council" (*L* 298). The Council further rules that a "New Constitution" should be written, one "founded on the Constitution and Procedure of Great Britain" (*L* 300). Finally, it is decided that "the Englishman, Rupert Sent Leger" should be Peter's "successor to follow the Voivode when God should call him" (*L* 299). Peter, in a rather stunning turn of events, refuses to accept rule in this new scheme, preferring instead that Rupert be named king. Peter's argument for Rupert's ascension to the throne reveals the imperial agenda of the novel, the fantasy of a compliant British client state in the Balkans:

> He comes of a great nation, wherein the principle of freedom is a vital principal that quickens all things. That nation has more than once shown to us its friendliness; and doubtless the very fact that an Englishman would become our King, and could carry into our Government the spirit and the customs which have made his own country great, would do much to restore the old friendship, and even to create a new one, which would in times of trouble bring British fleets to our waters, and British bayonets to support our own handjars [*L* 303].

Anticipating possible objections based on Rupert's British citizenship, Peter goes on to say that Rupert has sought and been granted permission from the "King of England himself, allowing him to be denaturalized in England, so that he can at once apply for naturalization here" (*L* 303).[36]

This move on Rupert's part would appear to run counter to Roger Melton's will, which encourages Rupert to maintain his ties to England and the king. But as the response of King Edward VII to Rupert's request reveals, Rupert will be inextricably tied to Britain no matter his nationality. When Mr. Bingham Trent, Roger Melton's executor, recounts for Rupert his audience with the king in furtherance of Rupert's desire to renounce his British citizenship, this fact becomes apparent:

> As that gentleman is settling himself in a part of the world which has been in the past, and may be again, united to this nation by some common interest, His Majesty wishes Mr Sent Leger to feel assured of the good-will of Great Britain to the Land of the Blue Mountains, and even of his own personal satisfaction that a gentleman of so distinguished a lineage and such approved personal character is about to be—within his own scope—a connecting link between the nations [*L* 290].

Rupert's renunciation of his British citizenship is, it would seem, but a stratagem to obscure the true purpose of his ascendancy in the political and military affairs of the Land of the Blue Mountains. Citizen or not, Rupert will serve to bind the interests of the Land of the Blue Mountain to those of Britain, performing duties similar to those of a colonial governor.

Rupert's coronation reinforces the close ties established with Britain. Although the ceremony takes place in the church of St. Sava, which was "built in the manner of old Greek churches," the building has been reconfigured "after the fashion of Westminster Abbey for the coronation of King Edward VII" (*L* 312). During the subsequent festivities celebrating the occasion, Edward VII arrives at the Blue Mouth, a harbor near Castle

Vissarion, on the "King's yacht" at the head of a squadron of "fifty of the finest ships in the world; the very latest expression of naval giants, each seemingly typical of its class–Dreadnoughts, cruisers, destroyers" (*L* 345). This "great Western fleet lay at their moorings" (*L* 349) while Edward VII is ferried ashore, a fact which would suggest a sizeable anchorage, one capable of providing docks and stores for refitting, refueling, and rearming a large naval force. It would not be unreasonable to assume that the Blue Mouth is being readied as a base of operations[37] for the British navy, something akin to Malta in the Mediterranean.[38] Perhaps in preparation for just this eventuality, Rupert has harnessed the labor and resources of the Land of the Blue Mountain for the production of armaments. He records in his journal that he has overseen the building of "great factories for war materials," tunneled "into the mountains, where are the greatest deposits of coal,"[39] and that the "cannon foundries are built and active" (*L* 323–324).

When Edward VII joins Rupert and Teuta, now his bride and queen, ashore, Teuta "kneeled before him with the gracious obeisance of a Blue Mountain hostess, and kissed his hand" (*L* 348). Undoubtedly, this is yet another act of supplication on the part of the nation to Britain, but, more significantly, the scene functions as a potent symbol of Rupert's and Britain's absolute dominion over the Land of the Blue Mountains, an authority deriving, in no small measure, from Teuta. When the National Council offers the crown to Rupert, thereby displacing Teuta from her rightful position in the line of succession, Teuta willingly abdicates her claim to the throne, citing Salic Law as justification. Her reliance on Salic Law to offset what Sage describes as the "morganatic nature of her marriage" (131) reveals her utter subjugation to Rupert:

> And it would ill become me, whom my husband honours— wife to a man whom you would honour — to take a part in changing the ancient custom which has been held in honour for all the thousand years, which is the glory of Blue Mountain womanhood. What an example such would be in an age when self-seeking women of other nations seem to forget their womanhood in the struggle to vie in equality with men! Men of the Blue Mountains, I speak for our women when I say that we hold of greatest price the glory of our men. To be their companions is our happiness; to be their wives is the completion of our lives; to be mothers of their children is our share of the glory that is theirs [*L* 307].

According to Hopkins, Teuta's reference to the "self-seeking women of other nations" suggests "that residual concern about the New Women's debate, which critics have detected as so forcibly present in *Dracula*, also informs *The Lady of the Shroud*" (143–144). Teuta, then, like Mina Harker, who enjoys shocking the "New Woman" (*D* 119), represents the appropriated, colonized Victorian woman, the absolute anti-type of the New Woman.[40]

Teuta and Mina, as would be imagined, share many common traits. Both, for example, are potential vampires and thereby threats to male sexuality. After finding Teuta asleep in a glass coffin in the Church of St. Sava, Rupert frets that she "might be a vampire" (L 139) just as Van Helsing and Seward worry about the effects of Dracula's attack on Mina. Moreover, Rupert and Jonathan Harker are willing to see their wives dead rather than have them appropriated — deracinated — by foreign men. Jonathan, for example, accedes to Mina's wish that he kill her should she become a vampire (D 391) while Rupert devises a rescue plan to save Teuta from "the harem of the Turk" where women are "no more than a sheep" (L 220) that will "kill her too" (L 229) should it fail.

Furthermore, Teuta and Mina recognize that as women they are inherently weak and dependent upon men. Just as Mina understands "all that brave honest men can do for a poor weak woman" (D 390), Teuta knows that she needs a "man's wit and experience" (L 241) to guide her. Cognizant of their weaknesses and reliance on men, both also assume the roles of pliant, deferential wives. Mina willingly accepts a subservient role as a secretary and helpmate to Jonathan (D 274), behaving like the docile "Angel in the House." Teuta, too, deprecates herself before Rupert. Once they are married, she leaves the church of St. Sava "holding [him] tightly by the left arm — which is the wife's arm" (L 196). She later addresses him with "the reverence that women owe to men" (L 232),[41] and, like "a good wife, she [obeys]" (L 242) all of Rupert's commands. And, finally, ever the willing facilitator of all Rupert's desires, Teuta conceives his child (L 322).[42]

Teuta, therefore, may be seen as a representation of what the Land of the Blue Mountains becomes by novel's end, a compliant subject of the patriarchal British Empire. Thus in *The Lady of the Shroud*, Stoker finalizes the project of imperial Gothic desire he started in *Dracula*. In the first novel, an Eastern, Russian menace is driven from English shores, pursued to his fortress, and eradicated. His castle and Balkan homeland are subsequently appropriated into the Baedeker world of English tourism. With *The Lady of the Shroud*, a permanent British colony is established in the Balkans to frustrate German economic and military ambitions by blocking Turkish expansion in the region and to keep a watchful eye on Russia. In real political and military terms, such a facile solution to British anxieties is beyond the reach of British power. Yet, in the world of fiction, British hegemony can spread anywhere, and British military power can vanquish all enemies.

# Conclusion

In 1903, a year after the settlement ending the Boer War, Stoker published another Imperial Gothic novel, *The Jewel of Seven Stars*. As in *Dracula* and *The Lady of the Shroud*, a young woman is threatened by an evil foreign power and must be saved by a group of middle-class male professionals, including a lawyer, two archeologists, and a physician, knowledgeable both in science and the occult. The woman in peril here is Margaret Trelawny, who has fallen under the spell of "Tera, Queen of the Egypts, daughter of Antef, Monarch of the North and the South" (*Jewel* 137). A figure adept in "statecraft" and "in ancient magic and ritual and all the Egyptian sciences" (Roth, *Bram Stoker* 68), Queen Tera suspends herself in time so as to ressurrect her empire centuries later. Therefore, she represents, in much the same way as do Dracula and the German-equipped Turks in *The Lady of the Shroud*, not only a mysterious occult danger, but also, more importantly, a foreign political threat to England and its North African empire.

*The Jewel of Seven Stars* enunciates, then, as do *Dracula* and other fin-de-siécle novels such as Richard Marsh's *The Beetle* and H. G. Well's *The War of the Worlds*, Victorian fears of what Arata identifies as a "reverse colonization" (623). As Judith Wilt has shown, "minor counter-attacks to Victorian imperialism — the Zulus, the dervishes, the Indian Mutiny, the Boxer Rebellion" created the anxiety that the Egyptians, Sudanese, Indians, Ghanans, and other "lesser" peoples ruthlessly subordinated to the commercial interests of England might one day wreak revenge not just on English colonists, but on the homeland itself. However, the "Great Counter-Attack, the one that hits the west itself, occurs nowhere but in the Victorian imagination," finding expression in "the great gothic and science fiction tales of the 80s and 90s" (Wilt 620). *Dracula, The Jewel of the Seven Stars*, and *The Lady of the Shroud*, it would seem, form a trilogy of sorts, conjoined by political and imperial themes. Nevertheless, *The Jewel of the Seven Stars* should be set off from the other two novels for two important reasons. One, it does not address the overarching imperial fear that animates the narrative in *Dracula* and to a lesser extent in *The Lady of the Shroud*: the threat posed by imperial Russia. Secondly, the invading force at work in *The Jewel of the Seven Stars* is far less threatening than those in the other novels because it springs from a land actually colonized and appropriated by England and is thus not an object of Imperial Gothic desire.

Since the genesis of the Eastern Question in the eighteenth century, Britain has contended with Russia over control of the Black Sea and the Balkans. From the time of the Napoleonic Wars to the Boer War of 1899, Britain supported Turkish dominion over the Slavic peoples of Bulgaria, Romania, and the Serbian homelands to protect commercial interests in Asia Minor and greater India. A succession of British governments turned a blind eye to Turkish injustices amongst the Orthodox Christians of the region so as to keep Russian warships out of the Black Sea and Mediterranean and thus halt the expansion of the Russian Empire. So committed to this strategy was Britain that in 1854 she sided with France, her erstwhile enemy, in a war to reverse Russian incursions in the Ottoman-controlled territories of Moldavia and Wallachia, roughly comprising present day Romania. Although the most technologically advanced nation in the world at the time, Britain fared poorly at the outset of the war. Incompetent military leadership coupled with indifferent governmental preparations for the war eventuated in tactical blunders and untold casualties resulting from deprivation, poor provisioning, and inept medical care. Even though French arms saved the day, the repercussions of the government's and military's mishandling of the war would transform those institutions as well as English society as a whole.

The great losers of the war were the aristocracy. Before the war was even over, middle-class professionals in business, medicine, and the sciences, both male and female, had wrested from aristocrats much of the control over governmental and military policies. Practical know how and business acumen attracted praise and approbation, not heritage, name, or title. Women, too, challenged the existing order and traditions. Following the lead of Florence Nightingale, many Victorian women sought educational and professional opportunities, hoping to achieve financial and social independence. By the end of the nineteenth century, the figure of the New Woman — educated, successful, sexually liberated — would become a force in England. Also, by century's end, the weaknesses in the military would be ameliorated, paving the way for colonial victories in Africa and Asia. Thus by 1890, Britain was the world's preeminent imperial power.

However, as continued Russian expansion in Central Asia, the locus of what came to be called the "Great Game," and the Boer War of 1899 proved, by the turn of the century continental powers such as Russia and Germany threatened not only to block the growth of the British Empire, but, more alarming, even to roll it back.

In this geopolitical environment, Stoker published *Dracula* and *The Lady of the Shroud*, novels that, I argue, provide a fictional means to assuage or to dissipate the anxieties engendered in the national/cultural conscience by the failures of the Crimean War, the ongoing threat of war with Russia, and, later, the emergence of a united and bellicose Germany. These works put the genie back in the bottle, so to speak, and secure the empire a Gibraltar[1] of sorts in the Balkans. Stephen Bann has written that "19th-century man did not simply discover history: he needed to discover history, or, as it were, to remake history on his own terms" (103). Stoker, in my thinking, is just such an historical revisionist, imagining a history that accommodates the political and commercial agendas of the British Empire. He well understood that to maintain its prestige and viability, the empire had to safeguard its colonial assets and secure access to raw materials. Yet, Stoker also comprehended that in a world where those colonial possessions and resources were increasingly objects of great power contention, fiction alone offered a world in which they could remain inviolate, one in which threats could be vanquished with no actual loss of blood, chance for defeat, or danger of reverse colonization.

Nevertheless, these "triumphalist" novels still manifest subtle suggestions about the very real threats that faced the empire. This is especially so in *The Lady of the Shroud*, which ends on what Hughes deems a "prophetic note":

> The flight of aeroplanes was a memorable sight. It helped to make history. Henceforth no nation with an eye for either defence or attack can hope for success without the mastery of the air [352].

For Hughes, these lines demonstrate that "the unchallenged role played by sea- and land-based combat [...] is drawing to a close" and that it is "but a matter of time, therefore, before other powers will seek" to acquire an air force to counter "the current supremacy of the conventional British navy" (*L* 351). Events of some five years hence would prove Stoker prescient. World War I would establish the importance of the airplane in modern warfare and demonstrate conclusively just how vulnerable land and naval forces were to it.

Stoker may also be credited with prescience in *The Lady of the Shroud* on yet another count. On June 28, 1914, Gavrilo Princip, a radical Bosnian Serb, assassinated Archduke Franz Ferdinand, heir to the Habsburg throne,

Yugoslavia, a confederation of Balkan states and nationalities cobbled together at Versailles after World War I, closely resembled Balka, the Balkan confederation imagined in *The Lady of the Shroud* (©2000 National Geographic Society. Used by permission).

and precipitated World War I. Princip was one of six conspirators who had been armed with weapons from Serbian government arsenals. At the time of his arrest, another of the assassins proudly proclaimed, "I am a Serbian hero" (qtd. in Jelavich, 2: 112). Something resembling Balka, the Serbian federation, modeled on the British Commonwealth, imagined in *The Lady of the Shroud*, did come into existence as a consequence of World War I:

Yugoslavia. Created by the victors, the newly formed kingdom included an unwieldy assortment of Serbs, Croats, and Slovenes. Though meant to satisfy the demands for independence and autonomy among the various Balkan nationalities, Yugoslavia would hold together as a nation less than a hundred years, eventually disintegrating shortly after the fall of the Soviet Union.

The ethnic violence between Serbs, Croats, and Bosnians that attended its demise shocked the world and drew comparisons to the mass killings perpetrated by the *Einsatzkommando* in the Baltic states and Russia during the early stages of the German invasion of Russia in 1941. In his 1999 memoir of his days reporting the fighting — a war travelogue, one might say — Anthony Loyd describes a scene in a forest near Srebrenica, a city in Bosnia-Herzegovina close to the border with Serbia, that recalls the bloody rampages of Hitler's killing units in Eastern Europe:

> The bones lay strewn for miles through this woodland, paperchasing a rough path eastwards across the hills from Srebrenica, the trail breaking then restarting in a jumbled profusion where a last stand had been made or a group of those too wounded or exhausted to go on had been found. The whole area was saturated with the legacy of the killing. There were mass graves in the valleys where prisoners had been herded, executed, then covered with a casual layer of earth which one year later was still heavy and reeking with decay. Elsewhere, more poignantly, there were solitary skeletons hidden in the undergrowth, individuals who had tried to make it out alone but had been hunted down and their lives chopped or shot from them. Even the roadsides bore tributes to the events of the previous summer. Beside one junction a skeleton in a pinstripe suit lay tangled around a concrete post. Among the bundle of collapsed bones fast being reclaimed to the earth by brambles and moss you could see that the man's arms had been bound to the post with wire. Whatever happened to him, it was unlikely to have been quick or painless [1–2].

Only direct intervention by NATO brought the fighting to a halt by 1995, but not before many thousands had died. In 1998, a similar scene began to play out in Albania as Serbian forces invested the province of Kosovo to halt efforts by Albanian Muslims to gain autonomy. Once again, only by force of NATO air strikes was the killing stopped in 1999. By the end of the century, it seems, Balkan Slavs were as bloodthirsty as their brethren described by George Stoker over a century earlier.

The sesquicentennial of the opening of the Crimean War has but recently passed, most of the old East-Bloc states have either joined or are attempting to join NATO and/or the European Union, and the Balkans are in a relative state of peace. However, Britain still confronts an Eastern menace. At this moment, it wears the face and attire of an Islamic fundamentalist or, as David Glover suggests, that of "the ageless Dr. Fu Manchu," with his "elongated fingers with their sharp pointed nails" (*Vampires, Mummies, and Liberals* 142). Both the Islamic and Chinese dangers owe much of their contemporary power to Russia. During the "Great Game," Russian agents curried favor with Afghan princes, enlisting them in the struggle with Britain for Central Asia. Later, the Soviet Union established diplomatic, military, and commercial links with Afghanistan, Egypt, Iraq, and Syria in the course of the Cold War with the West. The mujahedin of today became a viable force in response to the Soviet incursion in Afghanistan in 1979 (Meyer 115). Even Communist China is beholden to Russia, who armed and supported Mao during the revolution and for many years thence.

And, once again, Russia is increasingly at odds with Britain and her American patron. Although struggling to overcome the economic and environmental devastation of Soviet Communism, Russia is threatening to deploy a new generation of nuclear weapons against the West, fearful that the British and American military presence in the Middle East and the former Soviet republics of Central Asia is meant to encircle, isolate, and eventually emasculate the nation. Thus now, as in Stoker's time, a danger lurks in the East, and for all her wealth, prestige, and military might, England cannot dispel it. However, through the offices of the imagination — displayed in print or on screen — it can. As with Russia, Stoker's villainous creation continues, in the words of Joan Gordon and Veronica Hollinger, to "[enact] its familiar role as life-consuming threat" (Introduction 2). But, just as *Dracula* and *The Lady of the Shroud* provided British audiences with fictional palliatives to the threat, today's narratives, in film and print, offer a soothing, if illusory, balm for the troubled twenty-first century psyche.

# Notes

## Introduction

1. David Glover asserts that "In Stoker's romances the foot-loose adventurer, home from Australia, the Balkans, or South Africa, is a favorite device, and one of the most fascinating aspects of his fiction lies in its journeys." Glover goes on to write that for Stoker, "the pleasures of travel [...] shade into dreams of empire" (*Vampires, Mummies, and Liberals* 26).

2. In *Dracula: Sense & Nonsense*, Elizabeth Miller writes that in the travelogues Stoker consulted while researching the novel, "the geography [...] is intertwined with an imperialist attitude towards the more 'backward' regions of eastern Europe" (150).

3. A telling example of the vestiges of Russophobia in England today can be found in the wildly popular Harry Potter series. Specifically, in the fourth installment, *Harry Potter and the Goblet of Fire*, two characters of Bulgarian descent come in for particular derision: the headmaster, Professor Karkaroff, and the student participant, Viktor Krum, in the Triwizard Tournament from the Durmstrang School of Wizardry. In one scene, Hagrid, the gameskeeper at Hogswart, assaults Karkaroff for challenging the authority and integrity of Dumbledore, the headmaster at Hogwarts. Ordered by Dumbledore to leave to escort Harry to his dormitory, Hagrid chastises Harry for associating with the Durmstrang party and warns Harry to avoid them, saying, "The less you lot 'ave ter do with these foreigners, the happier yeh'll be. Yeh can' trust any of 'em" (563). Later, Cedric, a fellow student, evinces a similar disregard for the Durmstrang contingent. When Harry incapacitates Krum with a spell, he tells Cedric that he will signal for

someone to "collect him ... otherwise he'll probably be eaten by a skwert"; to this Cedric replies, "He'd deserve it" (627). Also of note, Professor Karkaroff is described as having "a fruity, unctuous voice, " a "rather weak chin," and "cold and shrewd" eyes (247). Interestingly, the ship on which the Durmstrang party arrives appears to be a ghost ship, much like the Russian schooner that brings Dracula to England's shores: "the ship rose out of the water, gleaming in the moonlight. It had a strangely skeletal look about it, as though it were a resurrected wreck, and the dim, misty lights shimmering at its portholes looked like ghostly eyes" (246). And, in a parallel with the Crimean War, the obviously French participants in the tournament are treated with deference and courtesy, reflecting the cooperation between the French and British allies opposed to Russia during the war.

4. To the best of my knowledge, other than copies held in private collections, only two copies are available to the general public. One may be found in the rare book collection of the Francis A. Countway Library of Medicine at Harvard Medical School. The other resides in the British Museum.

5. Glover documents the extent of the Stoker family's connection to the Irish Ascendancy and the Crown: "Bram's younger brother Thomas was also sent to Trinity College, but the other three boys, William, Richard, and George, went to medical school. William, his elder brother, became a venerable member of the Irish metropolitan elite: he was a trustee and governor of Ireland's National Gallery, president of the country's Royal College of Surgeons and of the Royal Academy of Medicine, and the recipient of a knighthood in 1895 and

a baronetcy in 1911 [...]. Thomas became an administrator in the Indian Civil Service and Richard joined the Indian Medical Service, while George became a doctor in London, working overseas as a surgeon during the wars in Turkey and the Balkans, and later in South Africa" (*Vampires, Mummies, and Liberals* 10).

6. Glover states that "Stoker described himself as a moderate or 'philosophical' advocate of Irish Home Rule" (V, M, and L 28) while Belford notes that "Stoker supported home rule but never spoke out loudly for it, probably because the apolitical Irving—playing devil's advocate—mocked him about it" (132).

7. Glover articulates a similar role for the novel *Dracula*, which "properly belongs within the Anglo-Irish Gothic tradition, a predominantly nineteenth century mode of writing which struggled obsessively with the cultural meaning of Ireland and Irishness. In this local subgenre the social and psychic fears that had been mobilized in the uncanny scenarios of English writers like Ann Radcliffe and Matthew 'Monk' Lewis were subtly inflected into a monstrous vision of Ireland as imagined through the eyes of some of the poorer members of the Protestant Ascendancy, the country's socially and culturally dominant elite" (*Vampires, Mummies, and Liberals* 25).

8. Bruce Haley, in *The Healthy Body and Victorian Culture*, contends that "Nothing occupies a nation's mind with the subject of health like a general contagion." Britain in the nineteenth century experienced successive waves of pestilence. Between 1831 and 1849, epidemics of influenza, cholera, typhus, typhoid, smallpox, and scarlet fever ravaged the populace: "That same year (1846), as the potato famine struck Ireland, a virulent form of typhus appeared, cutting down large numbers of even well-to-do families. As Irish workers moved to cities like Liverpool and Glasgow the 'Irish Fever' moved with them. By 1847 the contagion, not all of it connected with immigration, had spread throughout England and Wales, accounting for over thirty thousand deaths. As had happened a decade earlier, typhus occurred simultaneously with a severe influenza epidemic, one which carried off almost thirteen thousand. There was also widespread dysentery, and as if all this were not enough, cholera returned in the autumn of 1848, assailing especially those parts of the island hardest hit by typhus and leaving about as many dead as it had in 1831" (6–7).

9. Although part three of *Maud* clearly suggests Tennyson's approval of the war with Russia, something of a critical controversy surrounds the poem. For a discussion of the divergent readings of the poem's relationship to

British involvement in the Crimean War, see James R. Bennett, "The Historical Abuse of Literature: Tennyson's *Maud: A Monodrama* and the Crimean War," *English Studies* 62.1 (Jan. 1981) 34–45; Chris R.Vanden Bossche, "Realism versus Romance: the War of Cultural Codes in Tennyson's *Maud*," *Victorian Poetry* 24.1 (Spring 1986) 68–82; and Joseph Bristow, "Nation, Class, Gender: Tennyson's *Maud* and War, " *Genders* 9 (Fall 1990) 93–111.

10. During Queen Victoria's Jubilee in 1897, the same year as the publication of *Dracula*, Stoker expressed in an interview his devotion to the idea of empire: "'Everyone, ' he said, 'has been proud that the great day went off so successfully. We have had a magnificent survey of the Empire, and last week's procession brought home, as nothing else could have done, the sense of the immense variety of the Queen's dominions'" [Stoddard 488].

11. Stoker was well versed not only in the occult, but also the emerging disciplines of eugenics and physiognomy, which supposedly offered scientific evidence of the innate genetic inferiority of criminals and primitive peoples. As Glover notes, "From the inception of his career as a writer, Stoker regarded physiognomy as an eminently practical form of knowledge, and there are countless references to it scattered throughout his work. It has a foundational status in his writing, locating and attempting to stabilize the lines of difference and danger by marking out a highly deterministic order in which some agents can be shown to be so totally other that they pose a threat to human progress. Notwithstanding physiognomy's loss of influence in such divers fields as painting and medicine once scientists like Charles Bell and Darwin had begun to replace it with a proper psychology of human expression, Stoker continued to be a 'believer of the science' and at the time of his death he still owned a five-volume quarto edition of Johann Casper Lavater's *Essays on Physiognomy* (1789), the book which more than any other had been responsible for the modern revival of this age-old set of beliefs" (*Vampires, Mummies, and Liberals* 71–72).

## Chapter One

1. In the four part BBC/PBS documentary *Rebels and Redcoats: How Britain Lost America*, aired in June 2004, British historian Richard Holmes compared American rebels to the Viet Cong who were engaged in a civil war. Holmes asserts in the third episode, "The War Moves South," that like the Viet Cong, the rebels employed guerrilla tactics against both British troops and colonists loyal to the crown.

These included ambushes, hit and run attacks, and acts of terror against colonists loyal to Britain. Although Holmes's hypothesis holds up in regard to the conduct of the fighting in the American Revolution, it does not draw the distinction that the Revolutionary War was for all intents and purposes a "family" affair with colonists attempting to break away from the parent state. In Vietnam, as in the Crimea, however, foreign powers attacked a sovereign state.

2. In one intelligence-gathering ploy, Britain and Russia employed indigenous peoples as spies along the frontier separating Afghanistan and India. Peter Hopkirk, in *The Great Game: The Struggle for Empire in Central Asia*, describes just how this scheme worked: "Indian hillmen of exceptional intelligence and resource, specifically trained in clandestine surveying techniques, were dispatched across the frontier disguised as Muslim holy men or Buddhist pilgrims. In this way, often at great risk to their lives, they secretly mapped thousands of square miles of previously unexplored terrain with remarkable accuracy. For their part, the Russians used Mongolian Buddhists to penetrate regions considered too dangerous for Europeans" (5).

3. Reviewing three recently published works about the life of Florence Nightingale in the March 8, 2001, issue of *The New York Review of Books*, Helen Epstein makes the following statement: "From a public relations point of view, the Crimean War did not go well for Great Britain. The recent Limited Services act permitted ordinary middle-class men to spend short periods on military duty, and gentlemen could now see for themselves the horrors of war. Moreover, photographers and reporters for the first time sent firsthand dispatches from the front. Members of the British public, with the new political power they had gained from the expanded franchise under the Reform Bill of 1832, read with dismay in the daily papers as 'the best army that ever left these shores' succumbed to cannon fire, starvation, and disease, in a war fought in a faraway country, for obscure reasons'" (16).

4. In regards to Stoker's *Dracula*, a number of articles have treated the novel as a testament to English fears of moral and social degeneration at century's end. See Cannon Schmitt, "Mother *Dracula*: Orientalism, Degeneration, and Anglo-irish National Subjectivity at the Fin de Siecle," *Bucknell Review: Irishness and (Post) Modernism*, ed. John S. Rickard (London: Associated University Presses, 1994) 25–43; Rhys Garnett, "*Dracula* and *The Beetle*: Imperial and Sexual Guilt and Fear in Late Victorian Fantasy," *Science Fiction Roots and Branches*, ed. Rhys Garnett and R. J. Ellis (New York: St. Martin's Press, 1990) 30–54; Kathleen L. Spencer, "Purity and Danger: *Dracula*, the Urban Gothic, and the Late Victorian Degeneracy Crisis," *ELH* 59.1 (Spring 1992): 197–225; Troy Boone, "'He Is English and Therefore Adventurous': Politics, Decadence, and *Dracula*," *Studies in the Novel* 25.1 (Spring 1993): 76–91; and Laura Sagolla Croley, "The Rhetoric of Reform in Stoker's Dracula: Depravity, Decline, and the Fin-de-Siècle 'Residuum,'" *Criticism* 37.1 (Winter 1995): 85–108.

5. Aside from the revisionist films of the 1970's, such as *Rambo* and *Missing in Action*, a number of contemporary writers have issued similarly revisionist tracts. Most notable among these are Nelson DeMille's 2001 novel *Up Country* and Michael Lind's 1999 scholarly study *Vietnam: the Necessary War*.

6. The winter 2002 issue of the *Journal of the Russian Numismatic Society* featured an article by Richard Giedroyc titled "Moldavian-Russian History Intertwine Many Times." According to Giedroyc, "One important link between modern Moldova and Russia is the Eastern Orthodox Church. About 98.5 percent of the Moldovan population subscribe to this religion" (23). He goes on to note that "Moldova's first true relationship with Russia came when between the 11th and 13th centuries the territory became part of Kiev. The region was under the control of the Cumans in the 13th century when the Mongols invaded" (24). The coins Giedroyc describes further consolidate the historical links that existed between Russia, Moldavia, and Wallachia. The 1771 Moldavian-Wallachian coin for "one para/3 dengi (1 1/2 kopecks)" bears "the old Russian system of 3 dots (for 3 dengi) around the letters 'E II' (Catherine II)" (26). Coins of this period carried iconic symbols of the three states: either the Cyrillic "E" for Catherine II or the two-headed Romanov eagle representing Russia, a bull with a star between its horns signifying Moldavia, and a raven clutching a crucifix in its beak denominating Wallachia. And, as Clive Leatherdale notes in *Dracula: the Novel and the Legend*, the word Dracula is Wallachian for devil (95).

7. Though ostensibly an ally of France, Russia became a major irritant to Napoleon by 1811 because of her unwillingness to support the Continental System designed to dry up markets in Europe for British goods. According to Desmond Seward, author of *Napoleon and Hitler: A Comparative Biography*, Russian recalcitrance over this issue led Napoleon to confide to the Comte de Narbonne "that when Moscow had fallen and the Tsar had made peace or had been murdered by his subjects, or when a new state had taken the place of the Russian empire, a Franco-Russian army would

be able to march out from Tiflis, invade India and destroy British rule" (197–198).

8. Carol Senf, in *The Vampire in Nineteenth-Century English Literature*, argues that "Originating in the exotic past and in primitive cultures, the vampire enters English literature through Romantic poetry, where it remains an exotic supernatural creature" (30).

9. Joseph Boone suggests that the East provided Western travelers with an outlet for erotic, specifically homoerotic, desires as well. Such desires "echo throughout the writings of novelists, poets, journalists, travel writers, sociologists, and ethnographers whose pursuit of eros has brought them in Rana kabbani's phrase, 'to the Orient on the flying-carpet of Orientalism'(*Passionate Nomad* x)" (89).

10. As Hopkirk establishes, travel writing continued to stoke Russophobia. He comments that "British travellers returning from Russia insisted that Tsar Nicholas was aiming at nothing less than world domination. Robert Bremmer, in his *Excursions in the Interior of Russia*, published in 1839, warned that Nicholas was simply waiting for the most opportune moment to strike" (210). British voices were not the only ones raised in alarm: "A celebrated French observer, the Marquis de Custine, who toured Russia in 1839, returned with similar forebodings about St. Petersburg's ambitions. In his *La Russe en 1839*, a work still quoted by Kremlinologists today, he warned: 'They wish to rule the world by conquest. They mean to seize by armed force the countries accessible to them, and thence to oppress the rest of the world by terror. The extension of power they dream of […] if God grants it to them, will be for the woe of the world'" (211).

11. Soon after Jonathan Harker arrives at Castle Dracula, the count traces his heritage for the young barrister. Dracula proudly notes that he is descended from the Scythians, a point that will be discussed more fully later in this study.

12. Although the defeat of the Turkish flotilla at Sinope proved to be the spark that ignited the war, the British government had for some time pondered the means for neutralizing the naval presence Nicholas I had established at Sebastopol. As Meyer and Brysac stipulate, the Russian base at Sebastopol was viewed as a preparation in the process of capturing the Dardanelles and projecting Russian naval power into the Mediterranean, a consequence that "could threaten the main pillars of British foreign policy — maintaining the European balance of power, ensuring British supremacy at sea, and protecting the routes to India" (134).

13. According to A. J. Langguth, in *Our Vietnam: the War 1954–1975*, published in

2000, the North Vietnamese attack on the destroyer *Maddox* on August 2, 1964, that served as a pretext for passage of the Tonkin Gulf Resolution, which granted President Johnson authority to use military force directly against North Vietnam, is historically questionable at best. The *Maddox* was supporting commando raids against the North Vietnamese islands of Hon Me and Hon Nieu at the time of the supposed attack. Operating close to shore, the destroyer may have become involved in the North Vietnamese efforts to repulse the commando raids. Also, Langguth notes, an after-action report relayed from the *Maddox* the next day throws doubt on the attack altogether: "Review of action makes many reported contacts and torpedoes fired appear doubtful. Freak weather effects on radar and overeager sonar men may have accounted for many reports. No actual visual sighting by *Maddox*. Suggest complete evaluation before any further action taken" (299–301).

14. Phillip Knightley, in *The First Casualty: The War Correspondent as Hero and Myth-Maker from the Crimea to Kosovo*, recounts the public's approval of the declaration of war against Russia: "Britain's declaration of war had resulted in an upsurge of enthusiasm that had surprised everyone. 'The war,' Queen Victoria wrote, 'is popular beyond belief.' The workers, who genuinely hated Czarist absolutism, took to the streets shouting slogans and singing patriotic songs. Britain felt that Russia, ambitious to expand her empire, had to be stopped from establishing herself in Europe, and, since the British army was 'the finest, most powerful army in the modern world,' then it was up to her to undertake the task. Such a popular war created an unprecedented demand for news. 'The excitement, the painful excitement for information, beggars all description,' wrote one minister" (2).

15. Judith Halberstam's essay "Technologies of Monstrosity: Bram Stoker's *Dracula*" details how extensively Stoker both praises the scientific advancements of Victorian England yet simultaneously frets about the effects of such advancements on English society.

16. "Balaclava, while secure," writes Dossey, "was hardly suitable for supplying a huge field army. The only supply road from this tiny port rose 600' (9183m) up to the plateau above Sebastopol where the siege positions lay. Transporting supplies and casualties over this dirt track was difficult in good weather and nearly impossible in rain, sleet, and ice" (106).

17. As was often the case in most aspects of the Crimean War, the French bested the English in the treatment of the wounded. Russell makes this point emphatically in a letter to his editor at the *Times*: "The management is infa-

mous, and the contrast offered by our proceedings to the conduct of the French most painful. Could you believe it — the sick have not a bed to lie upon? They are landed and thrown into a rickety house without a chair or a table in it. The French with their ambulances, excellent commissariat staff and boulangerie etc., in every respect are immeasurably our superiors. While these things go on, Sir George Brown only seems anxious about the men being clean-shaved, their necks well stiffened and waist belts tight" (qtd. in Knightley 5–6).

In an October 13, 1854, *Times* article, Thomas Chenery echoes Russell's evaluation: "The worn-out pensioners who were brought out as an ambulance corps are totally useless, and not only are surgeons not to be had, but there are no dressers or nurses to carry out the surgeon's directions and to attend on the sick during intervals between his visits. Here the French are greatly our superiors. Their medical arrangements are extremely good, their surgeons more numerous, and they have also the help of the Sisters of Charity, who have accompanied the expedition in incredible numbers These devoted women are excellent nurses" (qtd. in Knightley 12–13).

18. In the estimation of Barbara Dossey, the "vermin-infested wards were as bad as the worst slums of London" (126).

19. Florence Nightingale was later to say of the Turkish Customs House that it was "a bottomless pit whence nothing ever issued of all that was thrown in" (qtd. in Dossey 126).

20. Hugh Small suggests that no such want would have existed among the officer ranks in the Crimea: "It is highly unlikely that any officers in the Crimea suffered from scurvy: being exclusively of wealthy private means, they were able to ride or send their servants to Balaclava to buy supplies from the many profiteering speculators who set up shop there, including the fruit and vegetables which would prevent scurvy. Many officers had hampers from Fortnum's delivered by private contractors to their huts. But the common soldiers in the trenches and tents round about suffered from the horrible symptoms of scurvy while cases of lime juice lay unused in the army's stores nearby" (64).

21. In one letter, Florence Nightingale wrote "I have never been able to join in the popular cry about the recklessness, sensuality, and helplessness of the soldiers. Give them suffering and they will bear it [...]. Give them work and they will do it. I would rather have to do with the army than with any other class I have every attempted to serve" (qtd in Small 26).

22. Soldiers in the Russian army fared even worse. In "The Negative Aspects of the Russian Soldier and Officer," a memorandum

written after the war, Leo Tolstoy, who had served at Sebastopol, complained that for the Russian soldier, death was a "blessing" because "privates are beaten if they smoke, seek to marry, or dare to notice when a superior pockets their pay [...]. We have not an army, but a crowd of oppressed, disciplined slaves..." (qtd. in Meyer and Brysac 135).

23. Here is another parallel to America's experiences in the Vietnam War. Harold G. Moore and Joseph L. Galloway recount in *We Were Soldiers Once ... And Young: Ia Drang — The Battle That Changed the War in Vietnam* that during the first major battle between American forces and North Vietnamese regulars, death notices to American families were delivered by taxi drivers. The army, in the rush to war, had overlooked the need to set up a system for handling death notices.

24. In another connection to *Dracula*, just as the wounded were susceptible to infection while under medical care during the first year of the campaign, so too are Lucy Westenra and Mina Harker prone to contamination by the Count even though Lucy is under the care of two physicians, Dr. Seward and Dr. Van Helsing, and Mina is housed in Carfax Sanitarium.

## Chapter Two

1. No less a figure than Edwin Lawrence Godkin of the *London Daily News*, Russell's rival in the Crimea, wrote this of Russell almost fifty years after the war: "If I were asked now what I thought the most important result of the Crimea War, I should say the creation and development of the 'special correspondents' of the newspapers.... The real beginning of newspaper correspondence was the arrival of 'Billy' Russell with the English Army in the Crimea. He was then a man of mature age, had had a long newspaper experience, and possessed just the social qualities that were needed for the place. In his hands correspondence from the field really became a power before which generals began to quail ... I cannot help thinking that the appearance of the special correspondent in the Crimea ... led to a real awakening of the official mind. It brought home to the War Office the fact that the public had something to say about the conduct of wars and that they are not the concern exclusively of sovereigns and statesmen" (qtd. in Knightley 16).

2. Bram Stoker, *Dracula, The Essential Dracula*, ed. Leonard Wolf (New York: Plume, 1993. 24–25). All further references to the book will appear parenthetically in the text preceded by the letter *D*.

3. The bloody fighting at the Battle of

Inkerman in November 1854 left Russell particularly incensed. In a letter to John Delane, his editor, Russell excoriated Raglan's command behavior: "He is a good brave soldier, I am sure, and a polished gentleman, but he is no more fit than I am to cope with any leader of strategic skill" (qtd. in Knightley 10).

4. The tragedy of command and supply in the Crimea left Russell despondent. In another letter to Delane, this one in 1855, Russell wrote "This army has melted away almost to a drop of miserable, washed-out, worn-out spiritless wretches, who muster out of 55,000 just 11,000 now fit to shoulder a musket, but certainly not fit to do duty against the enemy. Let no one at home attempt to throw dirt in your eyes. This army is to all intents and purposes, with the exception of a very few regiments, used up, destroyed and ruined [...]. My occupation is gone; there is nothing to record more of the British Expedition except its weakness and its misery — misery in every form and shape except that of defeat; and from that we are solely spared by the goodness of Heaven, which erects barriers of mud and snow between us and our enemies" (qtd. in Knightley 11).

5. According to Dossey, "It wasn't just Russell's vivid reporting that fueled public indignation against the army and the government; it was the full weight of the *Times* itself. With ten times the circulation of its nearest competitor, the London daily served the rising business and middle classes now coming to power in England. Its editor, John Thadeus Delane, was considered the greatest newspaperman of his era and had enormous influence. Outraged by Russell's detailed accounts, Delane thundered against the entrenched 'aristocracy' [...]" (142–143).

6. John Tilltson, editor of *Cassell's Illustrated Family Paper*, was said to have given the following instructions to a reporter headed to the Crimea: "You know the sort of thing we want. The popular claptrap about British valour, and a compliment a compliment to the Emperor [Napoleon III]" (qtd. in Patricia Anderson 98).

7. Knightley notes that when the Duke of Newcastle, the Secretary of War, visited the Crimea later in the war, he told Russell, "It was you who turned out the Government" (13).

8. According to Dossey, the problems the McNeill-Tulloch report identified "were precisely those that Nightingale had been writing about to Herbert since her arrival" (152).

9. Knightley points out that Fenton was well aware of the fact that his photographs did not present the war as it truly was: "Fenton's photographs, technically excellent though they are portray a war where everything looks shipshape and everyone happy. They show well-dressed officers and men eating, drinking, or smoking; ships in Balaclava Harbour; a convivial party between French and English troops; Lord Raglan, looking rather drawn; a group of happy Zouaves and Turks; quiet scenes at a mortar battery; and the interiors of captured forts after the bodies had been removed. Yet in the valley where the charge of the Light Brigade had taken place Fenton noticed, and described in a letter, this macabre reminder of what the war was really like: 'We came upon many skeletons half buried. One was lying as if he had raised himself upon his elbow, the bare skull sticking up with still enough flesh left in the muscles to prevent it falling from the shoulders. Another man's feet and hands were out of the ground, and shoes on the feet and the flesh gone'" (14).

10. Jane Stoddard, in "Mr. Bram Stoker: A Chat with the Author of *Dracula*," an interview published in *British Weekly* in 1897, reveals Stoker's familiarity with the literati of the time: "He has been in London for some nineteen years, and believes that London is the best possible place for a literary man. 'A writer will find a chance here if he is good for anything; and recognition is only a matter of time.' Mr. Stoker speaks of the generosity shown by literary men to one another in a tone which shows that he, at least, is not disposed to quarrel with critics" (185).

11. Meyer and Brysac employ the phrase "the British mystique of splendor in misfortune" to describe such revisionists depictions of military defeats (52).

12. Hopkirk cites the following reaction by the queen regarding the incident: "If the Russians reach Constantinople, the Queen would be so humiliated that she thinks she would abdicate at once." So wrote Queen Victoria to Disraeli, urging him to 'be bold.' To the Prince of Wales she declared: 'I don't believe that without fighting ... those detestable Russians ... any arrangements will be lasting, or that we shall ever be friends! They will always hate us and we can never trust them.'"

Hopkirk goes to state that her anger "was shared by the masses" and that "their mood was well summed up in the words of a jingoistic song which was then doing the rounds of the music halls." The lyric is unmistakably anti-Russian:

We don't want to fight,
But, by jingo, if we do,
We've got the men, we've got the ships,
We've got the money too.
We've fought the Bear before,
And while we're Britons true,
The Russians shall not have
    Constantinople [379].

13. Since September 11, 2001, notions of empire and a renewed Great Game have been pop-

ularized in the press. In March 2003, *Esquire* published "The Pentagon's New Map," an article by Thomas P. M. Barnett, a professor of warfare analysis at the U.S. Naval War College. A summary of the briefing he has given to numerous audiences at the Pentagon, the article sets forth why "engagement with Saddam Hussein's regime in Baghdad is not only necessary and inevitable, but good." Barnett goes on to identify the new American military empire, Washington's "ownership of strategic security in the age of globalization" (174). The February 16, 2004, issue of *The Nation* carried the article "Oil and the New 'Great Game'" by Lutz Kleveman. The same journal, in a July 5, 2004, review of Robert Cooper's book *The Breaking of Nations* written by Scott Malcomson, refers to "The New Liberal Imperialism" (58).

14. Meyer and Brysac suggest that The Great Mutiny of 1857 engendered similar reevaluations in India: "What Crimea was to Russia, The Great Mutiny was to British India, an analogous blow to a complacent ancien regime [...]. The British Parliament in August 1858, ended the [East India] Company's responsibility for governing India, transferring to the Crown its possessions and its civil military services. The Company's Board of Control and Court of Directors gave way to a fifteen-member Council that would advise the Secretary of State of India, to whom the Governor-General, now endowed with the grander title of Viceroy, would report" (151).

15. As Gillard notes, "For most Russians officially concerned with international problems, it was a fixed point that the British would try to exploit the region's instability and strife and, by developing diplomatic and commercial links with the khanates, make their own political influence predominate [...]. One uncontroversial method, used so effectively by the British, was the promotion of trade, especially as in the 1860's the raw materials and markets of central Asia were becoming of increasing value in themselves to the Russian economy" (121).

16. Proof of the involvement of the Royal Geographical Society in espionage is available in Rawlinson's 1875 study itself. In a footnote to chapter three, he writes "We would recommend to the special consideration of the Royal Geographical Society Major James's 'Report,' which extends to fifty paragraphs and gives a most interesting detail of Molla Abdul Mejid's outward and return journey through the regions between the Upper Oxus and Kokand, which regions in the best and latest map, that of Stanford, accompanying Mr. Mitchell's volume, are marked as 'unexplored.' (The most important portions of the 'Report' have since been published in the 'proceedings' of the Royal Geographical Society, vol. x p. 149; and

convey the only information yet available of the track across the Pamir plateau from South to North. The high road, however, from West to East has been repeatedly followed and described of late by Md. Amin, Major Montgomeries's Mirza, Feiz Bahksh, Irahim Khan, and finally by Col. Gordon's party, whose survey of the route on two lines leaves nothing to be desired.—1874)" (189).

Not to be outdone, Russia countered British espionage efforts in Central Asia through the efforts of her own Imperial Russian Geographical Society (Meyer and Brysac).

17. Hopkirk notes that in 1876, an English translation of the Anglophobic treatise *Russia and England in the Struggle for the Markets of Central Asia* by M.A. Terentiev became available in Calcutta. Terentiev charged Britain with "secretly distributing rifles among the Turcoman tribes for use against Russia. It also alleged that Sir John Lawrence, that staunch believer in masterly inactivity, had been sacked as Viceroy of India for not being sufficiently Russophobic. The Indian Mutiny, Terentiev maintained, had only failed because the Indians lacked a proper plan and outside support. They continued to suffer from British misrule and exploitation. 'Sick to death,' Terentiev went on, 'the natives are now waiting for a physician from the north.' Given such assistance, they had every chance of starting a conflagration to throw off the British yoke. In the event of such an uprising, the Russian claimed, the British would find themselves unable to rely on the support of their native troops, who formed the major part of their army in India" (363).

18. Some eight years later in 1883, J. R. Seeley wrote in *The Expansion of England*, a book which sold 80,000 copies, that "Every movement in Turkey, every new symptom in Egypt, any stirrings in Persia or Transoxia or Burmah or Afghanistan, we are obliged to watch with vigilance. The reason is that we have possession of India, and a leading interest in the affairs of all those countries which lie upon the route to India. This and only this involves us in that permanent rivalry with Russia, which is for England of the nineteenth century what the competition with France for the New World was to her in the eighteenth century" (qtd. in Meyer and Brysac, xix).

19. As Hopkirk notes, the crisis had global repercussions: "In America, where the news had rocked Wall Street, all talk was on the coming struggle between the two imperial giants. Beneath the banner headline ENGLAND AND RUSSIA TO FIGHT, the normally sober *New York Times* began its story with the words: 'It is war'" (429).

20. In *Personal Reminiscences of Henry Ir-*

*ving*, Bram Stoker praises Vambery as a "wonderful linguist" who "writes twelve languages, speaks freely sixteen, and knows over twenty" (1: 371)

21. Later in the book Vambery offers this scathing critique of the failures of liberal governments to protect the empire: "In concluding this chapter, treating of the means of defence left to England, I cannot leave unmentioned one point, to which, though seemingly out of place from a foreigner, I nevertheless must allude as to the *fons et origo malli*. I mean, party politics in England, which have, of late, so essentially injured the Imperial interests of that country, and which really have done so much harm to England's position in Asia, that the most strenuous efforts of very many years to come may scarcely be able to heal the wounds and restore the respect and consideration for England, so wantonly destroyed by the selfishness of one party in its struggle against the other. The frivolity and shortsightedness exhibited by a certain political party, of late years, culminating in the famous Egyptian ophthalmy, was really of such a nature as to make people despair of the results of constitutional life. In a superficial judgment one might have taken the statesmen, who have been deliberately deceived by Russia step by step in Asia, who have made all Europe an enemy to England, and who have shown cold indifference whilst the prestige of Great Britain was going to pieces all over the world, either as miscreants, or as men escaped from the lunatic asylum" (144–145).

22. Caine had been a guest in the Stoker household shortly before Stepniak's arrival and had informed Stoker of the Russian's political writings. At this time, Caine was preparing for a journey to Russia himself, and during his stay, he explained his theory for the great "Exodus" of Jews from Russian to England (*Reminiscences* 2: 53–54).

23. Vambery, too, it should be remembered, lay the blame for Britain's failure to actively oppose Russian expansion at the feet of liberal politicians.

24. By the end of Curzon's political career, the term "Curzonism" came to stand for all forms of interventionist foreign policy (Meyer and Brysac 433).

25. According to Andrew Rutherford, editor of *Rudyard Kipling: War Stories and Poems*, "Kipling's adolescence and young-manhood were passed in an era of minor but savagely fought wars on the frontiers of Empire, and these bulked large in his youthful awareness" (xiii).

26. Wilson records that in an 1885 letter from home, Lockwood Kipling wrote his son that "We are all agog about the prospect for war with Russia" (76).

27. In what Gilmour claims was his "most important assignment" as a journalist for the *Gazette*, Kipling attended a durbar, a state reception, in 1885 held by the recently appointed Viceroy of India, Lord Dufferin, for the Amir of Afghanistan, Abdur Rahman. Talk of Russia dominated the conversation: "Although largely ceremonial in intent, the meeting assumed political importance because it coincided with a crisis on the very indistinct frontier between Afghanistan and the Russian Empire. Dufferin was initially bellicose and heedless of Britain's history of disasters in Kabul, talked of marching through Afghanistan and confronting the Russians in Herat. He was supported by some Civilians as well as by army officers eager to do something virile to efface the humiliating memory of Khartoum where General Gordon had recently been killed" (27).

28. There is no evidence that Tennyson ever wrote such a poem.

29. George Mosse, in *Toward the Final Solution: A History of European Racism*, argues that racism became intertwined with notions of nationality and cultural vigor in this era: "Racism annexed every important idea and movement in the nineteenth and twentieth centuries and promised to protect each against all advesaries [...]. Such noble ideals as freedom, equality, and tolerance would become reality only if the race were perserved and its enemies defeated" (xxvi).

## Chapter Three

1. Robert Kaplan's 1993 account of his travels in the Balkans, *Balkan Ghosts: a Journey through History*, offers a most relevant and contemporary instance of Pratt's "monarch-of-all-I-survey" thesis. When describing the regions of Romania in which he sojourns, Kaplan invariably employs the tropes and images of his western cultural grounding, a practice that more often than not works to the disadvantage of his subject. Thus he finds quaint and alluring the "turbaned church domes, the absence of automobiles, the processions of horse-drawn peasant carts (called *leiterwagens* by Bram Stoker in *Dracula*)," images that might "have created a romantic traveler's picture of Europe meeting the Asian steppe." However, he immediately undercuts this attractive feature by noting that "all this existed on and under a film of mud and floodwater on which garbage floated, without a single paved street in sight" (118). Later in Bucovina, he falls into the same habit of description: "Among the wide ranks of beech trees, the soft hills were garlanded with pines, birches, and massive, black-pointed

firs. Poplars and linden trees lined the roads, and apple trees filled the adjacent fields. Enjoying the absence of polluting factories and the blessing of blue skies after days of rain, I felt as if the black-and-white part of my Romanian journey had suddenly ended and the Technicolor sequence had begun" (135).

2. Elizabeth Miller asserts that Belford's claim is "untenable," that there "is nothing in George Stoker's book about Transylvania: there is not one scrap of material in the opening chapters of *Dracula* that could have been taken from George's book. It is about Bulgaria, not Transylvania, and not even Romania" (147–148).

This may be so, but even if Miller is correct that Stoker has taken the locale for the novel explicitly from the sources listed in the working notes, it does not disprove that his descriptions could have been influenced by what he read in George's book. As I have noted earlier, Miller posits that "the geography in these source-books is intertwined with an imperialist attitude towards the more 'backward' regions of eastern Europe" (150). George's book is just such an imperialist travelogue, and if not the definitive source of exact locales, it nonetheless reinforces the abiding imperial attitudes toward the region popular in England in the nineteenth century, attitudes that Stoker most likely shared.

3. Gladstone drew heavily on the reporting of Januarius MacGahan, a reporter for *The New York Herald*, who in 1874 published a highly acclaimed and popular account of the Russian advance on Khiva, *Campaigning on the Oxus and the Fall of Khiva*. In 1876, the London *Daily News* commissioned MacGahan to report on the troubles in Turkish-occupied Bulgaria. In an account of the atrocities in the town of Batak, MacGahan documented how two hundred women who had been raped "were taken, in broad light of day, beneath the smiling canopy of heaven, coolly beheaded, then thrown in a heap, and left to rot" (Meyer and Brysac 159–162).

4. No less an Anglophobe and Pan-Slavist than Count Ignatiev was Russian ambassador in Constantinople in 1877 when the war began. Using Turkish atrocities in Bulgaria as a pretext, Ignatiev convinced Alexander II that war, not diplomacy, was necessary to protect the Orthodox Slavs of the Balkans (Meyer and Brysac 163).

5. Kaplan prefaces his observations of late twentieth century Romania with an overview of its often bloody past. One passage recounting the extent of Romanian participation in the Final Solution during World War II is particularly disturbing. Placed in the introduction, this chilling account cannot help but jaundice

the reader toward his subject: "On the night of January 22, 1941, the Legionnaires of the Archangel Michael — after singing Orthodox hymns, putting packets of Romanian soil around their necks, drinking each other's blood, and anointing themselves with holy water — abducted 200 men, women, and children from their homes. The Legionnaires packed the victims into trucks and drove them to the municipal slaughterhouse, a group of red brick buildings in the southern part of Bucharest near the Dimbovitsa River. They made the victims, all Jews, strip naked in the freezing dark and get down on all fours on the conveyor ramp. Whining in terror, the Jews were driven through all the automated stages of slaughter. Blood gushing from decapitated and limbless torsos, the Legionnaires thrust each on a hook and stamped it: 'fit for human consumption.' The trunk of a five-year-old girl they hung upside down, 'smeared with blood ... like a calf,' according to an eyewitness the next morning" (xviii).

6. According to Walter Baring, a British diplomat, the Turks slaughtered at least 12,000 Christians, and "at Batak a thousand were burned in a church" (Meyer and Brysac 163).

7. Just as war was about to commence, Captain Frederick Burnaby, author of *A Ride to Khiva: Travels and Adventures in Central Asia*, arrived in Constantinople. When Burnaby reached Erezeroum, he learned that the ever wary Count Ignatiev had advised the Russian consul in the town to keep a close watch on him (Hopkirk 378).

## Chapter Four

1. In the interview with Jane Stoddard, Stoker singles out two of his most useful sources: "I learned a good deal from E. Gerard's 'Essays on Roumanian Superstitions,' which first appeared in *The Nineteenth Century*, and were afterwards published in a couple of volumes. I also learned something from Mr. Barin-Gould's 'Were-Wolves.'"

2. According to McNally and Florescu, when Stoker was twelve, the union of Moldavia and Wallachia as part of a greater Romania occasioned a great deal of publicity in Britain. They contend that this event "was probably his initial introduction to that mysterious part of Europe" (137).

3. Bruce Haley draws attention to the emergence in nineteenth century England of the "'Viking or Berserker' ideal" that grew out of the practice of muscular Christianity. Perhaps the finest expression of this vision in print was Charles Kingsley's 1866 novel *Hereward*, whose title character is a "muscular wonder" and "also

Christian" (217). He is "stronger, cannier, and superficially nobler" and less "decadent" than the "Normans, Franks, or Frisians" (218–219) that he battles. David Glover also points out that "Stoker often gives his heroes some kind of Viking genealogy," but draws a distinct difference between the count and the "moral Viking" Quincy Morris. Quincy earns the appellation of "moral Viking" as opposed to "berserker" because, unlike the primitive Dracula, he understands the need for civilized self-restraint in the midst of adversity: "To bear oneself like 'a moral Viking' is precisely to display a measure of self-control conspicuously absent among those bellicose peoples who have not yet evolved out of the past. In short, the sublimation of human aggression requires the right combination of birth and upbringing if the march of human progress is to continue" (*Vampires, Mummies, and Liberals* 74).

4. Wilkinson observes that descendents from the original Slavs "went to the lower part of Dacia lying between the rivers Olt and Danube, where they fixed their habitations. They formed themselves into a nation, and chose for their chief one Bessarabba [...]. Their general system, however, consisted in making war against the Romans of the lower empire, in which they were seconded by the Slaves and Bulgarians of Maesie, whom they looked upon as their natural allies" (qtd. in Leatherdale, *The Origins of Dracula* 92–93).

5. Elizabeth Miller, echoing Clive Leatherdale, categorically refutes the assumption, advanced most famously by McNally and Florescu, that Vlad Tepes (a.k.a. Vlad the Impaler) was Stoker's model for Count Dracula. In *Dracula: Sense and Nonsense*, she writes, "To state this as fact is irresponsible. All we know for certain is that Stoker borrowed the name 'Dracula' and a few scraps of miscellaneous information about Wallachian history from William Wilkinson's *An Account of Wallachia and Moldavia* (1820). Out of such a mole-hill, mountains have emerged" (180).

As with her refutation of Vambery's pivotal influence on Stoker in crafting the Count, Miller rests her argument on the absence of any reference to Vlad Tepes or Vlad the Impaler in Stoker's working notes for the novel.

6. The illustrators at *Punch* would scarcely have known of this fact, but their repeated depictions of the czar adorned with the wings of a bat suggests at least the possibility that in the popular imagination, vampires, bats, and Russians might well have been lumped together.

7. McNally and Florescu contend that when Stoker read Joseph Sheridan Le Fanu's novel *Carmilla* in the 1870s, "he began thinking about writing his own Vampire tale." Additionally, they remark that "Le Fanu's descrip-

tion of how a person becomes a vampire is also based upon folk belief in Eastern Europe" (139).

8. Clive Leatherdale in the introduction to his definitive annotated edition of the novel, *Dracula Unearthed*, contends that of "all the popular misconceptions surrounding *Dracula*, none seems more entrenched as the idea that 'Dracula's Guest' is the excised opening chapter" (14). He rests his argument on the differences in the styles, narration, and characterization of Jonathan Harker between the two works. Leatherdale believes that "Dracula's Guest" was originally intended to be one in a set of three scenes taking place in Munich during Harker's trip east. Its excision from the final published novel means that it "fell under the author's or editor's axe," most likely the later, for "whole chunks of the early part of the novel were removed at a very late stage, *after* the manuscript had been submitted to the London publishers" (15).

9. Jean Chothia, in her introduction to *The New Woman and Other Emancipated Woman Plays*, describes the typical reaction in the press to the New Woman: "Throughout the 1890s, *Punch* both reflected and considerably shaped the habit of addressing female emancipation and educational success as subjects for glorious mirth, while, in September 1894, *The Idler* ran an Advanced Woman number with advice on how to court such creatures and invited eight women of different persuasions to comment on the species. Although much of the humour might seem feeble now, its omnipresence suggests that it answered a need" (x).

10. Clive Leatherdale posits that "Dracula's choice of alias has delicious irony, since the first five letters spell 'Devil.'" He goes on to state that Dracula "presumably reasons that, like Arthur, his title opens more doors than it closes" (*Dracula Unearthed* 375).

11. According to Nicholas Daly, Van Helsing is the embodiment of the new middle-class professional: "Van Helsing is the professional *ne plus ultra* [...]. In addition to his qualifications as a doctor and a scientist, we also learn he is a qualified lawyer [...]. Thus it is that this super-professional is the natural leader of this new social group composed largely of professional men" (39).

12. Daly argues that works such as *Dracula* should be "termed popular *middle-class* fiction, insofar as it was produced by, broadly speaking, middle-class writers for a middle-class reading public" (5). He further believes that the novel as well as its brethren "embodies the fantasies of this emerging professional group, whose power is based on their access to and control of certain forms of knowledge" (8).

13. Of Holmwood, Daly writes, he "is the

team's equivalent for the 'Sir John Paxton, the president of the Incorporated Law Society' who appears by proxy at Hawkin's funeral: his presence confers a suitable air of dignity and respectability on the business in which he is engaged, in this case the hunting of Dracula" (38).

14. Dracula, in Daly's thinking, threatens the corporate heroes of the novel because he represents "archaic or traditional individualism" that is at odds with "the emergence of monopoly capital, in the specific form that takes in the professional monopolies." The novel, he suggests, should be read to promote "the professional ideology of the self-regulating organization of experts, but also the more general collectivist ethos of the late nineteenth century" (43–45).

15. Both Leatherdale (419) and Wolf (364) note that the Kukri knife is the weapon of choice of the Gurkhas of Nepal, the most trustworthy and ferocious native troops in the imperial British army in India. Not only does the use of a Kukri knife reinforce the imperial overtones of the novel, but it also may be seen to signify the importance of India, described to no small extent by Vambery, in the British economy.

16. Jani Scandura argues that Dracula might also be said to resemble an undertaker, a marginalized professional often lumped in with "Jews and 'sexual inverts'": "The undertaker, as embalmer, literally sucks blood from the vessels of corpses, literally creates a corpse resistant to decay, literally obscures distasteful signs of death. And he survives on 'blood money,' income garnered by this pursuit. Gothic, androgynous, parasitic, the undertaker is a vampire without metaphoric disguise" (10). The unsavory aspects of the profession do not solely make it repellent to other middle-class professionals, but, as Scandura writes, it is that the undertaker "represents a socially and economically aspiring Other who scales the slippery façade of free enterprise, an Other whom members of the established bourgeoisie cannot readily distinguish from themselves" (26).

17. Daly wryly notes that contemporary readers may find it "easy to smile at this ... overdetermined reading," one "which tells us more about cold-war America than about Stoker's novel" (34).

18. In *Dracula Unearthed*, Clive Leatherdale notes that "Purfleet at the time was dotted with worn-out chalk quarries and the riverside was dominated by huge gunpowder magazines housed in reinforced silos. This high-security government arsenal, with attendant barracks, presented an ominous spectacle from the river, but provided work for much of the local population" (59–60).

19. In the two-volume *Medical and Surgical History of the British Army Which Served in Turkey and the Crimea During the War Against Russia in the Years 1854–55–56*, produced on order of Queen Victoria by Andrew Smith, Director-General of the Army Medical Department, and presented to both houses of parliament in May of 1858, Varna is prominently mentioned as a site where "Diarrhoea acquired considerable prevalence, Cholera soon appeared, and committed great ravages, and Fever and Dysentery were diseases of common occurrence" (1: 1).

20. According to Belford, Stoker was especially fearful of the disease because as a child he had often heard the gruesome tales of the cholera epidemic that swept through his mother's hometown of Sligo in 1832 (18).

21. In 1956, Bacil F. Kirtley posited that the original source for Dracula was the fifteenth-century Wallachian ruler Vlad Tsepesh. Kirtley bases this belief on parallels existing between Van Helsing's descriptions of Dracula and those of Vlad Tsepesh found in a little-know monastic manuscript. Kirtley notes that in "the monastery at Kirill-Belozersk, in northern Russia near the Finnish border, was found a manuscript which dates from the year 1490 and which is a copy of a document originally penned in 1486. The manuscript relates the story of Dracula (Rumanian for 'devil'), which is the name bestowed in horror by monkish chroniclers upon Vlad Tsepesh, Governor of Wallachia from the years 1456–1462 and again in the year 1476. The material of the Kirill-Belozersk manuscript was widely circulated among the monasteries of the Eastern Slavs, and by the middle of the 16th century had reached as far as Germany, a fact attested by the appearance of the Dracula story in the vernacular edition of Sebastian Munster's *Cosmographia universa* in 1541 (Latin edition, 1550)" (13).

Vlad Tsepesh's title as governor was "Voivod of Wallachia" (14). Also of interest is the fact that in *The Lady of the Shroud*, the narrator, Rupert Sent Leger, journeys to the Balkans to assist the ruler of the Land of the Blue Mountains, the Voivode Peter Vissarion.

22. According to Leatherdale, Stoker's working notes reveal that he took all five names from tombstones at Whitby (*Dracula Unearthed* 120).

23. In *The Struggle for Asia: 1828–1914*, David Gillard describes actions considered and taken by the British and the French in the Baltic in preparation for a strategic assault on St. Petersburg. These included a planned blockade of the Gulf of Finland that would preclude "some thirty Russian ships of the line from commerce raiding in the North Sea" and in-

duce the Russians to shift forces away from the Black Sea theater of operations. In preparation for this move, British and French forces bombarded the Aaland Islands and "Sveaborg, in the Gulf of Finland" (92).

24. Leatherdale notes that Russia had no consulate in Whitby and that Baltic trade with London was conducted through an office in London (*Dracula Unearthed* 140). In a footnote a few pages later, he explains why Stoker, who was usually quite fastidious about such details, contrived a Russian consular in Whitby: "Stoker needs a Russian-speaker in Whitby, otherwise the captain's log would not be translated. The Russian consul employs a clerk, who lends his services to the press and doubtless puts a pro-Russian slant on his translation. Russian ships, Russian log, part-Russian crew, Russian consuls and clerks. The Russian subtext in *Dracula* is extensive" (142). As regards this study, the last sentence is extraordinarily significant.

25. Warwick writes that the "mother/child relationship is often picked up in the vampire fantasies to focus monstrosity of the women; the children become the victims of their mothers' or other womens' infection. Where Dracula concentrates his attention on fully grown adults, the women turn to children" (212).

26. According to Warwick, the "metaphor of venereal disease is consolidated" in Dracula "by its origins 'abroad'" in "Eastern Europe" (210).

27. Belford suggests that the parallels between Svengali and Dracula are intentional. In 1890 the Stokers and Du Maurier were vacationing in Whitby at the same time. A *Punch* illustration that year, drawn by Du Maurier and titled "A Filial Reproof," depicts Bram, Florence, and their son, Noel, relaxing at a garden party. Belford notes "Du Maurier was completing his second novel, *Trilby* (published in 1894), which introduces the mesmerist Svengali, an enduring mythic character to rival Dracula. Surely the two writers had tea at the Spa and discussed their protagonists as the band played softly. Was Dracula born from Svengali, as critic Nina Auerback suggests, with his powers still further extended over time and space? There are striking parallels between the two novels. Both deal with the fear of female sexuality and the loss of innocence, and with brave men who rescue the mother figure from a foreigner's embrace. Trilby O'Ferrall has three suitors, Taffy, Sandy, and Little Billee; Lucy Westenra also has three. The tone-deaf, weak-willed Trilby becomes a great singer when hypnotized, and Lucy becomes voluptuous when bitten. Both books illustrate the male-bonding novels popular in the late 1880s, novels such as H. Rider Haggard's *King Solo-*

*mon's Mines* (1885) and Arthur Conan Doyle's *A Study in Scarlet* (1887)" (228).

28. Leatherdale writes that his association "with Jews made Dracula yet more despicable to the average 1890s reader. Stoker was typical of his time when it came to anti–Semitism, the prevalence of which is observable in Major Johnson's *On the Track of the Crescent*, listed among Stoker's source books" (*Dracula Unearthed* 473–474).

29. Joseph Boone has shown that the Orient, especially the Arab world, became "the psychic screen on which to project fantasies of illicit sexuality and unbridled excess." He also discusses the investigations of Sir Richard Burton, travel writer par excellence and Stoker's friend, into the sexual relations between men in the region. Burton contended that the vice spread east out of its original "Mediterranean 'belt'" to the Far East and the Americas and that it even gained a foothold in "our modern capitals, London, Berlin, and Paris" (93). Although Boone does not draw the connection, it is not untenable to suggest that Burton's ideas regarding the Orient may well have influenced Stoker's depiction of Dracula as both a physical (Jewish borne blood contagion) and moral (gender inversion and sexual license) threat.

30. George Stoker suggests a triumphal return by England to Varna in the following passage: "It was after dark when we arrived in Varna, and I fear the peaceful inhabitants must have thought another Crimean war was about to commence. An 'Italian from Cor-r-r-k,' who afterwards distinguished himself at Plevna, favoured us with 'The Wearing of the Green;' and to counterbalance the rebellious sentiments therein expressed we all sang, or rather howled, 'God save the Queen'" (*With the Unspeakables* 13).

Not only has Varna been occupied, but a subversive Irishman put in his place as well.

31. Kaplan describes the profound affinity that came to exist between Bulgaria and Russia as a consequence of the Russo-Turkish War: "A Russian army swept through Bulgaria in 1877 and 1878, liberating Bulgaria from Ottoman subjugation in order to create a pro-Russian, Bulgarian buffer state against the Turks. Although the 1878 Treaty of Berlin forced newly independent Bulgaria to cede Thrace and Macedonia back to Turkey — triggering a renewed outbreak of guerrilla war — Bulgarian gratitude to the Russians never entirely dissipated. The Russian liberation was one of the few happy moments in Bulgaria's history since the Middle Ages. Construction of the Aleksandar Nevski Memorial Church began in 1882, to honor the 200,000 Russian soldiers who died during the war" [206–207].

32. Here is another example of the anti–Semitic overtones of the novel. Hildesheim is described as having "a nose like a sheep" (*D* 413). Leatherdale notes that the "nose has always been a cultural indicator of inferiority or barbarity" (*Dracula Unearthed* 473). It should be remembered that Dracula has a similarly large and hooked nose.

33. As with Jonathan's Kukri knife, here is another example of imperial weapons at work, in this instance a weapon made famous by a former British colony and a contemporary ally.

34. Leatherdale echoes this view: "Stoker may have felt uncomfortable at the homoerotic idea of Dracula being phallically staked by men and then writhing and screeching in his orgasmic death-throes" (*Dracula Unearthed* 509).

35. Glover defines Mina's role thusly: "Ironically, it is only by becoming a man that the woman can ever come to deserve parity of esteem or cease to be other than a problem; but one condition of phallic womanhood is that it is almost immediately abandoned for the over-feminized maternal" (*Vampires, Mummies, and Liberals* 97).

36. Daly contends that Mina "may be seen as a soldier in the army of cheap (here, free) female labor that sustains the group." Although she "resembles a New Woman in her skills," she exhibits "no desire for equality" (40).

37. The choice of the name Quincey signifies, for Glover, a "form of hierogamy which subordinates American energy to the triumph of British breeding" (*Vampires, Mummies, and Liberals* 94).

## Chapter Five

1. Hopkins draws attention to Carol Senf's observation that "Stoker's granddaughter believes that Florence refused to have sexual relations with Bram after the birth of their child." Hopkins further suggests that the author's "strong-willed, proto-feminist mother provided a dominant and lasting influence on both his life and his writing" (146).

2. As David Glover notes, many of Stoker's novels have been "severely edited" since his death. *The Lady of the Shroud* has "suffered particularly badly, " with over a third of the original text excised in modern editions (8). The original version of this chapter (see "*The Lady of the Shroud:* A Novel of Balkan Anglicization," *Balkanistica* 12 (1999): 21–38) was based on just such an expurgated edition. Fortunately, William Hughes's 2001 unabridged and annotated edition has given me the material to expand and to refine the argument here.

3. Meyer and Brysac, describing the work of British and Indian surveyors and mapmakers who doubled as spies during the "Great Game" with Russia on India's northern frontier, argue that "maps are political, and, it may be ventured, all mapmakers are politicians." They go on to cite Matthew Edney, who argues in his 1997 study *Mapping the Empire* that "Imperialism and mapmaking intersect in the most basic manner" (204). Mapmaking, it would seem, is another variant of the imperialist practice Pratt describes in *Imperial Eyes* as the "monarch-of-all-I-survey."

4. The brutal occupation of Bosnia-Herzegovina in 1908 by Austro-Hungarian forces, with the blessing of Germany, garnered English sympathy for the Serbians. Stoker, who according to Leatherdale was "no political innocent" (*The Novel and the Legend* 215), was inspired by these events to pen *The Lady of the Shroud.* The *Bookman* reviewer makes much the same point, writing that the novel presents "in outline at least that Balkan Federation, which may or may not be feasible, but certainly seems essential to the curbing of Austrian ambitions on the one hand and Turkish pretensions on the other" (W. F. P. 155). Leatherdale concurs, suggesting that *The Lady of the Shroud* is "pure political allegory relating to the Balkan crisis" (*The Novel and the Legend* 215).

5. The ethnic cleansing that eventually precipitated United Nations military action against Serbia and the installation of peacekeepers in Kosovo and elsewhere in the Balkans at the end of the twentieth century lead Hughes to opine that the Balkans have become "a European Vietnam for a post–Cold War age" (10).

6. Victor Sage contends that the novel promotes the creation "of a Greater Serbia stretching from Bulgaria to the Adriatic in the south and from Bosnia to Albania, which wins back Bosnia-Herzegovina" (130).

7. Bram Stoker, *The Lady of the Shroud* 1909 (Westcliff-on-Sea, Essex, UK: Desert Island Books, Ltd., 2001) 19. All further references to the text will appear parenthetically preceded by the letter *L*.

8. Hughes offers the following description of the Adriatic in a footnote to this passage, a description highly relevant to the arguments advanced later in this chapter: "In 1907, the Adriatic Sea separated the eastern coast of Italy (unified in 1870) from the western coast of Austrian Protectorate of Bosnia and Herzegovina (annexed by Austria in 1908), Montenegro (an independent monarchy, absorbed into Serbia in 1918) and Albania (under Ottoman rule until 1913)" (19).

9. A recent posting to the Balkan Academic Newsletter, an online scholarly forum, about the location of Ilsin produced a number of revealing responses. One respondent reported that Stoker had been motivated by the plight of

the Montenegrins, the people of the Black Mountains who had fought the Turks for centuries, to write the novel. He went on to write that the novel will soon be translated into the Montenegrin dialect by a publisher established in the city of Ulcinji. Other respondents noted that the Slavic pronunciation of the name comes very close to the English approximation "Ilsin." As the writer notes, "The name which the Montenegrins of Serbian descent use and also the current official name of the town is Ulcinji, which in Serbo-Croat is pronounced similar to English for *ooll'tsi'nye* with the stress falling on the first syllable." Another pointed out that the Albanian pronunciation, *Oolchin*, is also quite close to the English equivalent. Finally, a number of respondents touched on Ulcinji's past as both a slave market and a stronghold of Mediterranean pirates as possible sources of interest to readers of romantic fiction.

10. At this point Hughes notes, "Clearly this is a border area and possibly represents the limit of reliable Blue Mountain rule. The Ottoman forces, if this building commemorates but 'one of the massacres of the invading Turks,' have made several incursions into the region and are likely to do so again if the chances of success appear favorable" (*L* 238).

11. Hughes suggests that Stoker may have conflated Dracula's castle with Castle Vissarion in the Land of the Blue Mountains. Outwardly, the castle is described as surrounded by a "frowning wall of black rock, of vast height and perpendicular steepness." Hughes suggests that this description is "reminiscent of Count Dracula's mountain fortress, located in the inland Balkan province of Transylvania" (*L* 80). To a subsequent passage describing Rupert's initial appraisal of his lavishly appointed new home, Hughes responds that "this description is again reminiscent of Harker's appreciation of Count Dracula's castle in *Dracula*" (*L* 83).

12. M. S. Anderson notes that in 1908, at the height of the crisis following the Austro-Hungarian annexation of Bosnia-Herzegovina, "British public opinion was still hostile (or believed by the government to be hostile) to the grant of free passage through the Straits to Russian warships, though the cabinet itself was willing to accept this" (282).

13. Apparently, either spelling — Gerbel or Guerbel — is acceptable, for Stoker employs the former in *Personal Reminiscences of Henry Irving*, but the latter in the dedication to *The Lady of the Shroud*.

14. Another instance of pro–Japanese sentiment occurs at the end of the novel when the newly appointed editor of the Blue Mountain *Official Gazette* is described, approvingly I might add, as "a chum of our Special in the Japanese and Russian War" (*L* 341–342).

15. Rupert Sent Leger shares a number of attributes with Stoker. Both are quite tall and are prodigious walkers. Moreover, their family backgrounds are very similar. On his father's side, Stoker's "ancestors had lived in Ireland since the seventeenth century. They were soldiers, farmers, tailors, shoemakers , and goldsmiths, eventually distinguishing themselves as physicians and medical researchers" (Belford 20). His mother's family, on the other hand, "traced their ancestors back to 1584, with branches in Cheshire and Derbyshire, England [...]. Most yeomen, a title given to those who farmed their own land, they eventually represented the trades of the time: weavers, wheelwrights, tailors, shoemakers, masons, and hatters. The men served in the army, a few marrying heiresses and increasing their acreage" (Belford 21).

16. Explaining Stoker's use of the name St. Leger, Hughes offers multiple possibilities. One possibility is that Stoker is employing a name familiar in Irish politics. Among the St. Legers who served the crown in Ireland, Hughes lists Sir Anthony Leger, "who acted as Lord Deputy of Ireland, suppressed many of the noble families of the nation, and who framed the Act which passed the government of Ireland to Henry VIII and his heirs" (*L* 25).

17. Meyer and Brysac point out as an example of the prevalence of India in "popular writing in the late Victorian years" that none other than Dr. John H. Watson, informal assistant to Sherlock Holmes, had "served as an Assistant Surgeon on the North-West Frontier and was wounded at Maiwand" (202). Rupert's family ties to India suggest another link to the Great Game and, perhaps, Stoker's awareness of and interest in the writings of Rudyard Kipling, a point discussed in chapter two.

18. Further in the text readers learn that Major-General MacKelpie wins a "Baronetcy" for his service in "the Frontier War in India," what Hughes describes as "one of the many border disputes between Britain, Russia and the buffer state of Afghanistan" (*L* 44). Here again is another link to India, the "Great Game," and, I would suggest, Kipling.

19. Book one of *The Lady of the Shroud* recounts the "Reading of the Will" of Uncle Roger Melton. As Roth notes, it is followed by a journal report of the event written by Rupert's cousin, Ernest Roger Halbard Melton, "a greedy, transparent figure" with aristocratic pretensions. He serves as a "foil to his cousin Rupert" (Bram Stoker 75), who is a thoroughly middle-class man. Returning to the anti-aristocrat theme so prevalent in *Dracula*, Stoker depicts cousin Ernest as the most detestable of figures. When he visits Rupert at Castle Vissarion, he outrages the natives by

first presumptuously kissing the wife of the wine steward, perhaps a vestige of the aristocratic *droit de seigneur*, and next by cowering "on his knees in a state of panic" when the aggrieved husband arrives wielding a handjar. Ernest is saved, appropriately, by his Cockney valet, who is reported to have "the heart of a man in him" (*L* 278). Ernest is no less contemptuous of foreign royalty, and when he is introduced to Tueta, he merely "put forward *one* finger" when she extends her hand in greeting (*L* 281). In his role as a special correspondent for *The London Messenger* assigned to report on the coronation that ends the novel, Ernest's account of the proceedings reveals him as nothing less than a self-indulgent, pampered, and silly aristocrat (*L* 309–310). Moreover, through the subplot involving Ernest Melton, Stoker once again draws attention to the inferior train service in the Slavic realms, a failing Harker had recorded in his diary. Rupert dispatches a fellow Englishman under his command to retrieve Ernest from the train depot in Fiume. He later reports in a letter to Rupert that he "went to meet the train from St. Peter, due 11.40. It was something late, arriving just as the clock was beginning to srike midnight" (*L* 276). Russian train service, it would seem, is no better than that in Hungary.

20. Stoker's interest in the occult is readily apparent in *The Lady of the Shroud*. For example, the novel is prefaced by a entry from *The Journal of Occultism* recounting a sighting off the Spear of Ivan of a woman — later identified as Teuta — dressed only in a death shroud sitting upright in a floating coffin. Moreover, many of Rupert's international adventures have come at the behest of the such journals as *The Magazine of Mystery, Occultism*, and *The Ghost World* (*L* 66). Finally, his aunt, Janet MacKelpie, is gifted with "Second Sight" (*L* 118). Rupert, who has travelled "in strange places amongst strange peoples with strange views of their own" (*L* 112), is thus a fit protagonist for yet another Imperial Gothic narrative, and his psychical investigations in the "dark places of the earth" (Brantlinger 246) are but thinly veiled manifestations of English imperial desire.

21. In the course of his psychical investigations, Rupert has spent time "in the far recesses of the Himalayas," apparently studying the origins of Buddhism (*L* 66–67). It is not inconceivable, also, that he may have served as a British spy in the region. In 1900 Curzon dispatched Major Francis Youngblood to the court of the Dalai Lama to normalize diplomatic relations between British India and Tibet and to forestall Russian gains in the region. Curzon had been alarmed by reports that an emissary from the Lama had visited St. Petersburg twice

and by stories in the St. Petersburg newspapers extolling the good relations between the two monarchs (Hopkirk 505–507).

22. About mid-way through the novel readers learn that, as is true of the Count and Quincey Morris in *Dracula*, Rupert has "Viking forbears" (*L* 207). Hughes notes that "though the Vikings are in part associated with violent and rapacious behaviour, such references at times emphasise their physical resourcefulness and racial superiority, the latter a genetic resource which is capable of surviving across the centuries [...] so Rupert may instinctively draw upon the racial inheritance of his warlike ancestors at this time of crisis" (*L* 207).

23. Roger Melton further stipulates that his grant of an estate in the Land of the Blue Mountains to Rupert is binding and final unless countermanded by an act of "Parliament" that is "endorsed by the King." In a footnote to this passage, Hughes perceives "a muted colonialist — if not integrationist — message": "Rupert, effectively, is here advised to treat an estate which is situated beyond the national boundaries of England as if it were actually within the British Isles" (*L* 70).

24. According to Hughes, this passage "mobilises a patriarchal fantasy of ownership and identity. Teuta is no longer the ward of her father, nor indeed the possessor of her own discrete and distinctive identity; rather she has become the chattel of her husband, taking his name and adopting his will as her own" (*L* 272). The "noble King" referenced here, Hughes comments later in the text, is Edward VII, under whose rule Britain "abandoned the Victorian policy of 'splendid isolation.'" Adopting the policies of the "forward school" of diplomacy, Edward formed an alliance with Japan in 1902 and constructed a "lasting *Entente*" with France (*L* 199). Although he attempted to mend fences with Russia, Edward put Britain in a stronger position diplomatically and militarily vis-à-vis her traditional imperial rival.

25. Rupert's acquaintance with Indian sages and holy men offers further proof of his having traveled in British India, possibly, as I have suggested earlier, as a British agent in the "Great Game," much as Kipling's *Kim* in the guise of a Hindu acolyte spies on Russian movements in northern Indian.

26. Hughes points out that St. James's Palace is "the official seat of the British Court, the monarchial Court of St. James's" (*L* 97).

27. As was the case in Montenegro in the nineteenth century, the basic social and political unit in the Land of the Blue Mountains is the tribe, loosely consolidated under the rule of the voivode. In the penultimate chapter of the novel, "The Flashing of the Handjar," the Na-

tional Council, made up of tribal representatives, establishes a monarchy and appoints a king. In the nineteenth century, Prince Nicholas, later King Nicholas, of Montenegro presided over a senate consisting of the twelve leaders of the major tribes (Jelavich, 2: 35).

28. To an earlier comparison of Rupert to a lion, Hughes notes that the creature is "one of the heraldic supporters of the monarchial arms of the British nation and a national symbol of great antiquity" (L 126).

29. Though a sickly child, Stoker blossomed into a champion athlete at Trinity. He played rugby, lifted weights, rowed, and excelled at long-distance walking, winning awards in both the five and seven-mile walk (Belford 30).

30. Rupert demonstrates similar "self-control" later in the novel when the National Council of the Land of the Blue Mountains offers him the "Crown and Kingship" of the realm, an offer that comes with PeterVissarion's blessing (L 305–306).

31. The use of modern weapons in the Land of the Blue Mountains recalls not only the modern weapons employed by the Crew of Light in *Dracula*, but also the weapons used by British forces in the Crimean War. In that conflict, the French Minie rifle proved as effective against the Russians as the Ingis-Malbron rifle does against the Turks in *The Lady of the Shroud*.

32. Once freed from his Turkish captors, Voivoide Peter Vissarion informs the High Council of the Land of the Blue Mountains that "this prince-merchant, the great English Roger Melton" has been a secret source of military funding for a number years (L 266).

33. These are the names of some of Britain's most famous designers of military hardware. Sir John Thornycroft designed a high-speed naval vessel and built torpedo boats for the British and Norwegian navies. Sir Charles Parsons built and developed marine turbine engines. Sir William Armstrong invented the rifled breech-loading gun and the mines deployed by the British navy during the Crimean War (Hughes, L 171).

34. The year prior to the publication of *The Lady of the Shroud*, 1908, the Wright brothers had achieved powered flight. Ludlam describes the plane Rupert flies as "a platformed machine with a light engine and carried bags of ballast which could be tipped over the side in an emergency. The pilot sat on a centre seat and 'manoeuvred steering gear,' while passengers on the platform clung tightly to a safety bar in front. The platform could be raised above the plane or lowered beneath it, as required" (142–143).

35. Responding to this passage, Hughes lays bare the not-so-subtle imperial agenda driving the narrative: "Colonel (*sic*) MacKelpie is making rather strong assumptions with regard to the politics of what is at present a neutral nation. Though some of the rhetoric exposed in the novel [...] might suggest that this neutrality will eventually change in Britain's favour, much is being taken for granted here, presumably because of Rupert's retention of British citizenship" (L 288).

36. At the end of the proceedings, which bring about the complete the overthrow of the political system of the Land of the Blue Mountains for one based on the British system, the member of the National Council cheer, appropriately, "'three times three' in British fashion" (L 308).

37. Hughes draws the opposite conclusion, arguing that the "Blue Mouth, the strategic harbour upon which Rupert proposes to center his adopted nation's strength, will thus be as impregnable to uninvited British Dreadnoughts as it will be to marauding Turkish ironclads" (Introduction 11). Hughes reads the exchange between Admiral Rooke and Edward VII at the end of the novel as evidence of Balka's determination to be independent of all external powers, even Britain. To close the ceremonies commemorating Rupert's coronation, a fleet of "aeroplanes" drop letters on the decks of the ships at anchor in the harbor. Of this amazing feat, Edward VII comments, "It must need some skill to drop a letter with such accuracy," to which Rooke responds, "It is easier to drop bombs, Your Majesty" (L 351). The possible implication, one favored by Hughes, is that Rooke's statement carries the weight of a warning that Balka has achieved military parity with the imperial powers by means of its air force and will brook no interference in its internal affairs. However, the references to Rupert's maintaining fealty to Britain and the significant role Britain and Edward VII play in reforming the government and military of the Land of the Blue Mountains clearly suggest that Britain will figure prominently in the future governance and foreign policy of Balka.

38. The incorporation of the Land of the Blue Mountains into a league aligned with Britain is expressed earlier in the text when Rupert records that he is "well into the subject of a great Balkan Federation" (L 325), a political entity that will coalesce the various Balkan nations into a conglomerate under the name of Balka, with, obviously, Rupert and the Land of the Blue Mountains in the lead. Hughes observes here that although "such a federated movement represents a novel idea for the frequently belligerent nations of the Balkans, the concept was already in popular circulation as an antidote to the problems of the widely spread British empire. By 1902 it was clear in

the minds of most politicians and investors that further expansion of British territory could only be achieved through protracted warfare with other developed powers […]. As Bernard Porter suggests, if Britain and the Empire were 'United as a single political and military unit it could defy the world.' This appears to be very much the sentiment behind Rupert's federal aspirations in *The Lady of the Shroud*" (*L* 325).

39. As was typically the case in Britain's far-flung empire, colonial authorities supported British firms in the identification and extraction of natural resources for use, primarily, at home. In an aside to Major-General MacKelpie, Teuta, the appropriated native consort of a British-born sovereign, outlines the commercial potential of the Land of the Blue Mountains: "Our mountains and their valleys are clad with trees of splendid growth, virgin forests of priceless worth; hard woods of all kinds, which have no superior throughout the world. In the rocks, though hidden as yet, is vast mineral wealth of many kinds […] whole mountain ranges simply teem with vast quantities of minerals, almost more precious for industry than gold and silver are for commerce — though, indeed, gold is not altogether lacking as a mineral. When once our work on the harbour is done, and the place has been made secure against any attempt at foreign aggression, we must try to find a way to bring this wealth of woods and ores down to the sea" (*L* 294–295).

Teuta's words describe the future commodification of her homeland. Aside from their potential laborers to extract these resources, she and her fellow Serbs of the Land of the Blue Mountains are also attractive to British colonial interests as potential customers for the goods manufactured from these resources. The following passage from the 1900 book *The Living Races of Mankind* describes the process: "We have begun to realize that the most promising fields of enterprise for our ever-increasing community, the most profitable markets for our wares, may some day be found in places which are now the darkest corners of the earth, and that half-clothed savages, just emerging from the brute condition, is a human being capable of being educated, in the near future, into a customer for British trade and a contributor to the world's wealth" (qtd. in Paul Rich 18).

40. Sage comes to much the same conclusion, positing that Stoker "is willing by the time of *The Lady of the Shroud* to dismantle even his own vampiric myth, banishing the occult and the uncanny from his text in order to mount a clarion call to a flaccid Edwardian bourgeoisie, advocating a return to patriarchy before it was too late" (131–132).

41. Hughes writes of Teuta's behavior here that "her submissive posture, her whole demeanour encode a Western fantasy about the woman, not as harem possession, but as idolater to a single man, his devoted servant and constant adoring companion" (*L* 232).

42. According to Said, nineteenth-century writers associated the "Orient with the escapism of sexual fantasy." Because of the "increasing *embourgeoisement*" of middle-class Victorian culture, "sex had been institutionalized to a very considerable degree. On the one had, there was no such thing as 'free' sex, and on the other, sex in society entailed a web of legal, moral, even political and economic obligations of a detailed and certainly encumbering sort. Just as the various colonial possessions — quite apart from their economic benefit to metropolitan Europe — were useful as places to send wayward sons, superfluous populations of delinquents, poor people, and other undesirables, so the Orient was a place where one could look for sexual experience unobtainable in Europe" [*Orientalism* 190].

As a colonized, Eastern, deracinated bride, Teuta offers the possibility of sex acts prohibited by Western culture. That sex is very much on Rupert's mind is obvious by his reaction to Teuta's refusal to stay with him on their wedding night: "'What?' I was all aghast, and I felt that my chagrin was expressed in the tone of horrified surprise in my voice. She went on quickly: 'Alas! It is impossible that I should go further — at present!' 'But what is to prevent you?' I queried. 'You are now my wife. This is our wedding-night; and surely your place is with me!'" [*L* 197].

Even though Teuta's not returning to her hiding place at St. Sava threatens her security and life, Rupert thinks of little more than the possibility of exotic sexual pleasures.

## Conclusion

1. Before the National Council of the Land of the Blue Mountains, Voivoice Peter Vissarion praises Rupert for having "undertaken the defence of the Blue Mouth at his own expense," exclaiming that when the improvements are complete, Rupert will have created an obstacle to incursions from the sea "stronger than Gibraltar" (*L* 304).

# Works Cited

Altick, Richard D. *Victorian People and Ideas*. New York: Norton, 1973.

Anderson, M. S. *The Eastern Question 1774–1923: A Study in International Relations*. New York: St. Martin's, 1966.

Anderson, Olive. *A Liberal State at War: English Politics and Economics During the Crimean War*. New York: St. Martin's, 1967.

Anderson, Patricia. *The Printed Image and the Transformation of Popular Culture, 1790–1860*. 1991. New York: Oxford UP, 1994.

Arata, Stephen D. "The Occidental Tourist: *Dracula* and the Anxiety of Reverse Colonization." *Victorian Studies* 33.4 (Summer 1990): 621–645.

Bann, Stephen. "The Sense of the Past: Image, Text, and Object in the Formation of Historical Consciousness in Nineteenth-Century Britain." *The New Historicism*. Ed. H. Aram Veeser. New York: Routledge, 1989. 102–115.

Barnett, Thomas P. M. "The Pentagon's New Map." *Esquire* March 2003: 174–179.

Belford, Barbara. *Bram Stoker: A Biography of the Author of Dracula*. New York: Knopf, 1996.

Bentley, Nicholas. Introduction. *Russell's Despatches from the Crimean War*. New York: Hill and Wang, 1966.

Blanton, Casey. *Travel Writing: The Self and the World*. New York: Routledge, 2002.

Boone, Joseph A. "Vacation Cruises; or, the Homoerotics of Orientalism." PMLA 110.1 (Jan. 1995): 89–107.

Boone, Troy. "'He Is English and Therefore Adventurous': Politics, Decadence, and Dracula." *Studies in the Novel* 25.1 (Spring 1993): 76–91.

Brantlinger, Patrick. *Rule of Darkness: British Literature and Imperialism, 1830–1914*. Ithaca, NY: Cornell UP, 1988.

Bratton, J. S. "Theatre of War: The Crimea on the London Stage 1854–55." *Performance and Politics in Popular Drama: Aspects of Popular Entertainment in Theatre, Film and Television 1800–1976*. Eds. David Bradby, Louis James, and Bernard Sharratt. Cambridge: Cambridge UP, 1980. 119–137.

Chothia, Jean. Introduction. *The New Woman and Other Emancipated Woman Plays*. Oxford: Oxford UP, 1998.

Clarkson, Jesse D. *A History of Russia*. 2nd ed. New York: Random House, 1969.

Clewing, Konrad, et al. "Query: Port of Ilsin, Bram Stoker, *Lady of the Shroud*." Online posting. 12 Jan. 2005. Balkan Academic News. 13 Jan. 2005. balkans@yahoogroups.com.

*The Columbia History of the World.* Eds. John A. Garraty and Peter Gay. 8th ed. New York: Harper and Row, 1987.

Craft, Christopher. "'Kiss Me with Those Red Lips': Gender and Inversion in Bram Stoker's *Dracula.*" *Dracula: The Vampire and the Critics.* Ed. Margaret L. Carter. Ann Arbor, MI: UMI Research Press, 1988. 167–194.

Cranny-Francis, Anne. "Sexual Politics and Political Repression in Bram Stoker's *Dracula.*" *Nineteenth-Century Suspense.* Eds. Bloom Clive, Brian Docherty, Jane Gibb, and Keith Shand. New York: St. Martin's, 1988. 64–79.

Croley, Laura Sagolla. "The Rhetoric of Reform in Stoker's *Dracula*: Depravity, Decline, and the Fin-de-siècle 'Residuum.'" *Criticism* 37.1 (Winter 1995): 85–108.

Daly, Nicholas. *Modernism, Romance and the fin de siecle: Popular Fiction and British Culture, 1880–1914.* Cambridge: Cambridge UP, 1999.

Dossey, Barbara M. *Florence Nightingale: Mystic, Visionary, Reformer.* Philadelphia: Lippincott Williams & Wilkins, 1999.

Dower, John W. *War without Mercy: Race and Power in the Pacific War.* New York: Pantheon Books, 1986.

Epstein, Helen. "The Mysterious Miss Nightingale." *The New York Review of Books.* 8 March 2001: 16–19.

Farson, Daniel. *The Man Who Wrote Dracula: A Biography of Bram Stoker.* London: Michael Joseph, 1975.

Fussell, Paul. *Abroad: British Literary Traveling between the Wars.* New York: Oxford UP, 1980.

_____. *The Norton Book of Travel.* New York: W.W. Norton, 1987.

Garnett, Rhys. "*Dracula* and *The Beetle*: Imperial and Sexual Guilt and Fear in Late Victorian Fantasy." *Science Fiction Roots and Branches.* Ed. Rhys Garnett and R. J. Ellis. New York: St. Martin's, 1990. 30–54.

Gartner, Lloyd P. *The Jewish Immigrant in England, 1870–1914.* Detroit: Wayne State UP, 1960.

Giedroyc, Richard. "Moldavian-Russian History Intertwine Many Times." *Journal of the Russian Numismatic Society* 73 (Winter 2002): 23–29.

Gillard, David. *The Struggle for Asia, 1828–1914.* New York: Holmes & Meier, 1977.

Gilman, Sander. "'I'm Down on Whores': Race and Gender in Victorian London." *Anatomy of Racism.* Ed. David Theo Goldberg. Minneapolis: U of Minnesota P, 1990. 146–170.

Gilmour, David. *The Long Recessional: The Imperial Life of Rudyard Kipling.* New York: Farrar, Straus and Giroux, 2003.

Gilroy, Amanda. Introduction. *Romantic Geographies: Discourses of Travel, 1775–1844.* Manchester: Manchester UP, 2000.

Gleason, John Howes. *The Genesis of Russophobia in Great Britain: A Study of the Interaction of Policy and Opinion.* 1950. New York: Octagon, 1972.

Glover, David. "Bram Stoker and the Crisis of the Liberal Subject." *New Literary History* 23.4 (Autumn 1992): 983–1002.

_____. *Vampires, Mummies and Liberals: Bram Stoker and the Politics of Popular Fiction.* London: Duke UP, 1996.

Goldfrank, David M. *The Origins of the Crimean War.* Origins of Modern War. London: Longman, 1994.

Gordon, Joan, and Veronica Hollinger. Introduction. *Blood Read: the Vampire as Metaphor in Contemporary Culture.* Philadelphia: University of Pennsylvania Press, 1997.

Halberstam, Judith. "Parasites and Perverts: Anti-Semitism and Sexuality in Nineteenth Century Gothic Fiction." Diss. University of Minnesota, 1991.

_____. "Technologies of Monstrosity: Bram Stoker's *Dracula.*" *Victorian Studies* 36.3 (Spring 1993): 333–352.

Haley, Bruce. *The Healthy Body and Victorian Culture.* Cambridge, MA: Harvard UP, 1978.

Haraszti, Eva H. *Kossuth as an English Journalist.* Boulder, CO: Social Science Monographs, 1990.

Hatlen, Burton. "The Return of the Repressed/Oppressed in Bram Stoker's *Dracula.*" Carter 117–135.

Holmes, Colin. *Anti-Semitism in British Society, 1876–1939.* New York: Holmes & Meier, 1979.

Holmes, Richard. "The War Moves South." *Rebels and Redcoats: How Britain Lost America.* Narr. Richard Holmes. Ex. Prod. Zvi Dor Nor. PBS. WNPT, 23 June 2004.

Hopkins, Lisa. "Crowning the King, Mourning his Mother: *The Jewel of Seven Stars* and *The Lady of the Shroud.*" *Bram Stoker: History, Psychoanalysis and the Gothic.* Ed. William Hughes and Andrew Smith. London: Macmillan, 1998. 134–50.

Hopkirk, Peter. *The Great Game: The Struggle for Empire in Central Asia.* 1990. New York: Kodansha International, 1994.

Howe, Irving. Introduction. *The Portable Kipling.* New York: Penguin, 1982.

Hughes, William, ed. *The Lady of the Shroud.* By Bram Stoker. 1909. Westcliff-on-Sea, Essex: Desert Island Books, 2001.

Jelavich, Barbara. *History of the Balkans: Eighteenth and Nineteenth Centuries.* 1983. Cambridge: Cambridge UP, 1995. 2 vols.

Kaplan, Robert D. *Balkan Ghosts: A Journey through History.* 1993. New York: Vintage Departures, 1994.

Karnow, Stanley. *Vietnam: A History.* New York: Viking, 1983.

Kipling, Rudyard. "Ave Imperatrix!" *Rudyard Kipling: Complete Verse.* Definitive ed. 1940. New York: Anchor Books, 1989. 168–169.

_____. "The Ballad of the King's Jest." *Rudyard Kipling: Complete Verse.* 245–248.

_____. *Kim.* 1901. Edward Said ed. London: Penguin, 1989.

_____. "The Last of the Light Brigade." *Rudyard Kipling: Complete Verse.* 200–201.

_____. "The Man Who Was." *Soldier Stories.* 1899. Freeport, NY: Books for Library Press, 1970. 78–100.

_____. "The Man Who Would Be King." *The Portable Kipling.* Irving Howe ed. London: Penguin, 1982. 28–67.

_____. "The Mutiny of the Mavericks." *Rudyard Kipling: War Stories and Poems.* Andrew Rutherford ed. Oxford: Oxford UP, 1999.

_____. "The Swelling of Jordan." *Soldier Three and Other Stories.* 1895. London: MacMillan & Co., 1965. 213–226.

_____. "The Taking of Lungtunpen." *Soldier Stories.* 182–190.

Kirtley, Bacil F. "*Dracula,* the Monastic Chronicles and Slavic Folklore." Carter 11–17.

Kleveman, Lutz. "Oil and the New 'Great Game.'" *The Nation* 16 Feb. 2004: 11–14.

Knightley, Phillip. *The First Casualty: The War Correspondent as Hero and Myth-Maker from the Crimea to Kosovo.* Baltimore: Johns Hopkins UP, 2002.

Kushner, Tony. *The Persistence of Prejudice: Antisemitism in British Society During the Second World War.* Manchester: Manchester UP, 1989.

Lalumia, Matthew Paul. *Realism and Politics in Victorian Art of the Crimean War.* Studies in the Fine Arts: Iconography, No. 9. Ann Arbor, MI: UMI Research Press, 1984.

Langguth, A. J. *Our Vietnam: the War 1954–1975.* New York: Simon & Schuster, 2000.

Leask, Nigel. "Francis Wilford and the Colonial Construction of Hindu Geography." Gilroy 204–222.

Leatherdale, Clive. *Dracula: The Novel and the Legend.* Wellingborough, Northamptonshire, UK: The Aquarian Press, 1985.

_____, ed. *Dracula Unearthed.* Westcliff-on-Sea, Essex, UK: Desert Island Books, 1998.

_____. *The Origins of Dracula: The Background to Bram Stoker's Gothic Masterpiece.* London: William Kimber, 1987.

Lind, Michael. *Vietnam: the Necessary War.* New York: Touchstone, 1999.

Longfellow, Henry Wadsworth. "Santa Filomena." 1857. *The Victorian Web: Literature, History, & Culture in the Age of Victoria.* Ed. Dr. Marjie Bloy. University Scholars Programme, National University of Singapore. 6 Apr. 2005. <http://www.victorianweb. org/history/crimea/filomena.html>.

Loyd, Anthony. *My War Gone By, I Miss It So.* 1999. London: Penguin, 2001.

Ludlam, Harry. *A Biography of Dracula: The Life of Bram Stoker.* London: Fireside Press, 1962.

Macintyre, Ben. *The Man Who Would Be King: The First American in Afghanistan.* New York: Farrar, Straus and Giroux, 2004.

Makdisi, Saree Samir. "Shelley's *Alastor*: Travel beyond the Limit." Gilroy 240–257.

Malcolmson, Scott. "Advise and Consent." Rev. of *The Breaking of Nations,* by Robert Cooper. *Nation* 5 July 2005. 56–60.

Martin, Kingsley. *The Triumph of Lord Palmerston.* 1924. London: Hutchinson, 1963.

Marx, Karl. *The Eastern Question: A Reprint of Letters Written 1853–1856 Dealing with the Events of the Crimean War.* Ed. Eleanor Marx Aveling and Edward Aveling. 1897. New York: Burt Franklin, 1968.

Matthew, H. C. G. "The Liberal Age (1851–1914)." *The Oxford Illustrated History of Britain.* Ed. Kenneth O. Morgan. Oxford: Oxford UP, 1989. 463–522.

McNally, Raymond, and Radu Florescu. *In Search of Dracula: the History of Dracula and Vampires.* 1972. Boston: Houghton Mifflin, 1994.

McWhir, Anne. "Pollution and Redemption in *Dracula.*" *Modern Language Studies* 17.3 (Summer 1987): 31–40.

Meyer, Karl E. *The Dust of Empire: The Race for Mastery in the Asian Heartland.* New York: Public Affairs, 2003.

_____, and Shareen Blair Brysac. *Tournament of Shadows: The Great Game and the Race for Empire in Central Asia.* Washington, D.C.: Counterpoint, 1999.

Mighall, Robert. *A Geography of Victorian Gothic Fiction: Mapping History's Nightmares.* Oxford: Oxford UP, 1999.

Miller, Elizabeth. *Dracula: Sense & Nonsense.* Westcliff-on-Sea, Essex, UK: Desert Island Books, 2000.

_____. *Reflections on Dracula.* White Rock, BC: Transylvania Press, 1997.

Moretti, Franco. "The Dialect of Fear." *New Left Review* 136 (Nov–Dec 1982): 67–85.

Morrison, Robert, and Chris Baldick, eds. Introduction. *The Vampyre and Other Tales of the Macabre.* Oxford: Oxford UP, 1998.

Mosse, George L. *Nationalism and Sexuality: Respectability and Abnormal Sexuality in Modern Europe.* New York: Howard Fertig, 1985.

_____. *Toward the Final Solution.* New York: Howard Fertig, 1978.

Nightingale, Florence. *A Contribution to the Sanitary History of the British Army During the Late War with Russia.* London: John W. Parker and Son, West Strand, 1859.

Oinas, Felix. "East European Vampires & Dracula." *Journal of Popular Culture* 16.1 (Summer 1982): 108–116.

*The Oxford Companion to English Literature.* Ed. Margaret Drabble. 5th ed. Oxford: Oxford UP, 1985.

*The Oxford Illustrated History of Britain.* Ed. Kenneth O. Morgan. Oxford: Oxford UP, 1989.

Pares, Bernard. *A History of Russia.* New York: Vintage, 1965.

Perry, Dennis R. "Whitman's Influence on Stoker's *Dracula.*" *Walt Whitman Quarterly Review* 3.3 (Winter 1986): 29–35.

Pick, Daniel. "'Terrors of the night': *Dracula* and 'degeneration' in the Late Nineteenth Century." *Critical Quarterly* 30.4 (Winter 1988): 71–87.

Polidori, John. "The Vampyre." *The Vampyre and Other Tales of the Macabre.* Eds. Robert Morrison and Chris Baldick. Oxford: Oxford UP, 1998. 3–23.

Poovey, Mary. *Uneven Developments*. Chicago: UP of Chicago, 1988.

Pratt, Mary Louise. *Imperialist Eyes: Travel Writing and Transculturation*. New York: Routledge, 1992.

Pynchon, Thomas. *V.* 1963. New York: Bantam, 1964.

Rawlinson, Sir Henry. *England and Russia in the East: The Political and Geographical Conditions*. New York: Praeger, 1875.

Rich, Norman. *Why the Crimean War? A Cautionary Tale*. London: UP of New England, 1985.

Rich, Paul B. *Race and Empire in British Politics*. Cambridge: Cambridge UP, 1986.

Robinson, Edwin Arlington. "Richard Cory." *An Introduction to Literature*. Ed. Sylvan Barnet, Morton Berman, and William Burto. 9th ed. Glenview, IL: Scott, Foresman, 1989. 22.

Roth, Phyllis A. *Bram Stoker*. Boston: Twayne Publishers, 1982.

_____. "Suddenly Sexual Women in Bram Stoker's *Dracula*." Carter 57–68.

Russell, William Howard. *Russell's Despatches from the Crimea 1854–56*. Ed. Nicolas Bentley. New York: Hill and Wang, 1966.

Rutherford, Andrew, ed. *Rudyard Kipling: War Stories and Poems*. Oxford: Oxford UP, 1999.

Sage, Victor. "Exchanging Fantasies: Sex and the Serbian Crisis in *The Lady of the Shroud*." *Bram Stoker: History, Psychoanalysis and the Gothic*. Ed. William Hughes and Andrew Smith. London; Macmillian, 1998. 116–33.

Said, Edward W. *Culture and Imperialism*. 1993. New York: Vintage Books, 1994.

_____. *Orientalism*. New York: Vintage Books, 1979.

Scandura, Jani. "Deadly Professions: *Dracula*, Undertakers, and the Embalmed Corpse." *Victorian Studies* Autumn (1996): 1–30.

Schivelbusch, Wolfgang. *The Culture of Defeat: on National Trauma, Mourning, and Recovery*. New York: Henry Holt, 2001.

Schmitt, Cannon. *Irishness and (Post) Modernism*. Ed. John S. Richard. *Bucknell Review*. London: Assoc. UP, 1994. 25–43.

Seaman, L. C. B. *Victorian England: Aspects of English and Imperial History 1837–1901*. London: Methuen & Co., 1973.

Senf, Carol A. "*Dracula*: Stoker's Response to the New Woman." *Victorian Studies* 26.1 (Autumn 1982): 33–49.

_____. "*Dracula*: The Unseen Face in the Mirror." Carter 93–103.

_____. "*The Lady of the Shroud*: Stoker's Successor to *Dracula*." *Essays in Arts and Sciences* 19 (May 1990): 82–96.

_____. *The Vampire in Nineteenth-Century English Literature*. Bowling Green, KY: Bowling Green University Popular Press, 1988.

Seward, Desmond. *Napoleon and Hitler: A Comparative Biography*. New York: Viking, 1989.

Showalter, Elaine. "Introduction." In *Trilby* by George Du Maurier. Oxford: Oxford UP, 1999.

_____. *Sexual Anarchy: Gender and Culture at the Fin de Siecle*. London: Penguin, 1990.

Small, Hugh. *Florence Nightingale: Avenging Angel*. New York: St. Martin's, 1998.

Smith, Andrew, M.D. *Medical and Surgical History of the British Army Which Served in Turkey and the Crimea During the War Against Ruissia in the Years 1854–55–56*. Vol. 2. London: Harrison and Sons, 1858. 2 vols.

Smith, Malcolm. "*Dracula* and the Victorian Frame of Mind." *Empire, Politics and Popular Culture: Essays in Eighteenth and Nineteenth Century British History*. Ed. C. C. Eldridge. *Trivium* 24 (1989): 76–97.

Spencer, Kathleen L. "Purity and Danger: *Dracula*, the Urban Gothic, and the Late Victorian Degeneracy Crisis." *ELH* 59.1 (Spring 1992): 197–225.

Spurr, David. *The Rhetoric of Empire: Colonial Discourse in Journalism, Travel Writings, and Imperial Administration*. Durham, NC: Duke UP, 1993.

Stabler, Jane. "Byron's Digressive Journey." Gilroy 223–239.

Stevenson, John Allen. "A Vampire in the Mirror: The Sexuality of *Dracula*." *PMLA* 103.2 (March 1988): 139–49.

Stewart, J. I. M. *Rudyard Kipling*. New York: Dodd, Mead, 1966.

Stoddard, Jane. "Mr. Bram Stoker. A Chat with the Author of *Dracula*." *British Weekly* 1 July 1897: 185.

Stoker, Bram. *Dracula*. *The Essential Dracula: The Definitive Annotated Edition of Bram Stoker's Classic Novel*. 1897. Ed. Leonard Wolf. 1975. New York: Plume, 1993.

_____. "Dracula's Guest." *The Essential Dracula: The Definitive Annotated Edition of Bram Stoker's Classic Novel*. 1897. Ed. Leonard Wolf. 1975. New York: Plume, 1993. 446–456.

_____. *The Jewel of Seven Stars*. 1903. New York: Carroll & Graf, 1992.

_____. *The Lady of the Shroud*. 1909. Ed. William Hughes. Westcliff-on-Sea, Essex: Desert Island Books, Ltd., 2001.

_____. *Personal Reminiscences of Henry Irving*. 2 vols. New York: Mcmillan, 1906.

Stoker, George. *With "The Unspeakables;" or, Two Years' Campaigning in European and Asiatic Turkey*. London: Chapman & Hall, 1878.

Strachey, Lytton. *Eminent Victorians*. New York: Harcourt Brace Jovanovich, 1918.

Vambery, Arminius. *The Coming Struggle for India*. London: Cassell, 1885.

Varma, Devendra P. "Dracula's Voyage: From Pontus to Hellespontus." Carter 207–213.

_____. "The Genesis of Dracula: A Re-Visit." Carter 39–50.

Ware, Kallistos. "Eastern Christendom." *The Oxford Illustrated History of Christianity*. Ed. John McManners. Oxford: Oxford UP, 1990.

Wasson, Richard. "The Politics of *Dracula*." Carter 19–23.

W. F. P. "Bram Stoker's Latest Novel." *Bookman* 37 (January 1910), 194. *The Critical Response to Bram Stoker*. Ed. Carol A. Senf. Westport, CT: Greenwood Press, 1993. 155–156.

Wicke, Jennifer. "Vampiric Typewriting: *Dracula* and Its Media." *ELH* 59.2 (Summer 1992): 467–493.

Wilson, Angus. *The Strange Ride of Rudyard Kipling*. New York: Viking Press, 1978.

Wolf, Leonard, ed. *The Essential Dracula: The Definitive Annotated Edition of Bram Stoker's Classic Novel*. 1975. New York: Plume, 1993.

Woodham-Smith, Cecil. *Florence Nightingale, 1820–1910*. New York: McGraw-Hill, 1951.

Zanger, Jules. "A Sympathetic Vibration: Dracula and the Jews." *English Literature in Translation* 34.1 (1991): 33–44.

# Index